A Part 1 Promotion Crammer for Sergeants and Inspectors – 2001

Tom Barron

No part of this publication may be reproduced No part of this publication may be reproduced or transmitted in any form or by any means, or stored in any retrieval system of any nature, without prior written permission, except the permitted fair dealing under the Copyright, Designs and Patents Act 1988, or in accordance with the terms of a licence issued by the Copyright Licensing Agency in respect of photocopying and/or reprographic reproduction.

Application for permission for other use of copyright material including permission to reproduce extracts in other published works shall be made to the publishers.

Full acknowledgement of author, publisher and source must be given.

© Jane's Information Group

3RD EDITION 2000

ISBN 07106 23682

Jane's Information Group
1st Floor
The Quadrangle
180 Wardour Street
London W1A 4YG

Produced by Hobbs the Printers, Totton, Hampshire

Whilst every care has been taken in compiling (and checking) the suggested answers and other information contained in this book, no responsibility can be accepted by the publishers or the author for any error, inaccuracy, or omission which remains, or for any loss or injury sustained to any (person/reader) as a result.

About the Author

Born in Glasgow in 1945, Tom Barron joined the army, aged 15, as a boy soldier. He subsequently saw service in Germany, Cyprus (United Nations), Singapore, Malaya and in Borneo where he saw active service with the Royal Corps Of Transport (Air Despatch).

He joined the Police Service in 1969 where he served for 27 years in many operational and training roles. Two years were spent teaching crammer courses for officials taking the sergeants' and inspectors' exams, followed by prosecuting in magistrates' courts in the West Country. He was also in charge of The Avon & Somerset Interview Technique training unit.

Tom has had a number of articles published, most notably in the *Daily Telegraph*, and an exclusive in the *Daily Mail*. He enjoys lecturing in colleges and universities on his subject, The Anatomy of a Lie. He is the author of The Special Constable's Manual.

**To my wife Isobel,
my raison d'etre**

Contents

THE RULES AND SYLLABUSES

Rules for the Sergeants' Exam
Rules for the Inspectors' Exam

On STUDYING

PART 1 - GENERAL POLICE DUTIES
Police 1
Police Powers 19
Powers of Entry 33
Public Order and Terrorism 43
Protection from Harassment 63
Communications 65
Firearms 69
Offensive Weapons 77
Nuisance 83
Animals 87
Offences Relating to Premises 93
Licensed Premises 101
Civil Disputes 111
Offences Involving Information 117

PART 2 - CRIME
Crime Introduction 119
Defences 123
Homicide 125
Misuse of Drugs 129
Pregnancy and Childbirth Offences 135
Offences Against the Person 139
Sexual Offences 147
Offences Against Children & Vulnerable Persons 157
Theft & Related Offences 169
Deception 181
Criminal Damage 189
Offences Against the Administration of Justice & Public Interest 195

CONTENTS

PART 3 - ROAD TRAFFIC
Standards of Driving 199
Notice of Intended Prosecution 205
Accidents 207
Drink Driving 209
Insurance 217
Traffic Safety Measures 219
Construction & Use 229
Traffic Signs 233
Driver Licensing 237
Excise & Registration 241
Goods Vehicles & Passenger Vehicles 243
Fixed Penalty System 249
Pedal Cycles 253
Forgery & Falsification of Documents 255

PART 4 - EVIDENCE & PROCEDURE
Summonses & Warrants 259
Court Procedure & Witnesses 263
Privilege & Public Policy 271
Evidence 273
Similar Fact Evidence 283
Disclosure of Evidence 287
Custody Officer Duties 293
Identification 309
Interviews 315
Superintendents 319

The Rules and Syllabuses

Rules for the sergeants' exam

1. Admission to the exam is restricted to constables who will have completed not less than 2 years service and the required probationary period by the 30th November of the year in which they take Part I of the exam.

2.. Part I will consist of a single, multiple choice paper, of two hours duration, which will normally be held in March. Candidates who pass Part I are required to take Part II at the first opportunity, i.e. within 12 months.

3. The pass mark for Part I of the exam is 75% of the available marks. Candidates who obtain less than 35% of the available marks will be ineligible to enter the exam the next time it is held.

4. Candidates who fail Part II may make one further attempt without retaking Part I during the next 3 years. Failure to pass Part II during this time means that the candidate must re-qualify in Part I again, before making a further attempt at Part II.

Notes.

1. In answering questions, candidates will be expected to draw upon their practical experience and training, and the questions will be framed to test knowledge of practice and procedure as well as law.

2. A knowledge of the more important decided cases is required.

3. The exam will be based on the most recent edition of the Blackstone's Police Manuals.

THE RULES AND SYLLABUSES

Rules for the inspectors' exam.

1. Admission to the exam is restricted to sergeants who are of substantive rank on lSf July of the year they take Part I of the exam.

2. Part I will consist of a single, multiple choice paper, of two hours duration, which will normally be held in September.

3. Candidates who pass Part I are required to take Part II at the first opportunity, e.g. within 12 months.

4. In order to pass Part I of the exam, a candidate must obtain a minimum of 75% of the available marks. Candidates who obtain less than 35% of the marks will be ineligible to enter the exam when it is next held.

5. A candidate who fails Part II may make one further attempt without retaking Part I during the subsequent three year period. Failure on this occasion means that the candidate must re-qualify in Part I.

Notes

1. Candidates are reminded that questions in the inspectors' exam will be based on more complex questions.

2. In answering questions candidates will be expected to draw upon their practical experience and training, and the questions will be framed to test knowledge on practice and procedure as well as the law.

3. A knowledge of the more important decided cases affecting police work and procedure is required. The exam will be based on the most recent edition of the Blackstone's Police Manuals.

Sergeants' and Inspectors' syllabus
[a summary]

Part 1
General Police Duties
Police
Police Powers
Powers of Entry
Public Order and Terrorism
Harassment
Offences involving communications
Firearms
Weapons
Nuisance
Animals
Offences relating to premises
Licensed Premises
Disputes
Offences involving information and data
Equal Opportunities and Discrimination

Part 2
Crime
State of Mind
Criminal Conduct
Incomplete Offences
Defences
Homicide
Misuse of Drugs
Pregnancy and Childbirth
Offences against the Person
Torture, Kidnapping etc
Sexual Offences
Offences against Children etc
Theft
Deception
Criminal Damage
Offences against the Administration of Justice and the Public Interest
Identification

Part 3
Road Traffic
Definitions
Standards of Driving
Notice of Intended Prosecution
Accidents
Drink, Drugs and Driving
Insurance
Safety Measures
Construction and Use Regulations
Traffic Signs
Driving Licensing
Excise and Registration
Goods and Passenger Vehicles
The Fixed Penalty System
Pedal Cycles
Forgery and Falsification of Documents

Part 4
Evidence and Procedure
Summonses and Warrants
Witnesses
Privilege and Public Policy
Evidence
Similar fact evidence
Exclusion of Evidence
Disclosure
Police Station Procedure
Identification

On Studying...

THE NEED TO KNOW PRINCIPLE

The need to know principle is summed up thus:

'If you don't need to know it, don't study it!'

This book is designed to help you pass the Sergeants' and Inspectors' exams at first attempt.

It is a 'no nonsense - no frills' book aimed at people who want to get as much as possible from their time spent studying, with all the verbiage thrown overboard together with everything else that seems to cloud the issues with facts, leaving only the bare bones of what you **need to** know to pass the exam. The bare bones are laid out in manageable bite-size portions which you can digest with relative ease and regurgitate when necessary. Why read the whole of the Bible if you can achieve a pass mark with a good knowledge only of the 10 Commandments? There are no semantic somersaults or linguistic limbo dancing in this book – just what you **need to know.**

MEMORY IS REPETITION

I know a three-year-old who can speak Chinese. Surprised? You shouldn't be, he lives in China.

We are all born with a blank sheet [our brain where we keep our memory]. That sheet has things imprinted on it, language say, and we learn the most difficult things possible, with apparent ease - how come? By repetition. By hearing the same thing over and over again we memorise something as difficult as a language. Police Officers fail exams, not because they have misunderstood a section of legislation when they **read it,** but because they did not **learn it.** Reading and learning are two different things. Learning takes place when you can remember or write down what you have read. By constant repetition information is memorised and when memorised it is learned. Why do you have to write down other people's telephone numbers but not your own. Repetition has caused you to memorise your number and therefore it is learned. Read this book over and over again until you reach a point whereby you know what's on the next page. When you reach that point

ON STUDYING...

you have learned it. The enormity of what you have to learn seems daunting. It actually begs the question 'How do you eat an elephant'?

Any elephant eater will tell you, one piece at a time. Learn 10 pages and have your partner test your knowledge. He or she needs no police knowledge in that the pages are set as questions and answers. Once you have satisfactorily mastered the first 10 pages, go onto the next. Remember, one piece at a time. Stick to basic facts, don't allow anything to cloud the issue with facts.

Do not stray from the concept of **KISS** - Keep it simple **stupid!**
And remember the elephant.

You need to score 75% to gain a pass mark - **GO FOR IT**

Tom Barron
Cannington
Somerset

Part I - General Police Duties

POLICE

Q What is the jurisdiction of a Police Officer?

A He has all the powers of a constable throughout England & Wales and the adjacent United Kingdom waters.   S 30 THE POLICE ACT 1996

Q What is the jurisdiction of a Special Constable?

A He has all the powers of a constable:

[a] in his own force area, and where there is a coast, the UK waters;
[b] in forces contiguous [next to] his own force area, and
[c] in other forces where he is sent as part of a mutual aid scheme,

and in the case of The City of London Police

[a] The City of London;
[b] The Metropolitan Police, and
[c] in forces next to The Metropolitan Police.

S 30[2] THE POLICE ACT 1996

Q Explain cross-border arrest without warrant?

A

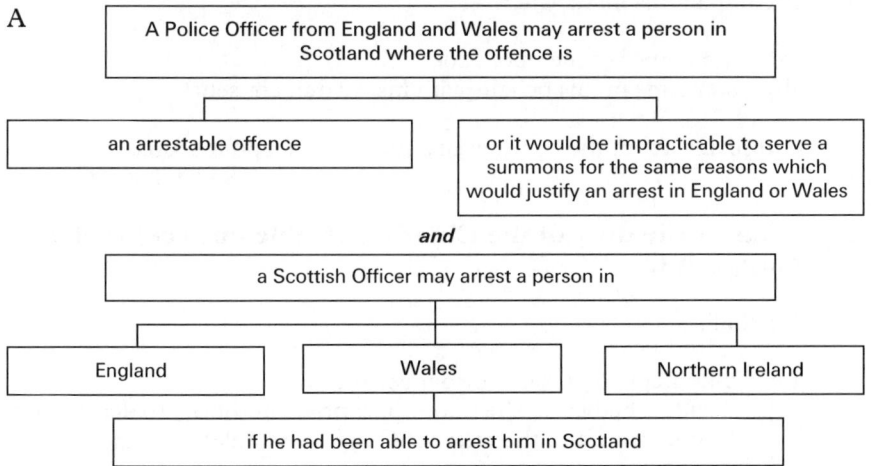

S 139 THE CRIMINAL JUSTICE AND PUBLIC ORDER ACT 1994

POLICE

Q   What is meant by Vicarious Liability of Chief Officer of Police?

A   The Chief Officer of Police is responsible for paying out damages arising from civil actions made against his officers, but not officers seconded to central services, e.g. National Crime Squad [when liability rests with the Home Office].

S 88 POLICE ACT 1996

Q   Can a Police Officer be a member of a Trade Union?

A   **No.** However, where he was a member before joining the police, the chief officer of police may consent to him remaining a member. Any police officer may be a member of the Police Federation.

S 64 POLICE ACT 1996

Q   What punishments are provided for under the disciplinary code?

A   Dismissal, requirement to resign, reduction in rank, reduction in pay, fine, reprimand and caution.

PACE ACT 1984

Q   What is meant by a complaint?

A   A complaint is made where

[a]   a member of the public, or
[b]   someone on his behalf [with his written consent]

complains about the conduct of a member of a police force

S 84[4] PACE ACT 1984

Q   What is the duty of the Chief Constable on receipt of a complaint?

A   He shall:

[a]   take steps to preserve evidence, and
[b]   decide whether he/she is the appropriate authority to deal with it. [if not, send it to the relevant Chief Constable]

POLICE

If he/she is the appropriate authority

[a] the complaint must be recorded, and
[b] a decision made as to whether the complaint is capable of informal resolution.

Q **When can a complaint be informally resolved?**

A The complainant must consent and, if proved, the chief must be satisfied it would not justify criminal or disciplinary proceedings.

Q **What if it is not suitable for informal resolution?**

A The Chief must appoint an investigating officer. If an officer had initially been appointed to informally resolve the complaint and found that it was incapable of informal resolution then he may not be appointed to investigate the complaint formally.

Q **When shall the Chief Constable refer complaints to the Police Complaints Authority?**

A Where a complaint alleges that the conduct of the officer resulted in:

[a] the death, or
[b] serious injury of any person.

S 89[I] PACE Act 1984

Q **When MAY the Chief Constable refer a matter to the Police Complaints Authority?**

A Where it appears that

[a] an officer may have committed a criminal offence, or
[b] he may have behaved in a manner justifying disciplinary proceedings,
[c] the matter is not the subject of a complaint, and

It appears to the Chief Constable that it ought to be referred by reason of:

[i] its gravity, or
[ii] exceptional circumstances.

S 88 PACE Act 1984

POLICE

Unsatisfactory Performance

The Police [Efficiency] Regulations 1999 apply as follows:

Apply to	Do not apply to
Constables	Cadets
Sergeants	Probationers
Inspectors	Chief Supt and above
Chief Inspectors	
Superintendents	

Q The Purpose of the Regulations

A To deal with matters of poor performance

Q Who are the players?

A The member: The officer subject to complaint
Reporting officer: The line manager [police or civilian]
Countersigning officer: Inspector, Chief Inspector or Superintendent. Where the reporting officer is a civilian he shall liase with a Police Officer

Q Unsatisfactory Performance - what happens first?

A 1. Evidence of unsatisfactory work is:
   [a] noted in the workplace, or
   [b] arises from a complaint by a member of the public.

2. In the event of a single or occasional act, advice may be given.

3. If there is a pattern of poor performance, formal action may be required.

4. The officer is given time and help to remedy the problem.

5. [a] If performance is improved - NFA,
   [b] If performance is not improved it shall be recorded and formal procedures started.

POLICE

The 1st Interview - procedure

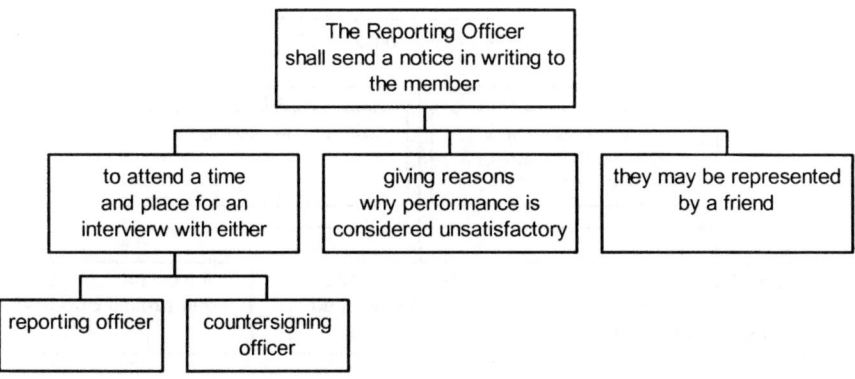

Q What if the reporting officer is a civilian?

A Where the member is a constable and his line manager is a civilian, a police officer will run the proceedings.

Q Reporting officer or countersigning officer - whose choice?

A The member may within seven days request that the interview be conducted by the countersigning officer.

Q Who is the friend?

A An officer of any rank can take the role of friend as long as they are not involved in the procedures. Their job is to advise and assist including speaking on the officer's behalf. They can call and question witnesses, produce witness statements, documentation or exhibits. They are on duty when attending meetings and may wear civilian clothes at a hearing.

POLICE

The 1ˢᵗ Interview

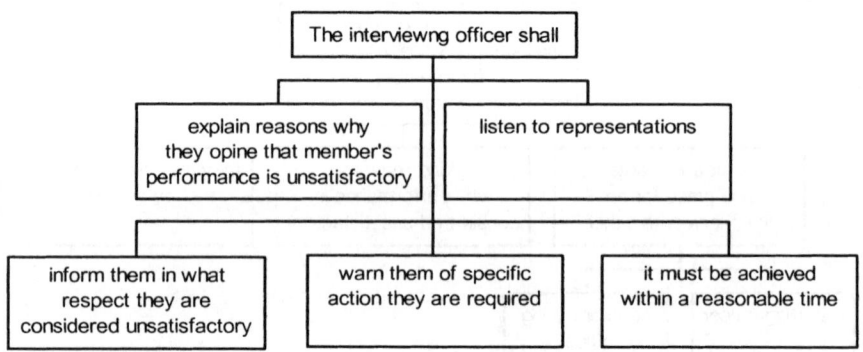

Representation
Representations can be made by the member or by their friend.

Q   What if they have a good explanation?

A   Where appropriate, NFA may be agreed.

Q   What is a reasonable time?

A   Between 3-6 months.

Recommendations
The interviewing officer may make recommendations that the member seeks assistance with health or welfare.

Record
Within seven days the interviewing officer shall make a record of the interview and send a copy to the member.

Member
Within seven may submit written comments or make no comment.

Expunge
The record shall be expunged after two years.

POLICE

Q   What are the interviewing officer's responsibilities concerning copies of the interview?

A   They must send copies of the interview and comments by the member to the:
- the senior manager, and
- the personnel officer

Q   What if the interview was conducted by the reporting officer?

A   A copy must be sent to the countersigning officer.

Q   What if the interview was conducted by the countersigning officer?

A   A copy must be sent to the reporting officer.

Q   What is meant by [a] the senior manager and [b] the personnel officer?

[a]   the supervisor of the countersigning officer

[b]   the police officer or civilian responsible for personnel.

The Decision to hold a 2nd Interview
Where the Reporting Officer opines that the member who was warned and at the end of the period has not made sufficient improvement they may refer the matter to the countersigning officer. The countersigning officer may, after consulting the personnel officer, order a 2nd interview.

2nd Interview - notices

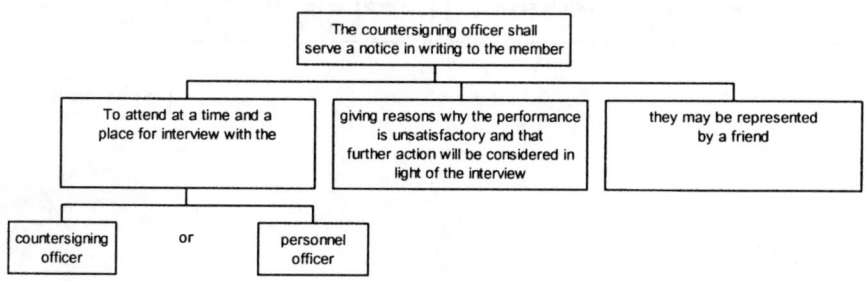

7

POLICE

On whom must copy notices be served ?
- reporting officer
- personnel officer
- senior manager

The 2nd Interview

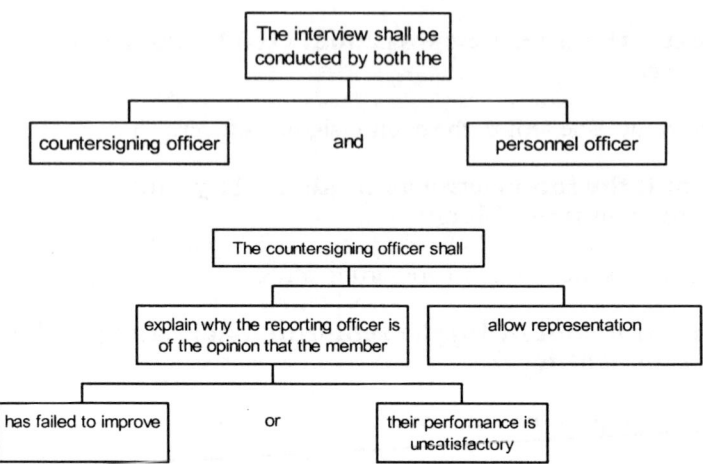

then...

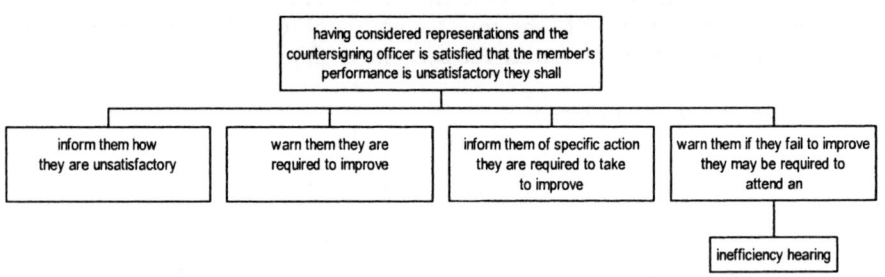

POLICE

Q   Who makes a copy of the record of interview?

A   It shall be made by the countersigning officer and the personnel officer.

Q   Who receives a copy?

A   The member and their friend together with a notice.

Q   What does the notice contain?

A   It confirms the warning and informs the member that they can [within seven days] submit written comments or not.

Q   Who else receives copies?

A   The countersigning officer shall send a copy of the record and written comments by the member to:
- the reporting officer
- personnel officer, and
- senior manager.

Assessment of Performance
Within 14 days of the specified period [3-6 months] the countersigning officer in consultation with the reporting officer shall assess the performance of the member and they shall inform the member in writing whether or not there has been a sufficient improvement in performance.

If the countersigning officer opines that there has been insufficient improvement the member must be informed that they may be required to attend an inefficiency hearing [not sooner than 21 or later than 56 days from notification]. The countersigning officer shall inform the senior manager who may direct that an inefficiency hearing be arranged.

POLICE

The Inefficiency Hearing

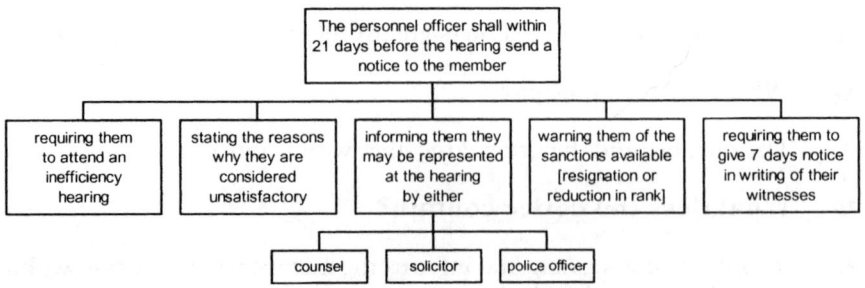

Q   Who conducts the Hearing?

A   City of London Police   Commander + 2 Superintendents

   Metropolitan Police   Commander + 2 Superintendents

   Provincial Forces   ACC + 2 Superintendents

The hearing must be in private unless the chairman and member agree to it being in public.

Documents to be made available

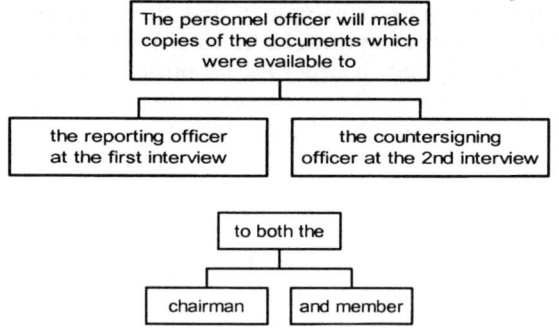

POLICE

Postponement and Adjournment

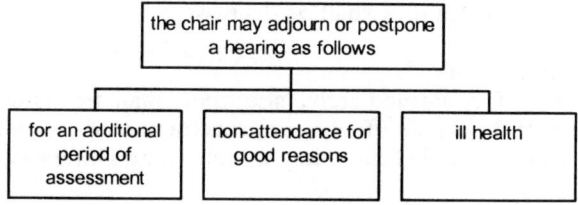

The Finding

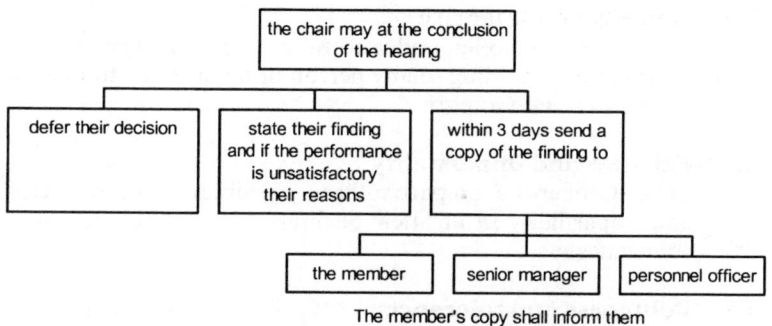

The Sanctions

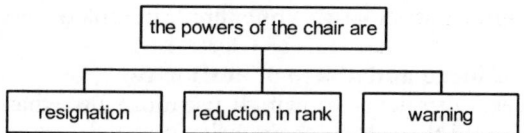

POLICE

Resignation
This means one month after receipt of the notice or a later date, where they refuse to resign they shall be dismissed.

Reduction in rank
This takes effect immediately, and they shall be issued a written warning that unless a sufficient improvement in their performance is made within a specified time they will face a first interview.

Discipline – the code of conduct

The Code of Conduct

1. **Honesty and integrity**
   Officers shall be open and truthful in their dealings; avoid being improperly beholding to any person or institution, and discharge their duties with integrity.

2. **Fairness and impartiality**
   Police Officers have a particular responsibility to act with fairness and impartiality in all their dealings with the public and their colleagues.

3. **Politeness and tolerance**
   Officers should treat members of the public and colleagues with courtesy and respect, avoiding abusive or deriding attitudes or behaviour. In particular, officers must avoid: favouritism of an individual or group; all forms of harassment, victimisation or unreasonable discrimination; and overbearing conduct to a colleague, particularly to one junior in rank or service.

4. **Use of force and abuse of authority**
   Officers must never knowingly use more force than is reasonable, nor should they abuse their authority.

5. **Performance of duties**
   Officers should be conscientious and diligent in the performance of their duties. Officers should attend work promptly when rostered for duty. If absent through sickness or injury, they should avoid activities likely to retard their return to duty.

POLICE

6. **Lawful orders**
   The police service is a disciplined body. Unless there is good and sufficient cause to do otherwise, officers must obey all lawful orders and abide by the provisions of Police Regulations. Officers should support their colleagues in the execution of their lawful duties, and oppose any improper behaviour, reporting it where appropriate.

7. **Confidentiality**
   Information that comes into the possession of the police should be treated as confidential. It should not be used for personal benefit and nor should it be divulged to other parties except in the proper course of police duty. Similarly, officers should respect, as confidential, information about force policy and operations unless authorised to disclose it in the course of their duties.

8. **Criminal offences**
   Officers must report any proceedings for a criminal offence taken against them. Conviction of a criminal offence may of itself result in further action being taken.

9. **Property**
   Officers must exercise reasonable care to prevent loss or damage to property excluding their own property but including police property.

10. **Sobriety**
    Whilst on duty officers must be sober. Officers should not consume alcohol when on duty unless specifically authorised to do so or it becomes necessary for the proper discharge of police duty.

11. **Appearance**
    Unless on duties which dictate otherwise, officers should always be well turned out, clean and tidy whilst on duty in uniform or in plain clothes.

12. **General conduct**
    Whether on or off duty, police officers should not behave in a way which is likely to bring discredit upon the police service.

POLICE

Schedule 1 of the Police [Conduct] Regulations, 1999

The superintendent who has had too much to drink: Home Office guidance suggests that superintendents will be classed as being on duty while they are 'on call'. They will not be on duty by reason only of their general 24-hour responsibility for their own area of command. The guidance further provides that an officer who is unexpectedly called out for duty should be able, at no risk of discredit, to say that he has had too much to drink.

Restrictions on Private Lives
A member of a police force:
1. shall at all times abstain from any activity which is likely to interfere with the impartial discharge of their duties or which is likely to give rise to the impression amongst members of the public that it may so interfere, and in particular a member of a police force shall not take any active part in politics. [They may however be a school governor]
2. shall not reside at premises not approved by the chief officer of police;
3. shall not, without the previous consent of the chief officer of police, take in a lodger in a house or quarters with which they are provided by the police authority, or sub-let any part of the house or quarters
4. shall not, unless they have given written notice to the chief officer of police, take in a lodger in a house in which they reside and in respect of which they receive rent allowance, or sub-let any part of such a house, and
5. shall not wilfully refuse or neglect to discharge lawful debts.

THE POLICE REGS 1995, SCH 2

Business Interests
If [a] a police officer, or [b] a relative,

propose to have, or have a 'business interest', the officer shall give written notice to the chief officer of police, [unless they did so when appointed]. The chief officer of police shall determine whether the interest is compatible with the officer remaining a police officer and shall notify them in writing.

POLICE

A business interest is where a police officer or relative:

1. holds any office or employment for hire or carries on any business
2. a shop [or like business] is carried on by the officer's spouse in the police area, or by a relative living with them, or
3. the officer, their spouse or relative living with them has a pecuniary interest in any licence or permit granted in relation to:
   a) liquor licensing
   b) refreshment house
   c) betting or gaming
   d) regulating places of entertainment

Relative includes spouse, parent, son, daughter, brother or sister.

Constables on Licensed Premises

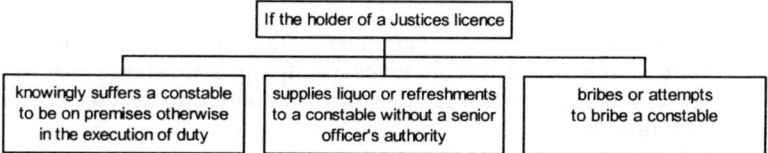

The meaning of knowingly suffering
The landlord's knowledge relates to him both [1] knowing they are a constable and [2] knowing that they are on duty.

Who is guilty?
Where a constable and sergeant visit licensed premises and accept a cup of coffee from the licensee, the PC commits no offence because they have a senior officer's authority [the Sergeant]. The Sergeant however commits the offence because they have no such authority!

POLICE

Impersonating a Police Officer

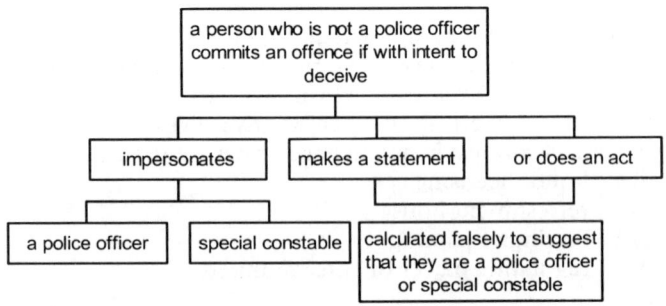

S 90[1], THE POLICE ACT, 1996

Wearing or Possessing Uniform
Any person who is not a police officer:

1. Wearing uniform – wears any article of police uniform in circumstances where it gives them an appearance so nearly resembling a police officer as to be calculated to deceive commits an offence.
2. Possessing uniform – has in their possession any article of police uniform shall, unless they prove that they obtained possession:
   a) lawfully, and
   b) has possession for a lawful purpose
   commits an offence.

S 90 THE POLICE ACT, 1996

What is an article?
An article of police uniforms means:

- uniform
- a distinctive badge or mark, or
- documents of identification.

Causing Disaffection
It is an offence to:

a) cause [or attempt], or do an act calculated to cause disaffection amongst the members of any police force, or
b) induce [or attempt] or do any act calculated to induce any member of a police force to withhold their services.

S91 THE POLICE ACT 1996

POLICE

Q **What is the offence of Constables being on licensed premises?**

A

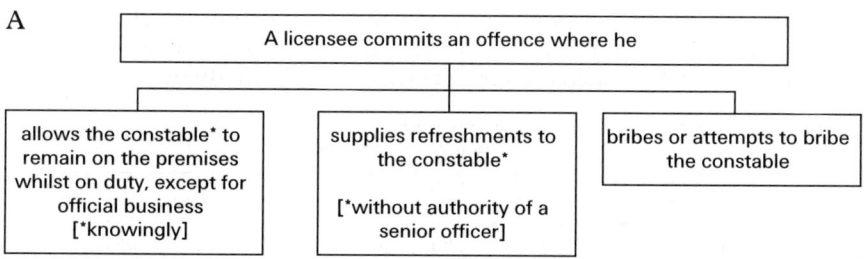

S 178 LICENSING ACT 1964

Q **What is the offence of impersonating a police officer?**

A

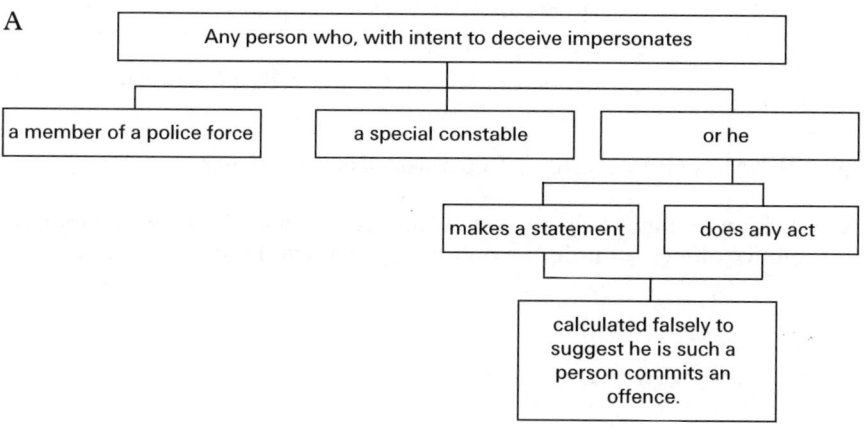

S 90[L] POLICE ACT 1996

POLICE

Q What is the offence of wearing/possessing a police uniform?

A Any person [not a police officer] who **wears any article** of police uniform in circumstances that give him the appearance of a police officer which is calculated to deceive, commits an offence.

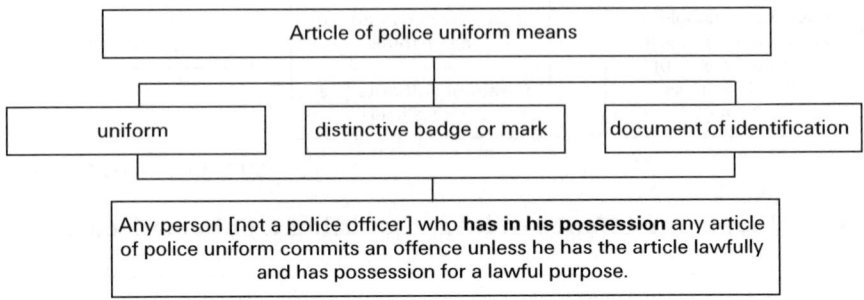

S 90[2] & [3] POLICE ACT 1996

Q What is the offence of causing disaffection?

A It is an offence to do any act calculated to cause disaffection amongst police officers or induce a police officer to withhold his services.

S 91[1] POLICE ACT 1996

POLICE POWERS

Q What are your powers to stop and search under S 1 PACE

A
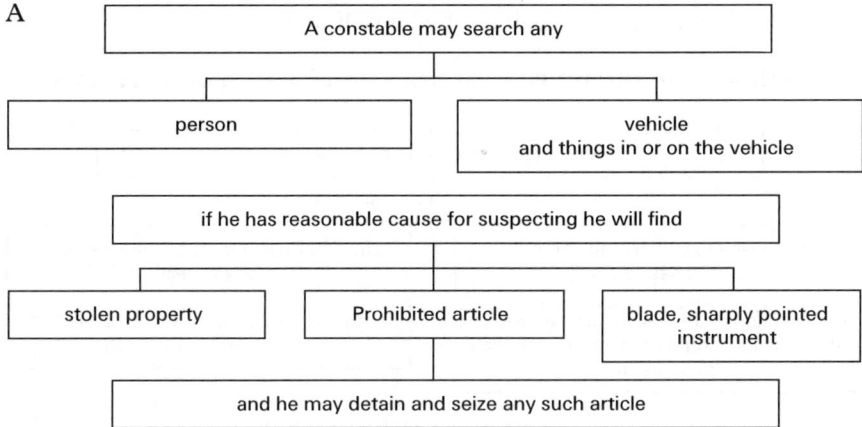

Q What is meant by a prohibited article?

A
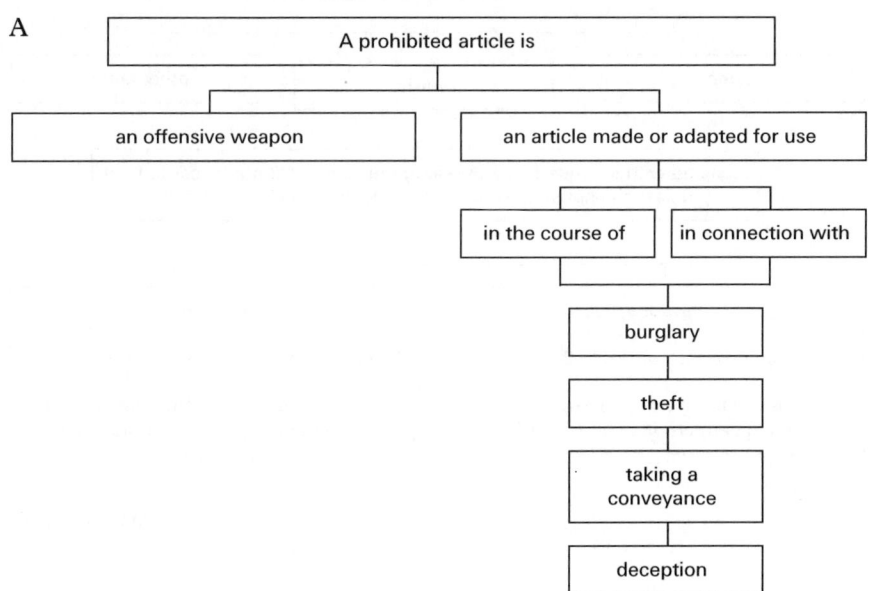

POLICE POWERS

Q **What is meant by an offensive weapon?**

A Offensive weapon means any article:

[a] made or adapted for use for causing injury to any person, or
[b] intending it for such use by himself or another.

Q **Where can the powers to Stop and Search be exercised?**

A

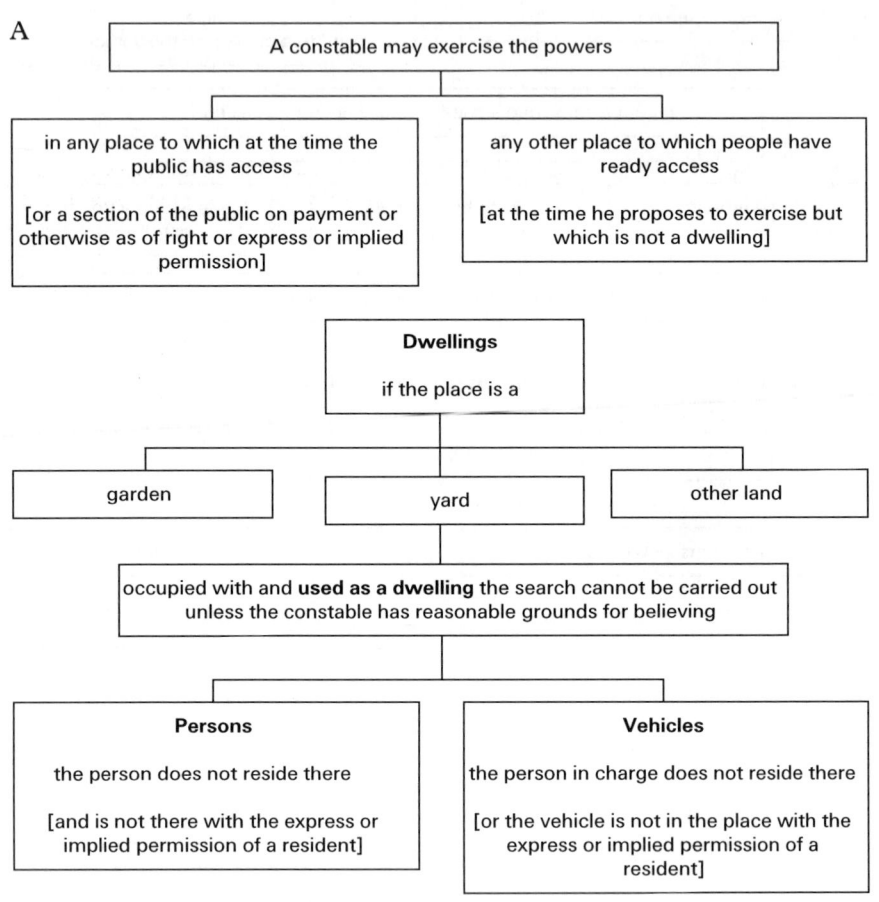

S 1 PACE Act 1984

POLICE POWERS

Q   What must be done before a search is carried out?

A
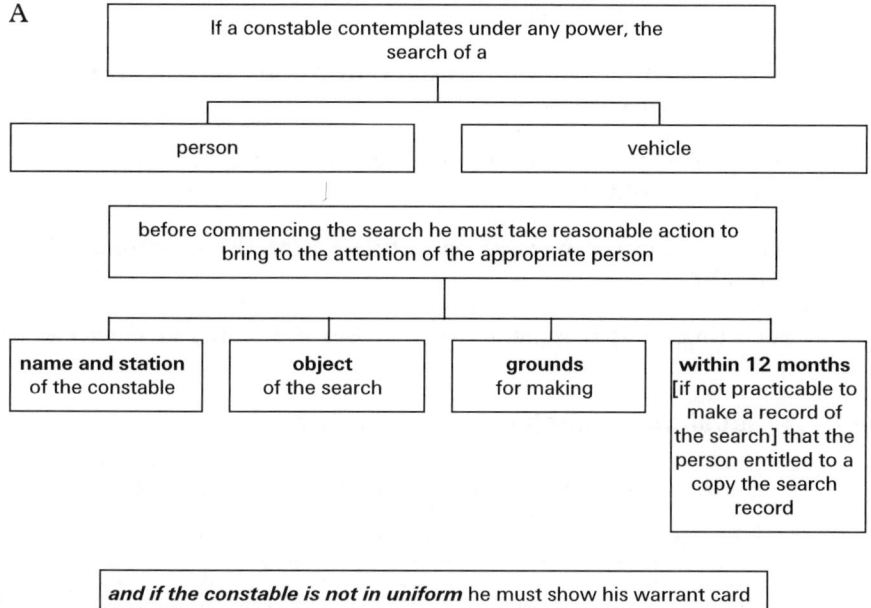

S 2/3 PACE Act 1984

Q   What is meant by the Appropriate Person?

A   [a]   where a person is searched, that person.
    [b]   where a vehicle is searched [or anything in or on it] the person in charge of the vehicle.

Q   What should be left on a Searched Unattended Vehicle?

A   A notice stating:

   [a]   the vehicle has been searched;
   [b]   the police station to which the officer is attached; [not his name]
   [c]   an application for compensation for damage to the vehicle which can be made at [b], and
   [d]   the owner and person in charge of the vehicle are entitled to a copy of the search record for up to 12 months.

POLICE POWERS

Q What does Vehicle include?

A Vessels, aircraft and hovercraft.

Q What clothing can be removed in public for the purpose of a Person Check?

A Outer coat, jacket and gloves. This restriction does not apply to searches elsewhere.

Q How long can a person be detained for the purposes of a search?

A Such time as is reasonable to carry out the search at the scene or nearby.

Q What shall a search record contain?

A

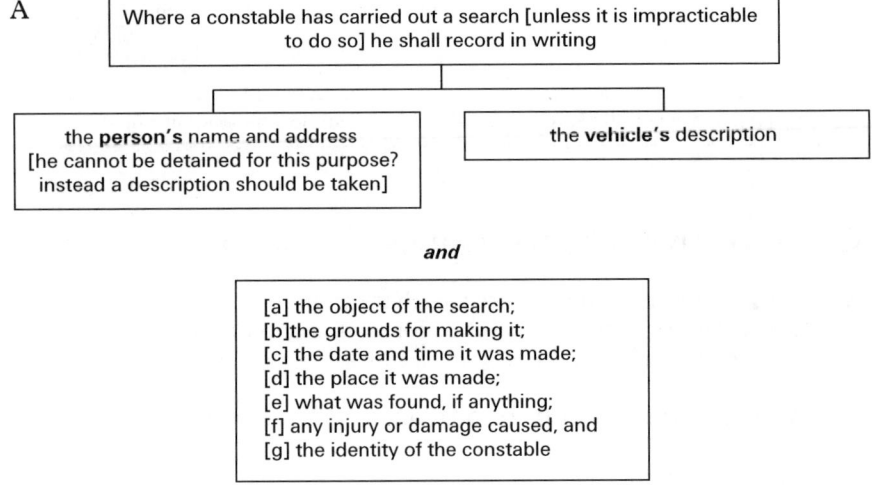

Where a constable has carried out a search [unless it is impracticable to do so] he shall record in writing

the **person's** name and address [he cannot be detained for this purpose? instead a description should be taken]

the **vehicle's** description

and

[a] the object of the search;
[b] the grounds for making it;
[c] the date and time it was made;
[d] the place it was made;
[e] what was found, if anything;
[f] any injury or damage caused, and
[g] the identity of the constable

POLICE POWERS

Q What record has to be kept when searching people entering Football Grounds?

A None. Nothing in the codes affects the routine searching of persons entering sports grounds or other premises with their consent, or, as a condition of entry.

Q What is a Road Check?

A

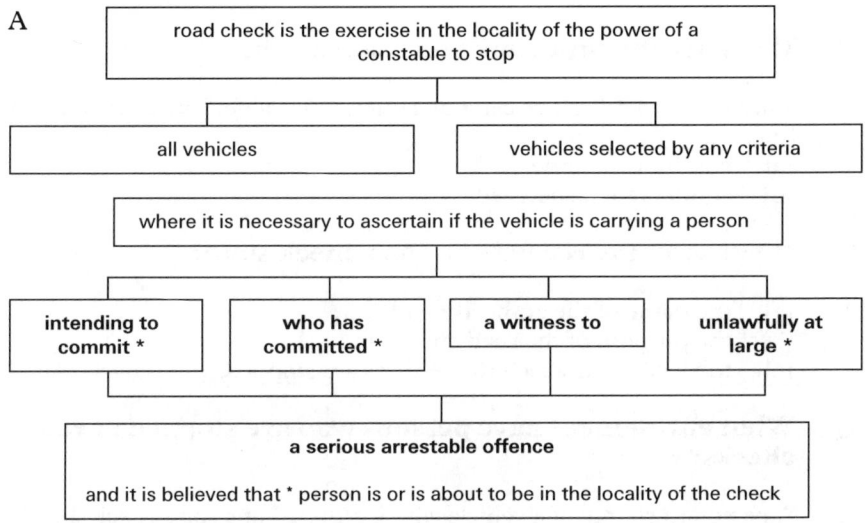

SEC 4 PACE ACT 1984

Q Give an example of vehicles stopped by any criteria

A Stopping all yellow Escorts carrying three youths ... all blue VWs ... all white vans. etc.

Q Who may authorise a road check?

A A **superintendent,** in writing, however an officer of **any rank in the case of urgency** in which case he must, as soon as possible, make a written record of the time he gives it and cause a superintendent to be informed.

POLICE POWERS

Q Can a superintendent discontinue the road check when reported to him?

A Yes, he may
[a] authorise it to continue, in writing, or discontinue the check and record in writing:

  [i] the fact that it took place, and
  [ii] its purpose.

Q What are the time limits on road checks?

A 7 **days,** which cannot be extended but is renewable. The check may be:

[a] continuous, or be
[b] conducted at specified times.

Q What shall the record of a road check state?

A [a] the name of the authorising officer;
[b] the purpose of the road check, and
[c] the locality in which the vehicles are stopped.

Q What entitlement have persons who are stopped at road checks?

A A person in charge of a vehicle who is stopped at a road check shall be entitled to a written statement of the purpose of the check if he applies for it not later than **12 months** from the date of being stopped.

Q What is not a road check?

A Stopping vehicles for road traffic offences, excise offences, or the stopping of vehicles for any purpose other than those mentioned in Section 4.

POLICE POWERS

Q What stop powers are there under the Criminal Justice & Public Order Act 1994?

A

> Where a **superintendent** reasonably believes incidents involving **serious violence** may take place in a locality in his area and it is expedient to prevent their occurrence, he may give authorisation to

- **stop**
  - Persons
- **search**
  - vehicles, drivers and passengers

for

- offensive weapons
- dangerous instruments

S 60 CJ & PO Act 1994

Q How long does the authorisation last?

A **24 hours.** It cannot be extended unless offences *have been* committed.

Q Who else can give the authorisation?

A An **inspector** who must then inform the superintendent.

Q Does the officer stopping and searching need reasonable suspicion to act?

A No. The authorisation to search is enough.

POLICE POWERS

Q **What are the Stop Search powers under the Prevention of Terrorism Act 1989?**

A

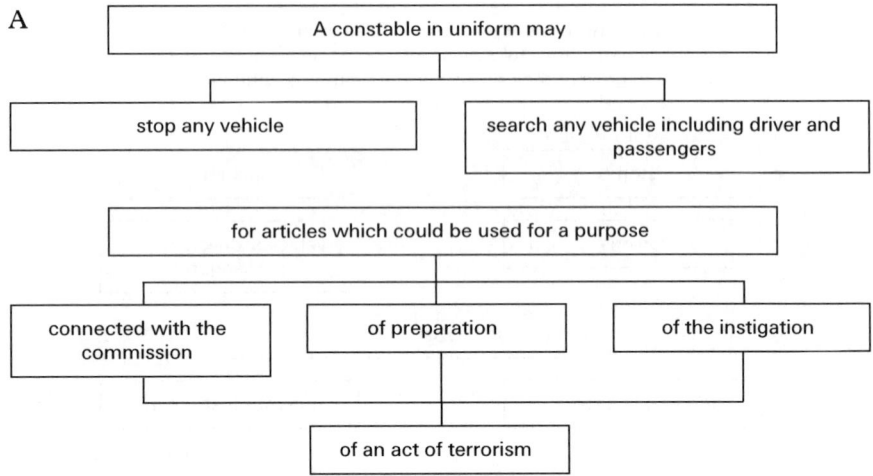

Q **What did the Prevention of Terrorism [Additional Powers] Act 1996 do?**

A   Extended the above to include pedestrians

Q **What is the power of arrest for an arrestable offence?**

A   **Any person** may arrest

   [a]   anyone **who is in the act** of committing an arrestable offence;
   [b]   anyone whom he has reasonable grounds for suspecting **to be committing** an arrestable offence.

   Where an arrestable offence **has been committed** any person may arrest:

   [a]   anyone **who is guilty** of the offence;
   [b]   anyone who he has reasonable grounds **for suspecting to be guilty** of it.

POLICE POWERS

A constable may arrest:

[a] where he has reasonable grounds for **suspecting** that an arrestable offence has been committed, any person whom he has reasonable grounds **for suspecting** to be guilty of the offence; and

[b] anyone who is **about to commit** an arrestable offence; and

[c] anyone who he has reasonable grounds **for suspecting to be about to commit** an arrestable offence.

S 24 PACE Act 1984

Q   What information must be given on arrest?

A   [a] the person is under arrest;
    [b] the grounds for arrest, however

the above does not apply if is impracticable to inform him by reason of his having escaped arrest.

Q   What did Christie v Leachinsky [1947] decide?

A   The reason for the arrest must be the **real reason** in the officer's mind at the time, and they must clearly indicate the reason for arrest at the time.

POLICE POWERS

Q What is an arrestable offence?

A

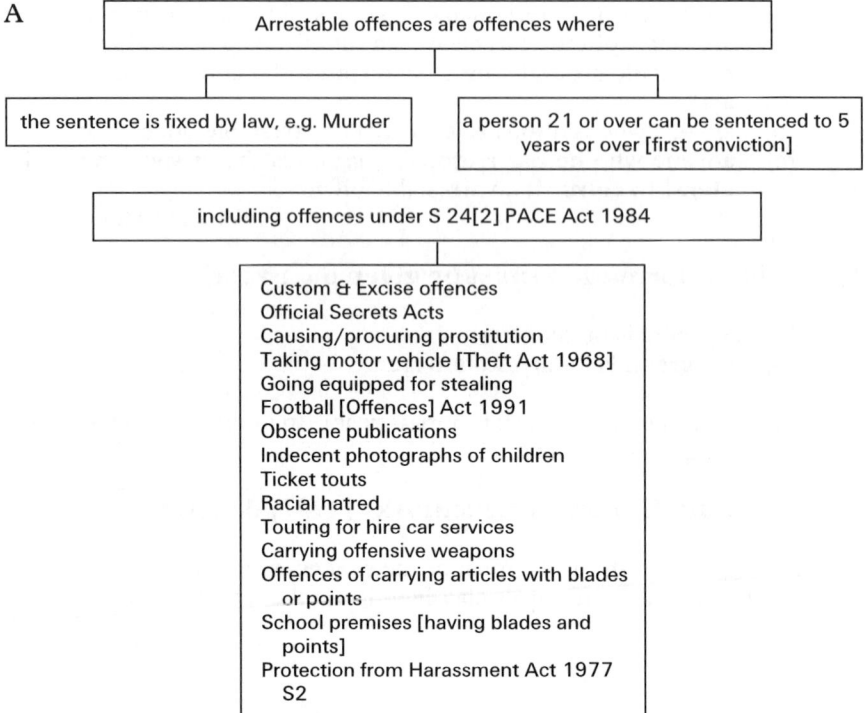

Q When does an Arrestable Offence become a Serious Arrestable Offence?

A Any arrestable offence will be serious if the commission would lead to, or is intended to lead to:

[a] serious harm to the security of the state or public order;
[b] serious interference with the administration of justice or with the investigation of offences;
[c] the death of any person;
[d] serious injury to any person;
[e] substantial financial gain to any person; and
[f] serious financial loss to any person.

S 116[6] PACE Act 1984

POLICE POWERS

Q **What is meant by serious loss?**

A This is based on the victim's circumstances, the test is subjective, 'is it serious for the person who suffers it'?

Q **What are the general arrest conditions?**

A

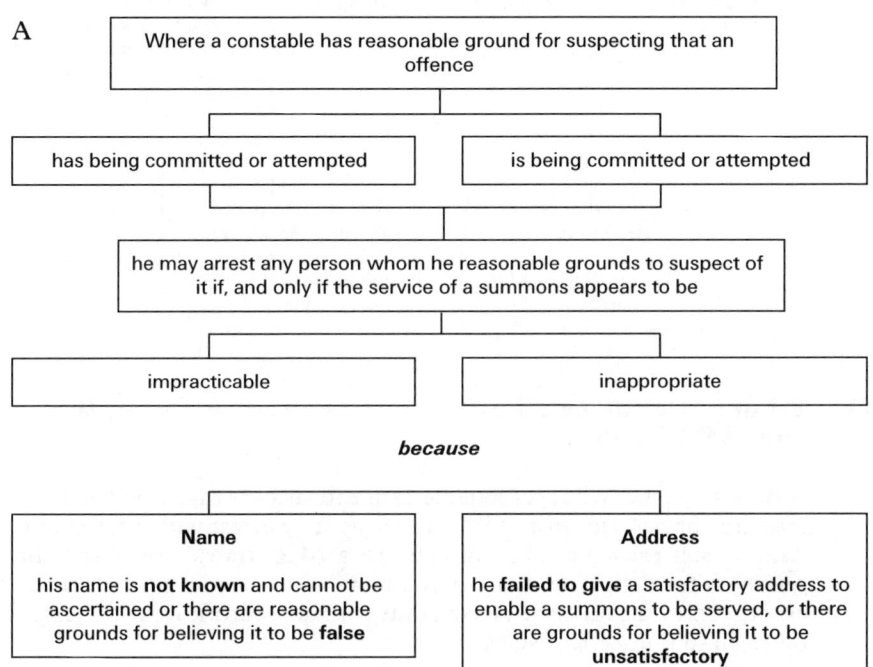

Note

An address is satisfactory if

[a] that person will be at the address long enough for the service of a summons; or
[b] that some other person specified will accept the summons on his behalf

POLICE POWERS

Q What power of arrest exists for absentees and deserters from HM Forces?

A Where a constable has reasonable cause to suspect that a person is an absentee or deserter from HM Forces he may arrest without warrant. The person must be taken directly to a Magistrates' court and the service informed. The court may remand in custody until a service escort can be arranged. The court must issue a certificate which must be given to the service escort.

POLICE POWERS

Q Explain the fingerprint recall provisions of PACE

A

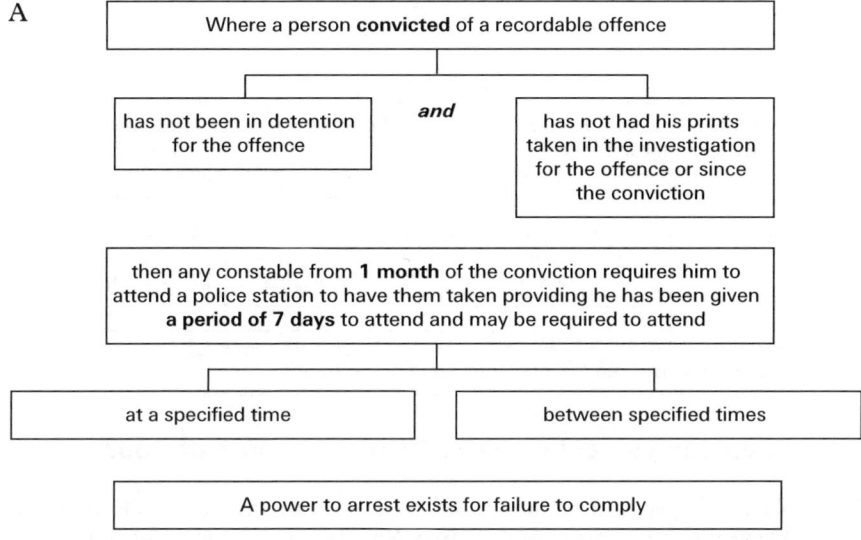

S 27 PACE Act 1084

Q What power of arrest exists for failure to answer police bail?

A Persons who are in breach of surrender to police bail may be arrested and taken to the original bailing police station where they will be treated as if arrested for the original offence.

Q What are the rules concerning voluntary attendance at a police station?

A Where a person voluntarily attends a police station [or anywhere where a constable is present] and is assisting with an investigation and is not under arrest he shall be:
  [a] entitled to leave at will, and
  [b] informed at once that he is under arrest if a decision has been made to prevent him from leaving, and
  [c] if he is under arrest at a police station and it appears that if he were released from that arrest, he would be liable to arrest for another offence, he shall be arrested for that other offence.

POLICE POWERS

Q After arrest, where shall a person be taken?

A
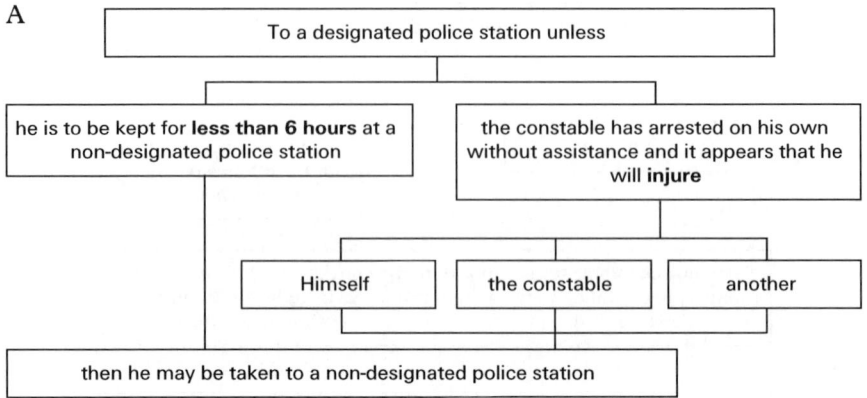

Q When can you delay taking him to a police station?

A When his presence is necessary to carry out investigations that are reasonable to carry out **immediately,** e.g. checking an alibi, recovering property etc.

S 30 PACE Act 1984

POWERS OF ENTRY

Q What provisions exist for the application of a search warrant?

A The application will be made by an **inspector** unless he is not available and the case is **urgent** when the senior officer on duty may make the application and he must state:

[a] the grounds for the application;
[b] the Act under which it would be issued;
[c] the premises to be searched;
[d] the identity of the articles/persons sought;

The application must be supported by written information.

Q How often can the same search warrant he executed?

A Once only, within 1 month.

Q What shall the warrant specify?

A [a] the name of the person applying for it;
[b] the date of issue;
[c] the Act under which it is issued;
[d] the premises to be searched, and
[e] identify the articles/persons sought [if possible].

Q What is the procedure for executing a search warrant?

A It shall be executed by a constable at a reasonable hour unless that would frustrate its purpose.

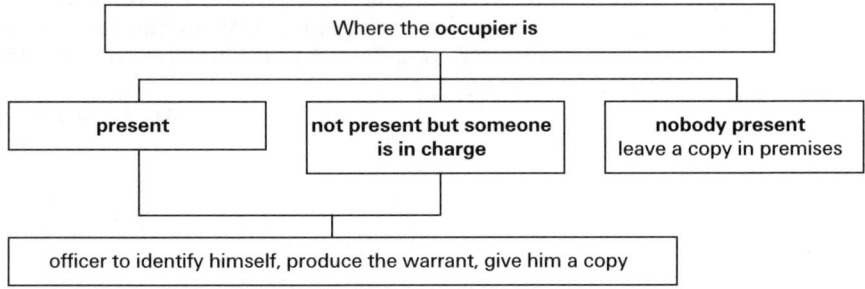

POWERS OF ENTRY

Q What shall be endorsed on the warrant?

A [a] whether the articles or persons were found;
[b] apart from what was sought, was anything else seized.

Q If a warrant is wrongly addressed can it be executed?

A No.

Q What are the provisions for a search warrant for a serious arrestable offence?

A The constable must satisfy a JP that there are reasonable grounds for believing:

[a] a serious arrestable offence has been committed; and
[b] there is material on the premises likely to be of substantial value to the investigation of the offence; and
[c] it is likely to be relevant evidence; and
[d] that it does not consist of:

[i] items subject to legal privilege;
[ii] excluded material; or
[iii] special procedural material, and
[iv] a condition at e] below applies, he may issue a starch warrant:

[e] [i] it is not practicable to communicate with any person entitled to grant **entry to the premises;**
[ii] a person at [i] can be found but it is not practicable to communicate with any person entitled to grant **access to the evidence;**
[iii] entry will not be granted unless a warrant is produced;
[iv] the search may be frustrated or seriously prejudiced unless the constable arriving at the premises can **secure immediate entry.**

S 8 PACE Act 1984

POWERS OF ENTRY

Q What is meant by an S 18 PACE [Inspectors] authority to search?

A

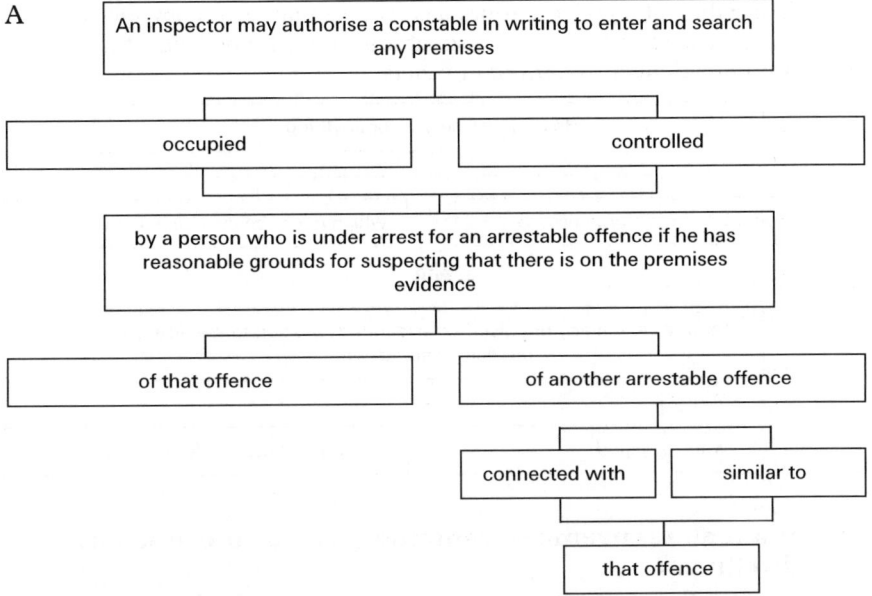

Q Can a constable conduct an S 18 search without authorisation?

A Yes. A constable can conduct the search before taking the person to the police station if his presence is necessary for the effective investigation of the offence. He must inform an inspector as soon as practicable after the search.

Q What must be recorded in writing regarding the search authority?

A The grounds for the search and the nature of the evidence sought.

POWERS OF ENTRY

Q What are your powers of entry under S 32 PACE following arrest?

A Other than at a police station, a constable may search any person who has been arrested if he has reasonable grounds for believing that he may present a danger to himself or others.

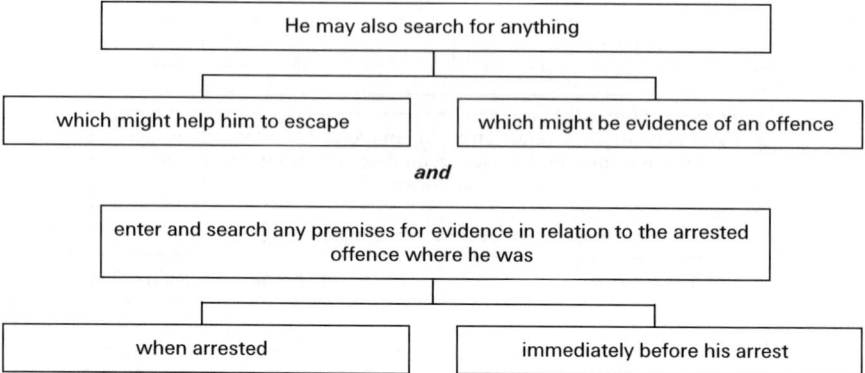

Q What about premises containing two or more separate dwellings?

A

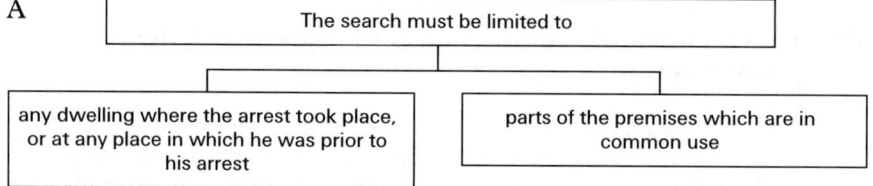

Q Outline your powers of entry under S 17 of PACE

A A constable may enter and search any premises for the purposes of:

[a] executing a warrant for arrest or committal;
[b] arresting for an arrestable offence;
[c] arresting for offences under:

[i] prohibition of uniforms Sl Public Order Act 1936;
[ii] offences of entering and remaining on property Criminal Law Act 1977;

POWERS OF ENTRY

    [iii] fear of provocation of violence S4 Public Order Act 1986;
    [iv] failing to comply with interim possession order;

[d] arresting any child or young person who is remanded to the care of the local authority;
[e] recapturing a person unlawfully at large;
[f] saving life and limb;
[g] preventing serious damage to property.

Q **Must the officer have reasonable grounds for believing the person is on the premises?**

A Yes, except in the case [f] & [g], above.

Q **Is there a power of entry for a breach of the peace?**

A Yes, if need be by force.

Q **What are your powers of entry in relation to fires?**

A Under the provisions of The Fire Services Act 1947 a constable may enter and if necessary break into any premises or place in which a fire has, or is reasonably believed to have, broken out or of protecting the premises from acts done for fire-fighting reasons.

Q **What are your powers of seizure under S 19 of PACE?**

A

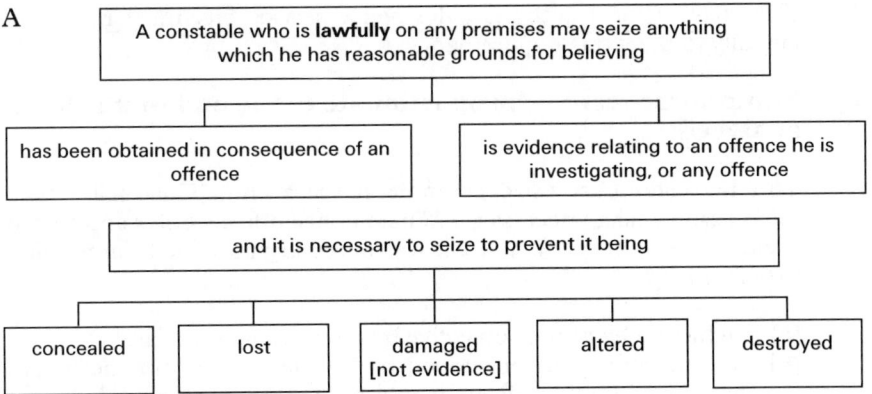

POWERS OF ENTRY

Q Which material cannot be seized?

A [a] Legally privileged material;
   [b] excluded material; and
   [c] special procedural material.

Q Under the Human Rights Act 1998, what is meant by the 3 tests ?

A The tests are :

   [a] Prescribed by law;
   [b] intended to achieve a legitimate objective, and
   [c] proportionate to the end that is to be achieved.

Q Summarise test 1 – 'prescribed by law'

A An individual has the right to ask "where did you get the power to act as you did"? and the state must be able to give an answer i.e. "from the Regulation of Investigatory Powers Act 2000". So that where an illegal telephone tap is made on a person at work, his employer may have breached his human rights.

Q Summarise test 2 – 'intended to achieve a legitimate objective'

A The state, a local authority, the police service etc, must be acting lawfully to meet this requirement.

Q Summarise test 3 – 'proportionate to the end that is to be achieved'

A The state cannot use a sledgehammer to crack a nut. The test is 'where the measures taken necessary'? Where police officers enter and search premises using more force than was necessary they might argue that they intended to :

   [a] achieve a legitimate objective by preventing crime, and
   [b] the objective was prescribed by law, ie PACE, but the means employed by the officers would have to be in proportion to the crime that was to be prevented.

POWERS OF ENTRY

Q Under the Human Rights Act 1998, when is a Public Authority acting unlawfully?

A It is unlawful for a public authority to act in a way that is incompatible with a convention right.

Q Under the Human Rights Act 1998, what is meant by a Public Authority?

A A public authority includes :

[a] a court or tribunal, including the House of Lords;
[b] police, fire and ambulance service, and
[c] any person whose functions are of a public nature, but does not include Parliament.

Q Under the Human Rights Act 1998, who can bring proceedings?

A Any person who is a victim of a breach of their rights

Q Under the Human Rights Act 1998, what are the time limits?

A **1 years** from the time of the act complained of, or longer period if the courts see fit.

Q Under the Human Rights Act 1998, what are the Convention Rights?

A 1. *The right to life.* A life may be taken only by :

[a] execution by order of a court;
[b] when it results from the use of force which is no more than absolutely necessary :
  [i] in defence of any person from unlawful violence;
  [ii] in order to effect a lawful arrest or prevent escape from lawful detention, or
  [iii] in action lawfully taken to quell a riot or insurrection.

2. *Freedom from torture.* No one shall be subjected to torture or to inhuman or degrading treatment or punishment. Oppressive interrogation techniques such as sleep deprivation, exposure to

POWERS OF ENTRY

continuous loud noise and forcing suspects to adopt uncomfortable postures has been held to be degrading and inhuman.

3. ***Freedom from slavery and forced labour.*** This does not include :

[a] work done in the ordinary course of detention;
[b] military service;
[c] service exacted during an emergency, or
[d] work done as a civic obligation.

4. ***The right to liberty and security.*** This does not include :

[a] lawful arrest, and
[b] lawful detention.

5. ***The right to a fair trial.*** Everyone is entitled to :

[a] a fair and public hearing;
[b] held within a reasonable time,
[c] by an independent and impartial legal tribunal

6. ***No punishment without crime.*** This effectively prohibits governments passing retrospective legislation making an offence of what was previously no offence, thus making criminals of otherwise lawful behaviour.

7. ***Right to a private life.*** This extends to a person's :

[a] private life.
[b] family life,
[c] home, and
[d] correspondence.

However these may be interfered with if the 3 tests can successfully be applied

[i] there is a legal authority allowing the interference;
[ii] there is a legitimate objective behind the actions and
[iii] there is a 'pressing social need' for the interference.

POWERS OF ENTRY

8. ***Freedom of thought.*** This gives people the right to freedom of:

[a] thought,
[b] conscience, and
[c] religion.

9. ***Freedom of expression.*** This gives people the right to the freedom :

[a] of expression,
[b] to have opinions, and
[c] to receive and impart information and ideas.

10. ***The right to marry.***

11. ***The right to an effective remedy.*** This applies equally to persons acting in an official capacity.

13. ***Prohibition in discrimination in conventional rights.*** This relates to :

[a] sex;
[b] race, colour;
[c] language,
[d] religion.
[e] political or other opinion,
[f] national or social origin,
[g] association with a national minority,
[h] property, birth or other status.

14. ***Derogation in time of emergency.*** This means that a State can derogate from some of its obligations under the convention during :

[a] times of **war**, or
[b] other public emergency **threatening the life of the nation.**

POWERS OF ENTRY

Q Summarise Articles 1,2 & 3 of Protocol 1

A **Article 1. *Protection of property.*** Every person is entitled to the peaceful enjoyment of his possessions. To breach this Article it must be shown that the State has :

[a] interfered with the applicant's peaceful enjoyment of his possessions, or
[b] deprived his of his possessions, or
[c] subjected those possessions to some sort of control.

Article 2. *The right to education.* No person shall be denied the right to education.
This provision requires the State to have regard to :

[a] religious, and
[b] philosophical convictions of the parents.

Article 3. *The right to free elections.* This Conventional right applies, not only to
the holding of elections, but also to rights of participation and to stand for election.

Q Summarise Protocol 6

A ***The Death Penalty.*** The death penalty is abolished **except in time of war**.

PUBLIC ORDER AND TERRORISM

Q Define a Breach of the Peace

A A breach is occasioned when an act is done or threatened which:

  [a] harms a person;
  [b] harms his property [in his presence];
  [c] is likely to cause harm; or
  [d] puts him in fear of harm.

There is no power to bail therefore he must be brought before the court to be bound over.

Q What is the power of arrest for a Breach of the Peace?

A
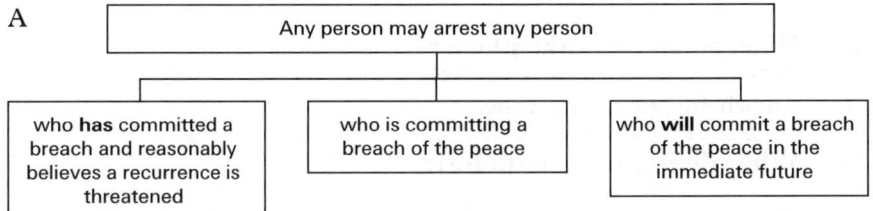

Q Where can the above power be exercised?

A Anywhere, public or private.

Q Who can arrest for Drunk and Disorderly Behaviour?

A Any person in a public place.

PUBLIC ORDER AND TERRORISM

Q   Define riot

A

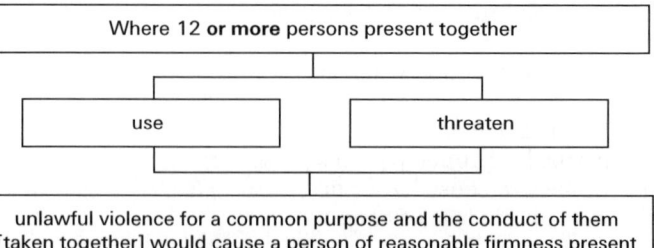

Q   Whose consent is required for the prosecution of riot?

A   DPP.

Q   Where can riot take place?

A   Anywhere, public or private.

Q   What does violence include?

A   Violence towards persons and property.

Q   Can drunkenness be a defence?

A   No, unless it was not self-induced or taken as a medicine.

Q   Define violent disorder

A

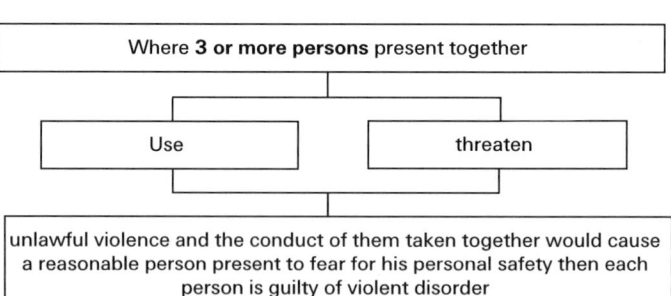

PUBLIC ORDER AND TERRORISM

Q **Define affray**

A
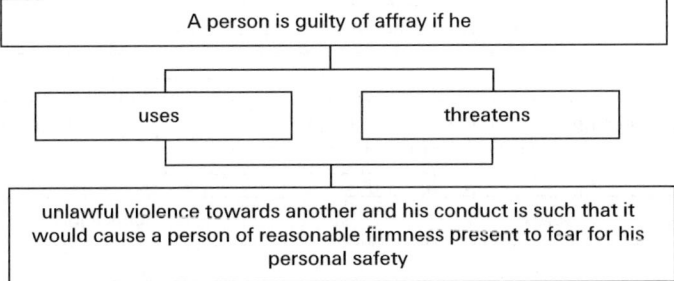

Q **Can words alone constitute a threat?**

A No.

Q **Compare riot, violent disorder and affray**

Attribute	Riot	Violent disorder	Affray
Minimum number	12	3	1
Present together	Yes	Yes	N/A
Common purpose	Yes	Not required	N/A
Unlawful violence	Person or property	Person or property	Personal only
Reasonable person	Need not be present	Need not be present	Need not be present
Who is guilty?	Actually use violence	Use or threaten violence	Use or threaten violence
Awareness/ intoxication	Provisions apply	Provisions apply	Provisions apply
Private or public	Yes	Yes	Yes
Arrest	Arrestable offence	Arrestable offence	Statutory power

PUBLIC ORDER AND TERRORISM

Q Define fear or provocation of violence

A

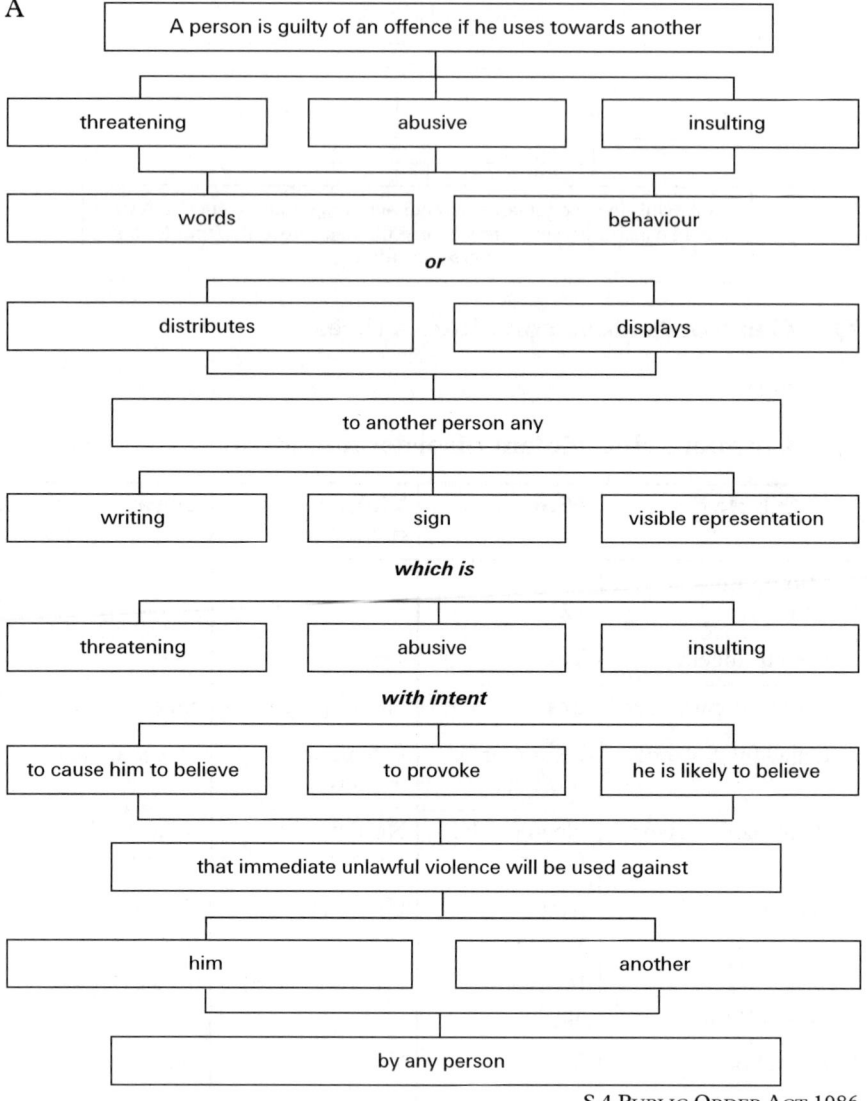

S 4 Public Order Act 1986

No **offence** where the things are done inside a dwelling and the other person is inside that or another dwelling.

PUBLIC ORDER AND TERRORISM

Q **Define a dwelling**

A Any structure or part thereof **occupied as a person's home** or as living accommodation.
Structure includes tent, caravan, vehicle, vessel or other temporary or moveable structure.

Q **What is the power of arrest for the Section 4 offence?**

A A constable may arrest anyone he reasonably suspects is committing the offence.

Q **Define the S 4A intentional harassment, alarm or distress offence**

A It is an offence, if **with intent** to cause a person harassment, alarm or distress, to:
  [a] use threatening, abusive or insulting words or behaviour, or disorderly behaviour, or
  [b] display any writing, sign or other visible representation which is threatening, abusive or insulting, thereby causing a person harassment, alarm or distress.

Defence. To prove that he was inside a dwelling and had no reason to believe that the activities would be heard or seen by a person outside that or any other dwelling, or his conduct was reasonable.

S 4A PUBLIC ORDER ACT 1986

Q **Define the S 5 harassment, alarm or distress offence**

A It is an offence to:

  [a] use threatening, abusive or insulting words or behaviour, or disorderly conduct;
  [b] display any writing, sign or other visible representation which is threatening, abusive or insulting **within the hearing or sight** of a person likely to be caused harassment, alarm or distress.

Mens rea. The offender must **intend** his actions or **he aware** of their consequences.

No **offence** if the activity is by a person **inside a dwelling** and the other person is inside that or another dwelling.

PUBLIC ORDER AND TERRORISM

Defence:
- [a] he had no reason to believe that anyone could **hear or see** his activities;
- [b] he was **inside a dwelling** and he had no reason to believe would be heard or seen by anyone outside the dwelling; or
- [c] his conduct was reasonable.

Power of arrest. Where he engages in offensive conduct which a constable **warns him to stop** and he engages in further offensive conduct immediately or shortly afterwards.

Q What effect has the Crime and Disorder Act 1998 made to racially aggravated offences ?

A The act does not create new offences but instead sets out the circumstances when an offence is racially aggravated.

Q What powers does the Powers of Criminal Courts [Sentencing] Act 2000 relate to the above ?

A The Act can increase the penalties for offences where they are shown to be racially aggravated.

Q Which offences can be deemed to be racially aggravated?

A
- [a] wounding and GBH;
- [b] ABH;
- [c] common assault;
- [d] simple criminal damage;
- [e] causing fear of provocation;
- [f] intentional harassment, alarm or distress;
- [g] causing harassment, alarm or distress;
- [h] harassment and putting in fear of violence [Protection from Harassment Act]1997.

Q Define racially aggravated

A [a] a **demonstration of hostility** by the defendant based on the victim's membership of a racial group:
- [i] immediately before the offence;
- [ii] at the time of the offence, or
- [iii] immediately after committing the offence, or

PUBLIC ORDER AND TERRORISM

[b] **motivation by hostility** by the defendant based on the victim's membership of a racial group.

Note : A purely religious group such as **Rastafarians** are not a racial group.

Q **Who can apply for an Anti-Social Behaviour Order [ASBO]?**

A Either :
[a] The chief officer of police, or
[b] the local authority, **but** they must **consult each other** before making the application.

Q **At what age can an ASBO be applied for?**

A 10 years.

Q **What is the purpose of the ASBO?**

A To protect persons in which the harassment, alarm or distress was caused **or was likely** to be caused from further anti-social acts.

Q **Can an ASBO be applied for by someone in the same household?**

A No, this means that the ASBO cannot be used to solve domestic disputes.

Q **At which court must the application for an ASBO be made?**

A The court in the area where the harassment etc, took place. So that if a person in Wiltshire makes telephone threats to a person in Bristol, the proper court to make the application would be in Bristol.

Q **How long does an ASBO last?**

A 2 years. It may be discharged before then with the consent of **both parties.**

PUBLIC ORDER AND TERRORISM

Q What can the ASBO prohibit?

A Anything prohibiting the defendant from doing anything described in the order.

Q Is there a power of arrest for breaching an ASBO?

A Yes.

Q Who can appeal in the case of an ASBO?

A Only the defendant. The applicant cannot appeal against a refusal to make an order.

Q Define S 18 racial hatred offence

A A person who uses threatening, abusive or insulting words or behaviour, or displays any written material which is threatening, abusive or insulting commits an offence if:

[a] **he intends** to stir up racial hatred, or
[b] **is likely** to stir up racial hatred.

No **offence** where the activity is **inside a dwelling** and is not heard or seen except by persons in that or another dwelling.

Power of arrest. A constable may arrest anyone he reasonably suspects is committing.

Q Define the S 19 Racial Hatred - publishing, distributing written material offence

A A person who publishes, or distributes written material which is threatening, abusive or insulting commits an offence if:

[a] **he intends** to stir up racial hatred, or
[b] **is likely** to stir up racial hatred.

Defence. For a person who is not shown to have intended to stir up racial hatred to prove **he was not aware of the contents** of the material and did not suspect, or have a reason to suspect, it was threatening, abusive or insulting.

PUBLIC ORDER AND TERRORISM

Q Define the racial hatred public performance of a play offence

A If the public performance of a play is given which involves the use of threatening, abusive or insulting words or behaviour, any person who **presents or directs** it is guilty of an offence if:

[a] **he intends** to stir up racial hatred, or
[b] **it is likely** to stir up racial hatred.

No **offence,** for rehearsals, recording the performance or enabling it to be included in a programme service, **unless** it is attended by the public.

Defence. If a person presenting or directing the performance is **not shown to have intended to stir up racial hatred** then it is a defence to prove:

[a] he did not know and had no reason to suspect that the performance would involve the use of the offending words or behaviour; or
[b] they were threatening, abusive or insulting, or
[c] racial hatred would be likely to be stirred up.

Q Define the racial hatred distributing, showing or playing a recording offence

A A person who distributes, shows or plays, a recording of visual images or sounds which are threatening, abusive or insulting is guilty of an offence if:

[a] **he intends** to stir up racial hatred, or
[b] **it is likely** to stir up racial hatred.

Defence. If a person is not shown to have intended to stir up racial hatred, it is a defence for him to prove **he was not aware of the contents of the recording,** and had no reason to suspect that it was threatening, abusive or insulting.

PUBLIC ORDER AND TERRORISM

Q What are the requirements of the written notice to be given for public processions.

A

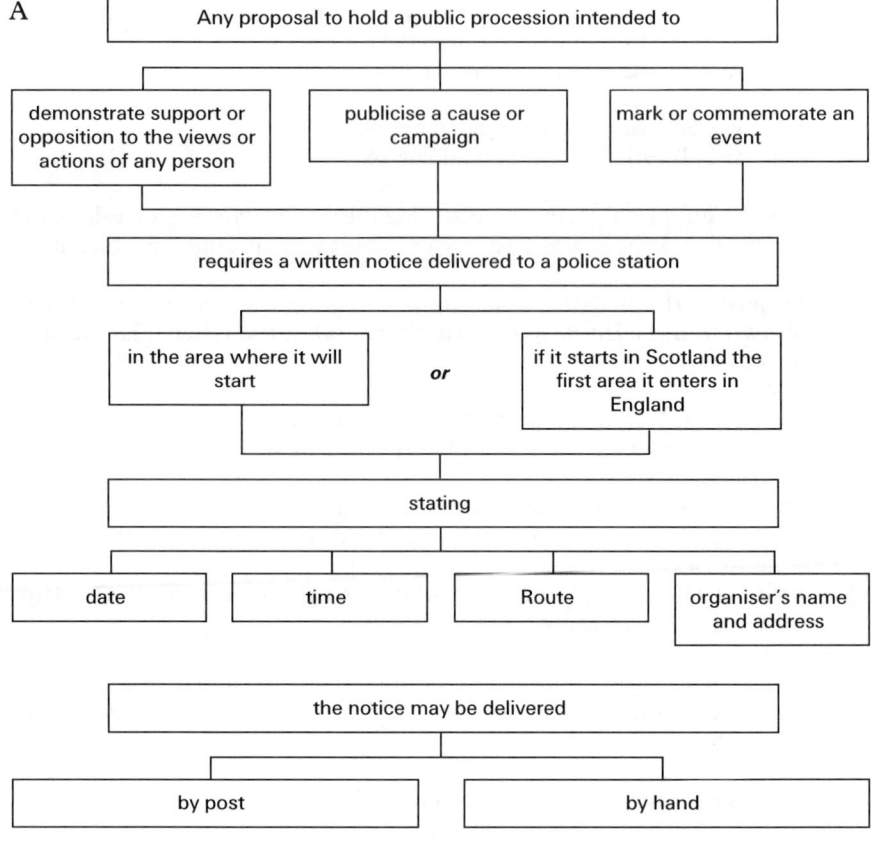

By post. Not less than **6 clear days** by **recorded delivery.** [S 7 of the Interpretation Act 1978 under which a document sent by post is deemed to have been served when posted and to have been delivered in the ordinary course of post does not apply]; or

By hand. Not less than **6 clear days,** or as soon as is practicable.

Offence. Not to comply with the above.

PUBLIC ORDER AND TERRORISM

Defence. To prove that he did not know of the failure to satisfy the requirements. In the case of date, time, route, something happens beyond his control or with the agreement of a police officer.

Q What condition under S 12 can a senior police officer make?

A

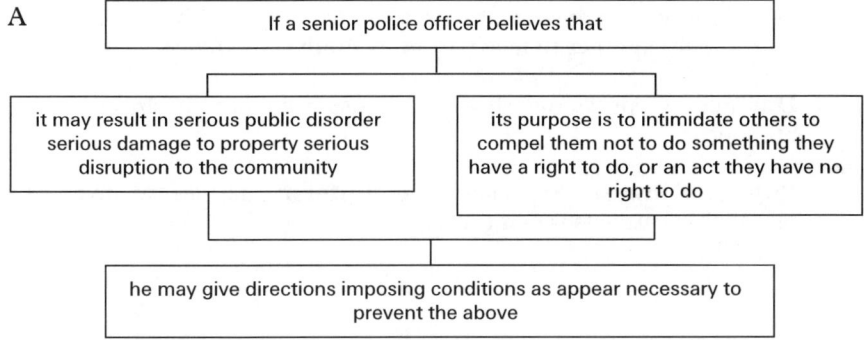

A senior police officer means the chief officer of police, unless it is in the process of being held, e.g. people forming up etc, the **senior police officer present.**

Power of arrest. A constable **in uniform** may arrest anyone he reasonably suspects is committing.

Q Define the offence under S 13 of taking part in a prohibited procession

A Any person who:

[a] organises a prohibited procession; or
[b] who takes part in, or
[c] incites another to take part in, commits an offence.

Power of arrest. A constable **in uniform** may arrest anyone he reasonably suspects is committing.

PUBLIC ORDER AND TERRORISM

Q **Define the offence under S 14 of organising a public assembly**

A   Any person who:

[a]   organises a public assembly and fails to comply with a condition; or
[b]   takes part in an assembly and fails to comply with a condition, or
[c]   incites another to take part in, commits an offence.

Defence. To prove that the failure arose from circumstances beyond his control.

Power of arrest. A constable **in uniform** may arrest anyone he reasonably suspects is committing.

PUBLIC ORDER AND TERRORISM

Q **Outline the offence under S 148 of trespassory assembly**

A

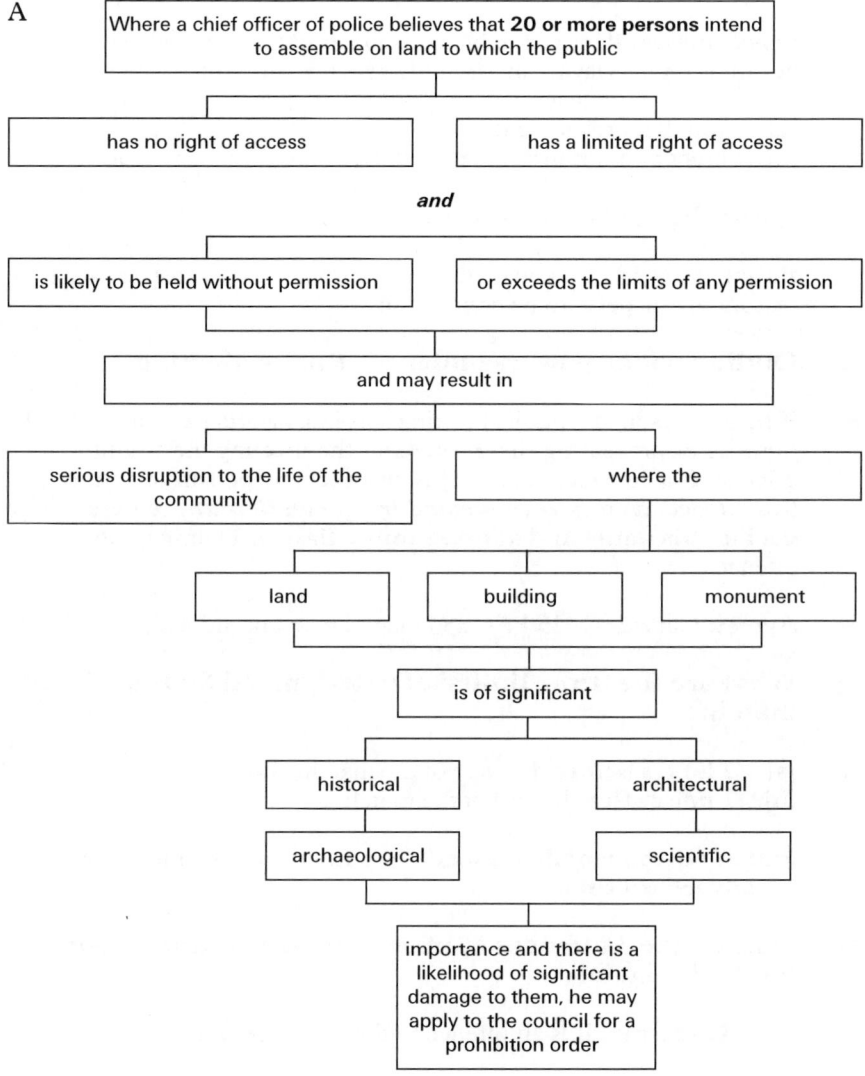

The order. Shall not exceed **4 days** within a 5 mile radius

PUBLIC ORDER AND TERRORISM

Power of arrest. A constable in uniform may arrest anyone he reasonably suspects to be committing.

Police powers. If a constable in uniform reasonably believes that a person is on his way to an assembly which is prohibited, he may:

[a] stop that person; and
[b] direct him not to proceed in the direction of the assembly.

Offence. Failure to comply is an offence.

Police powers. A constable **in uniform** may arrest anyone he reasonably suspects to be committing.

Q Outline police powers under S 1 Public Meeting Act 1908

A   Where a person at a public meeting acts in a disorderly manner for the purpose of preventing the business of the meeting, he is guilty of an offence. If a constable reasonably suspects any person of committing this offence, he may *if requested by the chairman,* require him to **declare his name and address immediately.** Failure to do so is an offence.

Arrest. Consider S 25 PACE General arrest conditions.

Q What are the 'time limits' of a designated football match:

A   [a] **2 hours before** the start of the match, and
    [b] **1 hour after** the end of the match.

Match postponed/abandoned. Two hours before, and 1 hour after the **advertised time**

Q Outline the 3 offences of misbehaviour at designated football matches

A   [a] **Throwing.** It is an offence to throw anything at:

   [i] the playing area or adjacent to it where spectators are not admitted.
   [ii] any area at which spectators may by present [without lawful authority or reasonable excuse - onus of proof lies on him].

PUBLIC ORDER AND TERRORISM

[b] **Chanting.** It is an offence to take part in chanting of an **indecent or racist** nature, and chant means:

   [i] the repeated uttering of words or sounds in concert with others; and
   [ii] racist nature means threatening, abusive or insulting to a person by reason of colour, race, nationality or ethnic origins.

[c] **Entering playing area.** It is an offence to go onto the playing area or place adjacent to it where spectators are not normally allowed [without lawful authority or reasonable excuse - onus of proof lies on him].

Power of arrest. All 3 are arrestable offences.

Q To which vehicles does the Sporting Events [Alcohol] Act 1985 apply?

A **PSVs and trains** used for the main purpose of carrying passengers to or from a sporting event.

Q Who commits alcohol related offences in relation to vehicles?

A Any person who knowingly causes or permits alcohol to be carried in the case of:

PSV, the operator; or **Hired vehicles,** the hirer, [and their servants or agents].

Q Who else commits alcohol related offences in relation to vehicles?

A A person who has alcohol in his **possession** or is **drunk** while on a vehicle.

PUBLIC ORDER AND TERRORISM

Q Outline the alcohol related offences at Sports Grounds

A
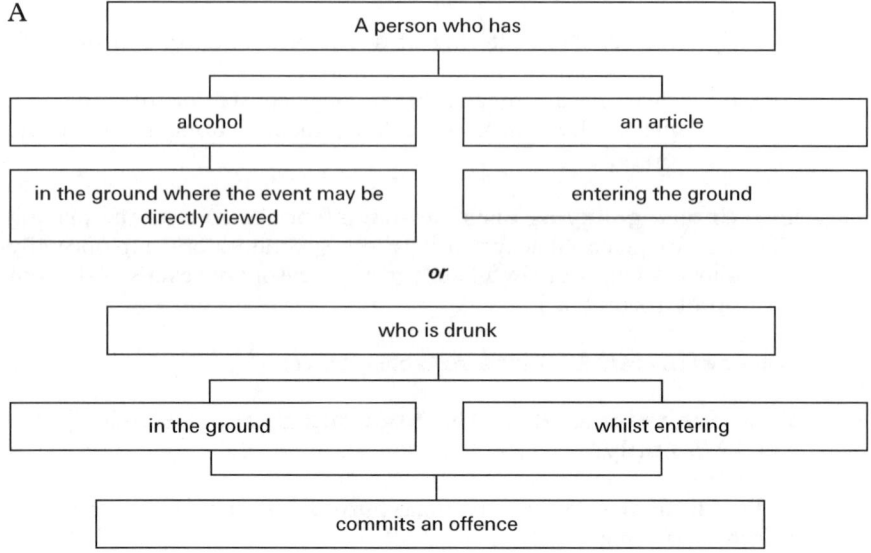

Q Define an article

A It must be capable of **causing injury** to a person struck by it, being:

   [a] a bottle, can or portable container, or part of [whether crushed or broken] which

   [i] is for holding drink, and
   [ii] is discarded when empty.

   But not. Medical containers.

Q Define the offence of Ticket Touts

A It is an offence for **an unauthorised person** to sell [offer/expose] a ticket for a designated football match in a public place [or any place in the course of a business].

   Who is unauthorised. Anyone who does not have written authorisation from the home club or organisers.

PUBLIC ORDER AND TERRORISM

Power of arrest. Arrestable offence [S 24 PACE].

Search. The power to search extends to vehicles believed to be used by touts.

Ticket. Means anything which purports to be a ticket.

Q **What is the purpose of the Football [Disorder] Act 2000?**

A Courts will be under a duty to pass an order where they believe they will help prevent violence or disorder at a designated/prescribed football match. In addition to a sentence the court can issue a banning order even if the offence is dealt with by way of a conditional or absolute discharge.

Q **Who can apply for a banning order?**

A The chief officer of police where the person has caused or contributed to violence or disorder in the UK or elsewhere.

Q **What power has the court in relation to banning orders?**

A The court can impose conditions and [when the Act is in force] **must** request the **surrender of his passport** in connection with matches **outside the UK.**

Q **When must a person who is the subject of a banning order first report to a police station?**

A Within 5 days.

Q **Is there a power of arrest for breaching a banning order?**

A Arrestable offence.

Q **What are the time limits for a banning order where a person has been imprisoned?**

A [a] Between **10 and 6 years**, if sentenced to immediate imprisonment;
[b] between **5 and 3 years**, in any other case, and
[c] **2 years,** where the application is brought by the police.

PUBLIC ORDER AND TERRORISM

Q Terrorism. Outline the offence of Membership of a proscribed organisation

A

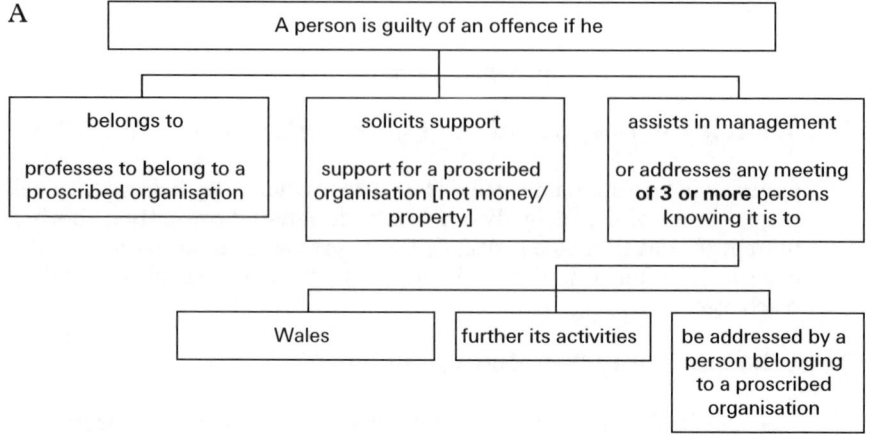

Arrest. Serious arrestable offence.

S 2 PREVENTION OF TERRORISM ACT 1989

Q Outline the offence of Display of Support for a proscribed organisation

A   It is an offence for any person in a public place to:

[a] wear any item of dress; or
[b] wear, carry or display any article,
in a way as to arouse apprehension that he is a member of a proscribed organisation.

Q What is the offence of Possession of Articles for terrorism?

A   A person is guilty of an offence if he has any article in his possession which gives rise to reasonable suspicion that it is in his possession for a purpose connected with:

the commission;
preparation or instigation of an act of terrorism connected with Northern Ireland

Arrest. Serious arrestable 0ffence. S 16A Prevention of Terrorism Act 1989

PUBLIC ORDER AND TERRORISM

Q What is the offence of Collection of Information in relation to terrorism?

A No person shall, without lawful authority or reasonable excuse [onus of proof lies on him]

　[a]　collect/record information which is likely to be useful to a terrorist;
　　　or
　[b]　possess any record/document which contains the above.

Record information will include taking photographs.

Arrest. Serious arrestable offence.

S 16B Prevention of Terrorism Act 1989

Q Outline the offence of Soliciting Funds for Terrorism

A A person is guilty of an offence if he:

　[a]　gives, lends or makes available money or property; or
　[b]　is concerned in an arrangement whereby money or property is to be made available:

　　knowing or suspecting it is in connection with acts of terrorism.

Arrest. Serious arrestable offence.

S 9 Prevention of Terrorism Act, 1989

Q Outline the offence of Causing Explosion likely to Endanger Life/Property

A A person in the UK or Republic of Ireland who unlawfully and maliciously causes an explosion which is likely to endanger life or serious injury to property is guilty of an offence.

Arrest. Serious arrestable offence.
Explosive. Includes fireworks and petrol bombs.

S2 Explosive Substances Act 1883

PUBLIC ORDER AND TERRORISM

Q **Outline the offence of Attempting to Cause an Explosion**

A   A person in the UK or elsewhere who unlawfully and maliciously:

[a]   does any act with intent to cause an explosion likely to endanger life or cause serious damage to property; or

[b]   makes, has in his possession or under his control, any explosive with intent to endanger life or cause serious damage to property or

[c]   enables another to do so, commits an offence.

Arrest. Arrestable offence.

S 3 Explosive Substances Act 1883

Q **Outline the offence of Possessing Explosives under Suspicious Circumstances**

A   Any person who knowingly has in his possession or under his control any explosive under circumstances as to give rise to a reasonable suspicion that it is **not for a lawful object** [onus of proof lies on him] commits an offence.

Arrest. Arrestable offence.

S 4 Explosive Substances Act 1883

PROTECTION FROM HARRASSMENT

Q   Define the offence of Protection from Harassment

A
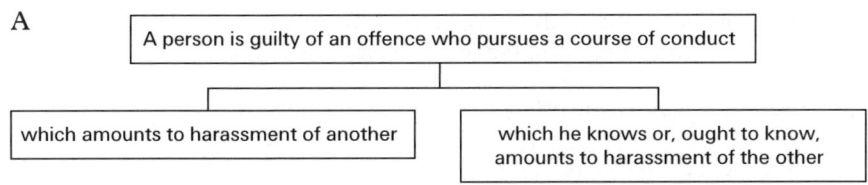

How many occasions. At least 2.

The test. If the course of conduct is in question, the person 'ought to know' if a reasonable person in possession of the same information would think it amounted to harassment.

No offence. If done for the purposes of preventing or detecting crime, under a rule of law or the conduct was reasonable.

Arrest. Arrestable 0ffence.

S 1 & 2 Protection from Harassment Act 1997

Q   Outline the offence of Putting People in Fear of Violence

A   A person whose course of conduct causes another to fear, on at least **2 occasions** that violence will be used against him is guilty of an offence if he knows or ought to know that his course of conduct will cause the other to fear on each occasion.

The test. If the course of conduct is in question, the person 'ought to know' if a reasonable person in possession of the same information would think it amounted to harassment.

Defence. If done for the purposes of preventing or detecting crime, under a rule of law, or for the **protection of himself/another** or **protection of property of self/another.**

PROTECTION FROM HARRASSMENT

Secretary of State may issue a certificate that a specified person on a specified occasion relating to:

[a] national security;
[b] the economic well-being of the UK, or
[c] the prevention and detection of serious crime

thereby negating the offence.

Arrest. Arrestable offence.

S 4 Protection from Harassment Act 1997

COMMUNICATIONS

Q **Outline the offence of Bomb Threats**

A
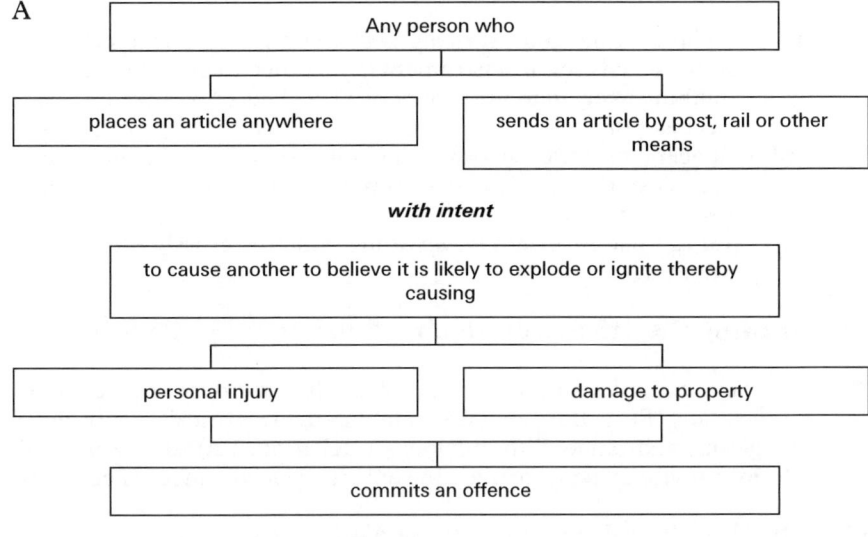

Arrest. Arrestable offence

S 51 Criminal Law Act 1997

Q **Define the offence of Communicating Bomb Threats**

A   A person who communicates information which he knows or believes to be false intending to induce in any person a belief that a bomb or anything liable to explode is in any place, commits an offence.

Arrest. Arrestable offence.

Q **Outline the offence of Taking or Opening Mail Bags under the Post Office Act 1953**

A   If any person unlawfully takes or opens a mail bag or opens a postal packet he commits an offence.

Arrest. Arrestable offence.

COMMUNICATIONS

Q   Outline the offence of Sending Prohibited Articles by Post

A   It is an offence to **send** or **procure to be sent** a postal packet which contains:

   [a]   explosives, dangerous, noxious or deleterious substances, filth, unprotected sharp instruments, noxious living creatures, or anything likely to injure other postal packets or persons on postal business; or
   [b]   indecent or obscene prints, painting, photograph, lithograph, engraving, film, book, card or communication, or any indecent or obscene article; or
   [c]   [on the packet or cover] anything which is grossly offensive or indecent.

Q   Outline the offence of Placing Substances in Post Boxes

A   A person commits an offence who places [or attempts to place] in or against any Post Box any fire, match, light, explosive substance, dangerous substance, filth, noxious or deleterious substance or fluid. Or does anything likely to injure the box, its appurtenances or contents.

Q   Outline the offence under the Malicious Communications Act 1988

A   Any person who sends to another a letter or other article which he intends should cause distress or anxiety to the recipient or another conveying:

   [a]   a message which is indecent or grossly offensive;
   [b]   a threat, or
   [c]   information which he knows is false

Defence. It is a defence to prove that the threat was used to reinforce a demand which he had reasonable grounds for making and the threat was the proper means of reinforcing demand.

Q   Define the offence of Mating a Threat to Kill

A   A person who without lawful excuse makes a threat to kill a person or a 3rd person intending that he would fear it would be carried out, commits an offence.

   Arrest. Arrestable offence. S 16 Offences Against the Person Act 1861

COMMUNICATIONS

Q **Outline the offence of Improper Use of Public Telecommunication Systems**

A A person who:

    [a]   sends by means of a **public** telecommunication system, a message or matter that is grossly offensive or indecent, obscene or menacing; or

    [b]   for the purpose of causing annoyance, inconvenience or needless anxiety to another, sends a message or matter that he knows to be false, or persistently does so, commits an offence

Q **Outline the offence of Interception of Messages**

A Otherwise than as his duty as a crown servant it is an offence to:

    [a]   use a wireless intending to **obtain information** of any message about the sender, the contents, or the recipient which he is not authorised to receive, or

    [b]   disclose such information which would not have come to his knowledge without his interception

FIREARMS

Q Define a firearm

A

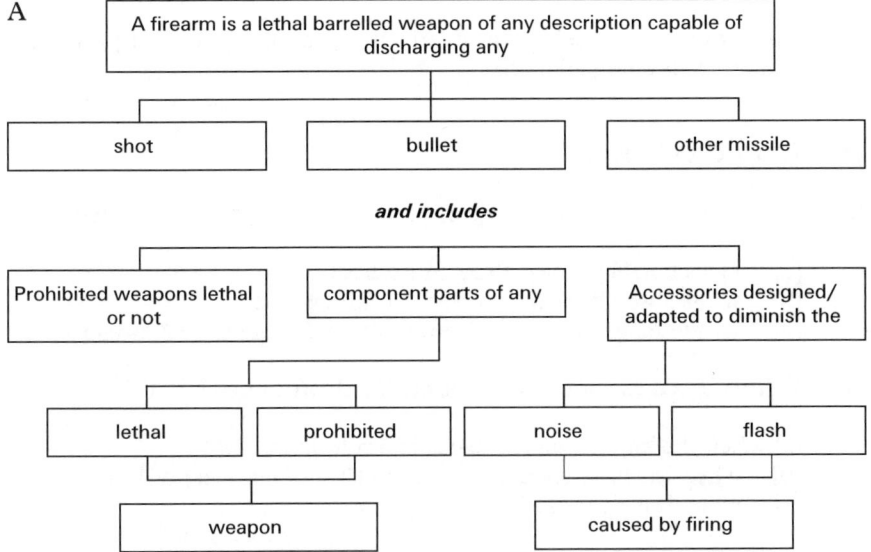

Component parts such as triggers, barrel etc are included.

Q When is a firearm not a firearm?

A   It may cease to be a firearm if it is de-activated by proving:

   [a]   it bears a mark [approved by the Secretary of State] denoting the fact that it has been de-activated by an approved company; and
   [b]   the company has certified in writing that the work has been carried out in an approved manner for rendering it incapable.

Q Summarise the list of prohibited weapons

A   [a]   automatic weapons;
   [b]   most self-loading or pump-action weapons;
   [c]   any firearm which is less than 60 ems long or whose barrel is less than **30 cms** long **e.g. [most handguns]**;
   [d]   most smooth-bore revolvers;

FIREARMS

    [e]   any weapon designed or adapted for the discharge of noxious liquid, gas or thing.
    [f]   military weapons and ammunition, including grenades and mortars.

Empty washing up bottles filled with noxious liquid [acid] does not amount to it being adapted.

Firearms Acts 1968 & 1997

Q   **Define a shotgun**

A   A shotgun is a smooth-bore gun [not air weapon or revolver] which:

    [a]   has a barrel not less than **24 inches;**
    [b]   whose bore does not exceed **2 inches;** and
    [c]   whose magazine [if any] does not hold more than **2 cartridges.**

Q   **When is an air weapon specially dangerous?**

A   [a]   when the kinetic energy exceeds 6 ft lb [air pistol];
    [b]   when the kinetic energy exceeds 12 ft lb [air weapon]; or
    [c]   when it is disguised as another object.

Note. [b] does not apply to underwater guns.

Q   **What ammunition is exempt as Section 1 Firearms?**

A   [a]   cartridges containing 5 or more shots, none bigger than **0.36 inch** diameter;
    [b]   ammunition for an airgun, air rifle or air pistol; and
    [c]   blank cartridges not more than **1 inch** diameter.

FIREARMS

Q Outline the offence of Possessing a Firearm/Ammo without a Certificate

A

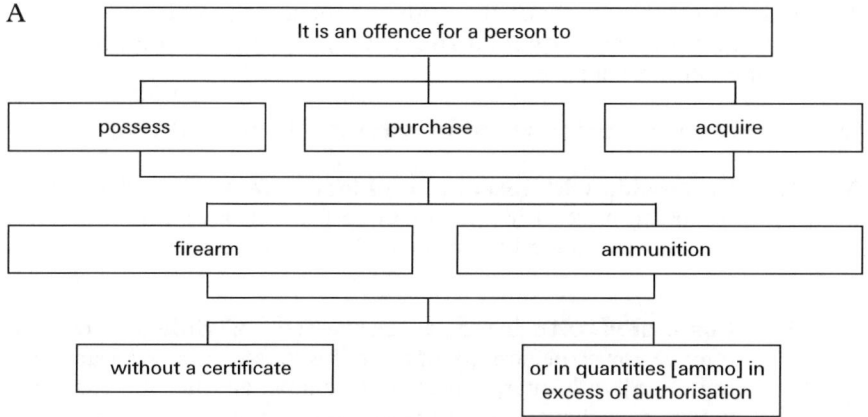

Q Summarise who is generally exempt from holding a firearms certificate

A [a] police permit holders;
[b] clubs, athletics and sporting purposes;
[c] borrowed rifle on private premises;
[d] holders of visitors permits;
[e] antiques as ornaments or curiosities;
[f] authorised firearm dealers;
[g] auctioneers, carriers or warehouse staff;
[h] licensed slaughterers;
[i] theatrical performers;
[j] ship or aircraft equipment;
[k] crown servants;
[l] proof houses; and
[m] museum licences.

Q What are the 2 main shotgun offences?

A [a] It is an offence to possess, purchase or acquire a shotgun without a certificate; and
[b] to fail to comply with a condition.

FIREARMS

Q Define the offence of Possessing or Distributing Prohibited Weapons

A It is an offence, without the authority of the Secretary of State to possess, purchase, acquire, manufacture, sell or transfer a prohibited weapon or ammunition.

Q Outline the 6 offences of Firearms - Criminal Use

A 1. **Possession with intent to endanger life.** It is an offence for a person to have in his possession a firearm or ammunition with intent to endanger life or to enable another to do so.
Sec 16.

2. **Possession with intent to cause fear of violence.** It is an offence for a person to have in his possession a firearm [or imitation] with intent to cause, or enable another to cause, any person to believe that **unlawful violence** will be used against him or another.
Sec 16A.

3. Using a firearm to resist arrest. It is an offence for a person to make [or attempt] use of a firearm [or imitation] to prevent the lawful arrest of himself or another. See 17[i].

4. **Possession of a firearm while committing/being arrested for a Sch 1 offence.** If a person, at the time of committing or being arrested for an offence in Schedule 1 to the Act, has in his possession a firearm [or imitation] he commits an offence unless he can show he has it for a **lawful object.** Sec 17[ii].
Schedule 1 offences are:

   [a] Criminal damage;
   [b] theft, robbery, blackmail, burglary, taking conveyance;
   [c] Bassaults and wounding;
   [d] rape and taking out of possession;
   [e] child abduction
   [f] aiding and abetting above.

5. **Having a firearm with intent to commit indictable offence or resist arrest.** It is an offence to have a firearm [or imitation] with intent to commit an indictable offence, or resist or prevent arrest of another.
Sec 18.

FIREARMS

6. **Having a loaded firearm in a public place.** A person commits an offence if, without lawful authority or reasonable excuse [onus of proof lies on him], he has in a public place, a loaded shotgun, a loaded air weapon, or any other **firearm** [loaded or not] **together with ammunition** for it.

Sec 19.

Q Outline Firearms and ages

A FIREARMS - AGES

Age	Firearm & ammo	Shotgun	Air weapon
under 14	**cannot possess** except 1. Carrying for another for a sporting purpose 2. Member of a cadet corps 3. At a shooting gallery or miniature range 4. A member of a gun club		**cannot have with him [anywhere]** except Supervised by a person who is 21 or over in a private place. If a missile is fired beyond those premises both juvenile and adult commit an offence
under 15		**cannot have with him an assembled shotgun [anywhere]** except 1. With a supervisor who is 21 or over 2. The shotgun is covered so it cannot be fired	

FIREARMS

FIREARMS - AGES (cont)

Age	Firearm & ammo	Shotgun	Air weapon
under 17			**cannot possess in a public place** except 1. At a shooting gallery or miniature rifle range 2. Member of a gun club 3. Securely fastened in gun cover so it cannot be fired

FIREARMS ACT 1968

Q   What are Police Stop and Search powers under S 47 Firearms Act 1968?

A

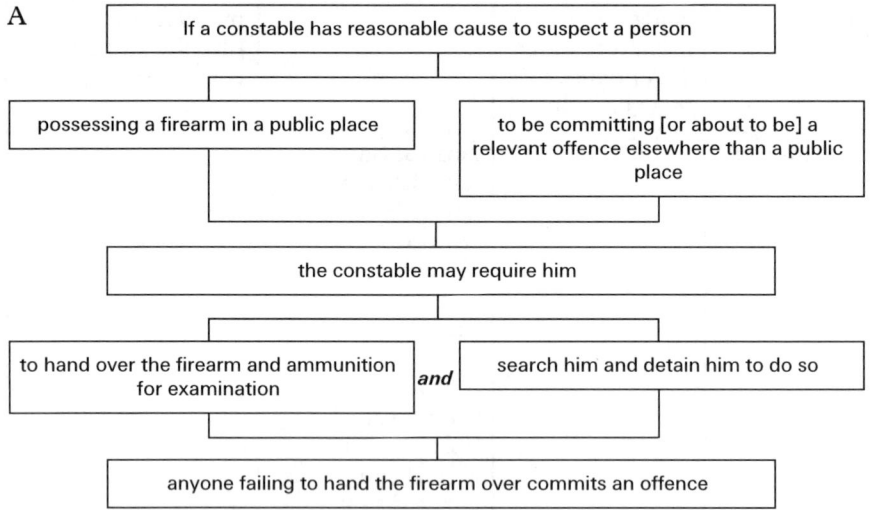

FIREARMS

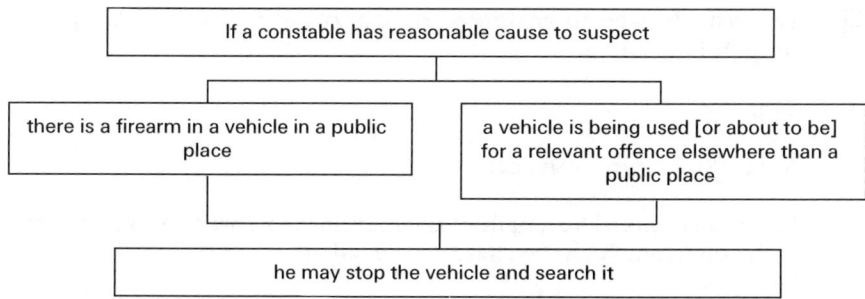

Q   What are police powers to demand certificates under S 48 Firearms Act 1968?

A

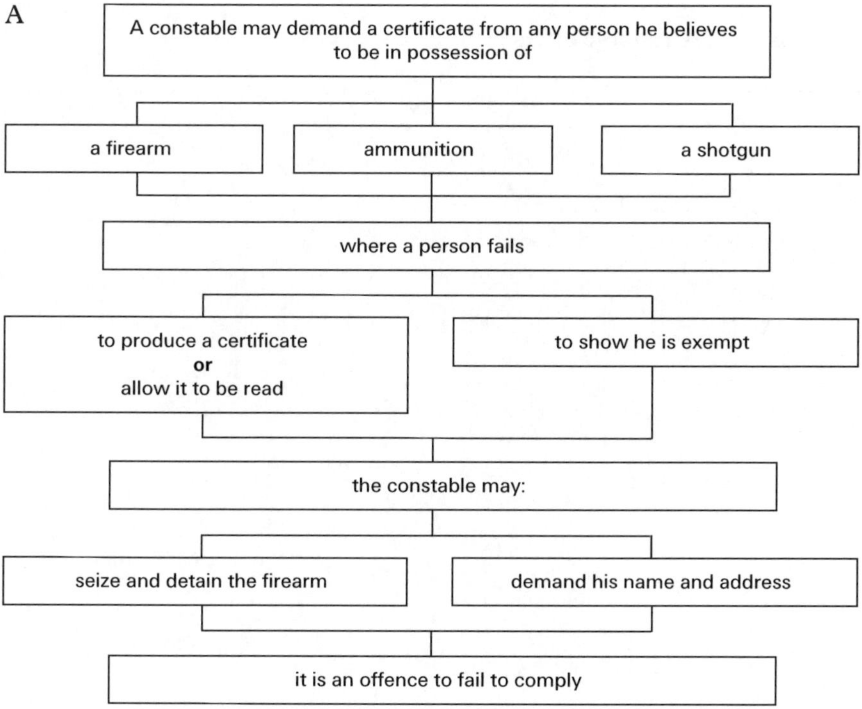

FIREARMS

Q **It is an offence to shorten the barrel of a shotgun to a length less than?**

A 24 inches.

   Arrest. Arrestable offence.

   Measurement. The length of the barrel is measured from its muzzle to the point at which the charge is exploded.

Q **Define the offence of Converting an Imitation Firearm**

A It is an offence for a person [other than a firearms dealer] to convert an imitation firearm into a firearm.

   Arrest. Arrestable offence.

OFFENSIVE WEAPONS

Q Outline the offence of Having an Offensive Weapon in a Public Place

A

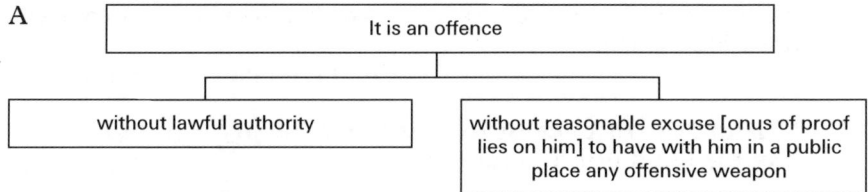

Arrest. Arrestable offence.

Lawful authority. Police officers, members of the military. **Not security guards** who may have reasonable excuse.

Reasonable excuse. Possession of tools of your trade, fancy dress incorporating say a policeman's truncheon. It is **not reasonable** to carry an offensive weapon 'just in case'. It may be reasonable if you have good grounds for fearing an unlawful attack, e.g. whilst guarding money in transit.

Has with him. Means actual physical possession or at least readily accessible.

Q Define an Offensive Weapon

A

Offensive per se. An article made for causing injury, e.g. a knuckle duster, swordstick, bayonet, flick-knives etc are offensive per se [without further proof] and there is no need for the prosecution to show further proof of intent, possession is enough.

OFFENSIVE WEAPONS

Adapted. Where an article is adapted for causing injury, broken bottle, chair leg containing nails, etc, the prosecution must show that injury was intended.

Inoffensive articles. An article which is inoffensive in itself, e.g. an umbrella, which is intended for use as an offensive weapon becomes an offensive weapon.

SEC 1 PREVENTION OF CRIME ACT 1953

Q **Outline the offence of Blades and Sharply Pointed Articles in a public place**

A

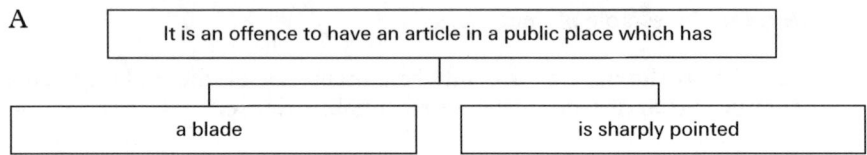

Blade. Folding pocket knives with a blade which does not exceed 3 inches are exempt. If the folding pocket knife locks in the open position, it is not exempt.

Defence.

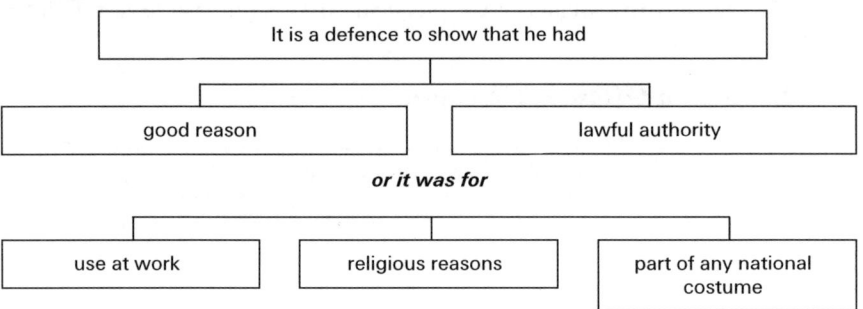

Religious reasons. A member of the Sikh religion may carry a small knife.

National costume. Someone in Highland dress with a skean dhu, [knife in sock].

Arrest. Arrestable offence.

OFFENSIVE WEAPONS

Q Define the offence of Weapons on School Premises

A
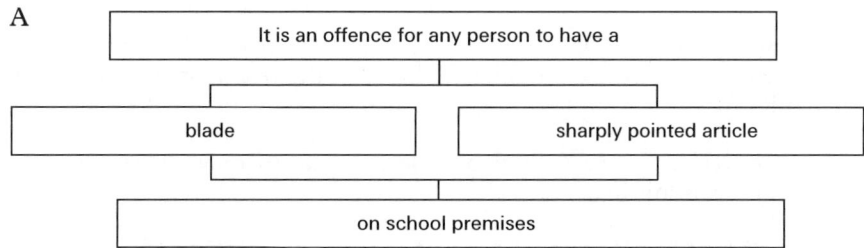

School premises means. Primary or secondary education. Not higher education.

Defence. It is a defence to show that he had good reason or lawful authority or that he had it for use at work, for religious reasons or as part of any national costume.

Arrest. Arrestable offence.

Q What is the power of entry for the above offence?

A
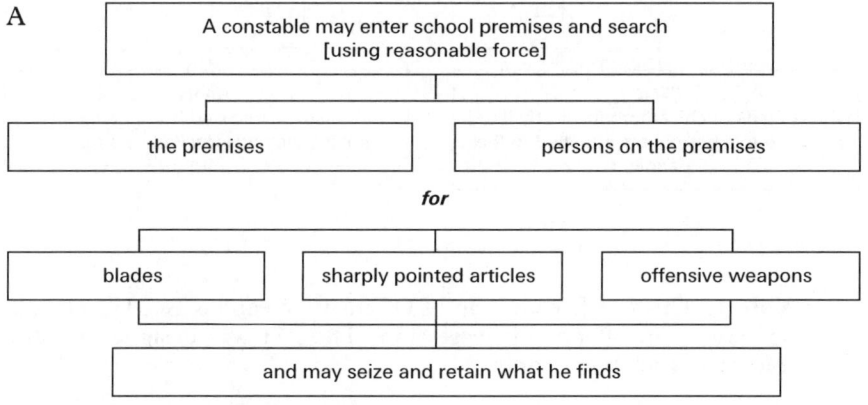

Arrest. Arrestable offence.

School premises. Means land used for school purposes, but not land occupied solely as a dwelling by a person employed by the school.

OFFENSIVE WEAPONS

Q **Define the offence of Trespassing with an Offensive Weapon**

A Any person who, without lawful authority or reasonable excuse is on premises as a trespasser, has with him an offensive weapon commits an offence.

Conditional arrest. A constable in uniform may arrest someone found committing.

Q **Define the offence of Manufacture, Sale/Hire of Weapons**

A

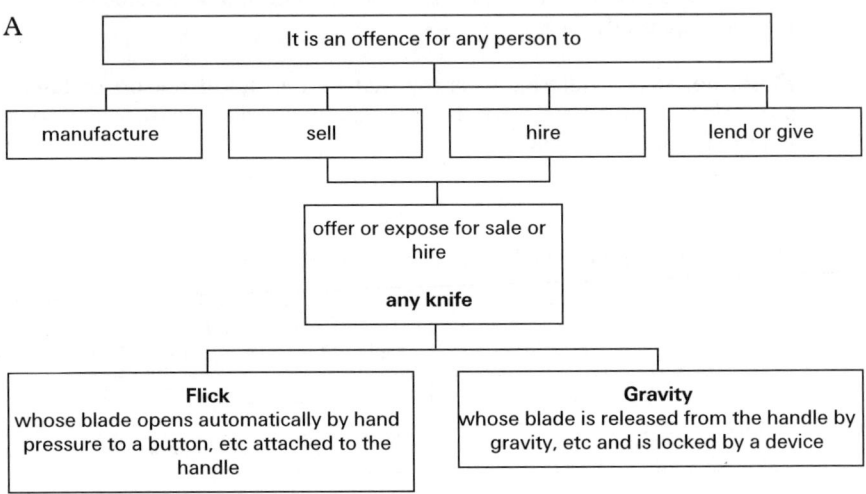

Note 1. This Act [Restriction of Offensive Weapons Act 1959] does not create an offence of possession. The Act was designed to stop trading in such knives only.

Note 2. S 141 of the Criminal Justice Act 1988 makes similar provisions for a whole range of Martial Arts weapons.

OFFENSIVE WEAPONS

Q What is the offence of Selling Knives and Articles to under 16s?

A
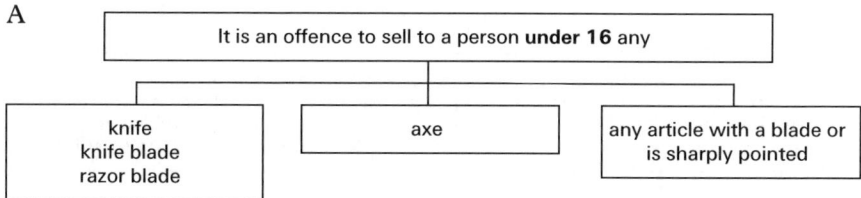

Defence. To prove that he took all reasonable precautions and exercised due diligence to avoid committing the offence.

Q Outline the offence of Unlawful Marketing of Knives. S 1 Knives Act 1997

A
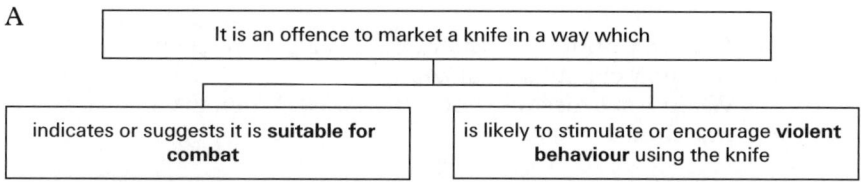

Market. Includes selling, hiring [offering or exposing] and possession for marketing.

Q Outline the offence of Publishing Marketing Material. S 2 Knives Act 1997

A [a] the knife was marketed for use by the armed forces of any country or as an antique or curio; and it was reasonable to market it that way; and
[b] there were no reasonable grounds for believing it would be used unlawfully.

It is also a defence to prove that he did not know or suspect that the way in which the knife was marketed [published] indicated that it was **suitable for combat** or would stimulate or encourage **violent behaviour** using the knife as a weapon, or that he took reasonable precautions and exercised due diligence to avoid committing the offence.

OFFENSIVE WEAPONS

Q **Outline the 3 offences of Crossbows and persons under 17 years of age**

A 1.

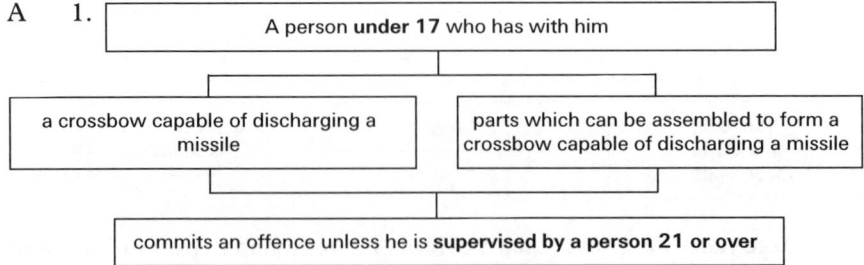

2. It is an offence to sell or hire a crossbow or a part of a crossbow to a person **under 17,** unless he has grounds for believing he is 17 or over.

3. A person **under 17** who buys or hires a crossbow or part of a crossbow commits an offence.
When is a crossbow not a crossbow. When the draw weight is less than 1.4 kgs.

NUISANCE

Q Outline the offences of Dangerous Activities on Highways

A [a] Any person who [without lawful authority or excuse] **deposits** anything on a highway whereby a user is **injured or endangered** commits an offence;

[b] any person who [without lawful authority or excuse] **lights a fire, discharges a firearm or firework, within 50 feet** of the centre of the highway whereby a user is **injured, interrupted or endangered** commits an offence;

[c] any person who plays **games** on a highway to the **annoyance** of a user commits an offence;

[d] any person who [without lawful authority or excuse] allows **offensive matter** to flow onto a highway from adjoining premises commits an offence;

[e] any person who **lights a fire on land [not a highway]**, or directs or permits it whereby a user is **injured, interrupted or endangered** by the fire or smoke, commits an offence; and

[f] any person who places any **rope, wire or anything** across a highway whereby it is likely to cause **danger** to a user commits an offence, unless he proves he has given adequate warning of the danger.

Fire defence. At the time the fire was lit he was satisfied that it was unlikely that users would be injured, interrupted or endangered by the fire or smoke and either :

[i] both before and after the fire was lit he did what he reasonably could to prevent users being injured etc, or

[ii] he had a reasonable excuse for not doing so.

Q Define the offences on Educational Premises

A Any person without lawful authority is present on school premises and causes or permits nuisance or disturbance to the annoyance of persons who use those premises [present or not] commits an offence.

Schools. Maintained by a local authority, grant maintained and institutions maintained by the local authority and providing higher or further education.

NUISANCE

Premises. Include playgrounds, playing fields, and other premises for outdoor play.

Q **What powers do the police have to Remove Persons ?**

A A constable [or authorised person] who has reasonable cause to suspect that any person is offending under the section, may remove him from the premises.

Q **Define the offence of Exceeding Noise Level after Service of Notice**

A Where a warning notice has been served in respect of noise from a dwelling, any person responsible for noise which is emitted from the dwelling during the **period specified** and exceeding the prescribed limit **measured from the complainant's dwelling,** commits an offence.

Defence. To show that there was a reasonable excuse for the noise.

Q **Define the offence of Leaving Litter**

A

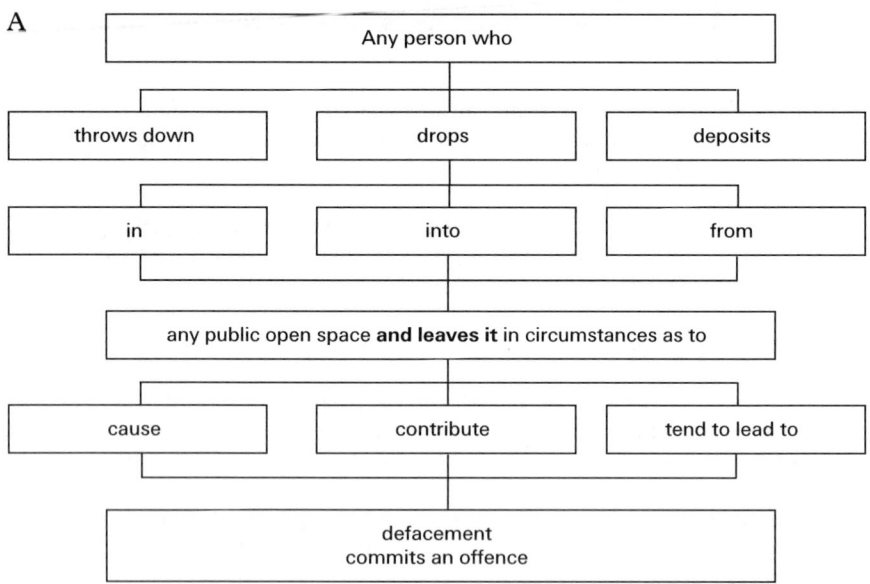

NUISANCE

Public open space. Means where the public are entitled to access **without payment** and any **covered space** open to the public **open to the air on at least one side.**

Note. This offence can also be committed on relevant land belonging to : Local authority, the Crown, Statutory undertakers, [railway, tramway, docks etc] and designated educational institutions.

Defence. When authorised by law or the consent of the owner.

ANIMALS

Q Define the offence of Failing to Keep a Dog under Proper Control

A If a dog is dangerously out of control in a public place:

[a] the owner, and
[b] if different, the person in charge of the dog

commits an offence. If the dog **injures** anyone the offence becomes aggravated.

Q What if the dog is trespassing in a private place?

A If the dog is trespassing in a **private place** and it injures any person or there are grounds for believing it will do so, an offence is committed, and if the dog **injures** any person the offence becomes aggravated.

Q What does Dangerously Out of Control mean?

A When there are grounds for reasonable apprehension that the dog will injure any person. This does not apply to a Police dog handler or a Crown dog handler.

Q What if the owner's dog is under 16?

A Then the head of the household commits the offence as well as the owner.

Q What is the defence for the owner if a different person is in charge of the dog?

A That he reasonably believed that the person was a fit and proper person to be in charge of the dog.

Q What is the offence of Breeding, Selling, etc Dogs of a Type Controlled?

A No person shall:

[a] breed, or breed from such a dog;
[b] sell, exchange, advertise a sale or exchange;

ANIMALS

[c] give, or advertise such a dog as a gift;
[d] allow the dog in a public place without being **muzzled and on a lead;** or
[e] abandon such a dog, or allow it to stray.

Type controlled. Are dogs of the type known as pit bull terriers, etc. This legislation is designed to ensure that such dogs die out.

Q What can a court presume in relation to the Type of dog?

A That the dog is a Type known as a pit bull terrier unless the contrary is proved by the defendant who must give the court **14 days notice** of his intention to prove his claim.

Q What is meant by Muzzled and Kept on a Lead?

A Securely fitted muzzle and securely held on a lead by a person who is 16 **or over.**

Q What is the power to seize dogs?

A A constable [or Council's dog warden] may seize a dog which is held unlawfully or which is un-muzzled or off its lead in public.

Q Outline the offences of Advertising Animal Fights and Attending a Fight

A Any person **present,** without reasonable excuse, when animals are fighting commits an offence, and a person who knowingly **publishes an advert** for animal fighting commits an offence.

Q Define a Guard Dog

A A guard dog is a dog which is being used to protect:

[a] premises;
[b] property kept on premises, or
[c] people guarding premises or property.

GUARD DOGS ACT 1975

Q When can a guard dog be used?

A When the handler is present on the premises and the dog is under his control, unless the dog is securely tied up.

ANIMALS

Q When is the handler no longer a handler?

A [a] when the dog is under the control **of another handler;** or
[b] when it is secured so that it is not at liberty to go freely about premises.

Q What notices must be exhibited in relation to guard dogs?

A A notice containing a warning that a guard dog is present shall be clearly exhibited at **each entrance** to the premises.

Q When is a guard dog not a guard dog?

A When it is being used to protect houses or agricultural land.

Q Define the offence of Dogs Worrying Livestock

A Where a dog worries livestock on agricultural land, the owner and person in charge at the time commit an offence, **except** where the livestock are **trespassing** on the land and the dog is owned by the occupier. The exception does not apply if the person causes the dog to attack the livestock.

Defence. If the owner is charged it is a defence to prove that at the time the dog was in the charge of another whom he reasonably believed to be a fit and proper person to have charge of it.

Q What is meant by the term Worrying livestock?

A [a] attacking livestock;
[b] chasing livestock in a way to cause injury or suffering, or abortion or loss of or diminution of their produce; or
[c] in the case of **sheep,** not being on a lead or under close control in a field or enclosure.

Q What is meant by the term 'Chases'?

A It is only necessary to prove that the dog ran among the livestock so as to cause them to panic and run. **Except,** in a field of **sheep** the following dogs are exempt:

Police dogs, guide dogs, trained sheep dogs, working gun dogs and hounds in a pack.

ANIMALS

Q What are the police powers to seize the dog?

A Where a dog is found on agricultural land by a constable:

[a] and the officer has reason to believe the dog has been worrying livestock, and
[b] no person is present who admits to owning/being in charge of the dog, then

the constable can seize and detain it in order to discover its owner.

Q What are the Farmer's Rights?

A A person may protect livestock from dogs which may result in the dog being shot. In civil proceedings for killing or injuring a dog it will be a **defence** to prove:

[a] he acted to protect the livestock and he was entitled to do so; and
[b] that **within 48 hours** he gave notice to an officer in charge of a police station

S 9 Dogs [Protection of Livestock] Act 1953

Q Outline police powers in relation to Rabies

A

A constable may arrest any person whom he, with reasonable cause, suspects to have committed or be in the act of committing

landing an animal in contravention of the Rabies laws	by a person in charge of boat or vessel failing to abide by the rabies laws	moving any animal in, within or out of a rabies area

Q Define the offences of Cruelty to Animals

A Any person who causes or procures the cruel treatment of an animal commits an offence if he:

[a] cruelly treats, beats, kicks, etc;
[b] does, or omits to do something so as to cause unnecessary suffering;
[c] conveys the animal so as to cause unnecessary suffering;
[d] subjects the animal to an operation performed without due care or humanity;

ANIMALS

[e] administers injurious poison or drugs without reasonable cause or excuse;

[f] tethers any horse, ass or mule, causing unnecessary suffering.

Q What are police powers in relation to Cruelty?

A A constable may arrest without warrant any person whom he has reasonable cause to believe is guilty of an offence, which is **punishable by imprisonment** without the option of a fine [e.g neglect of animal] if:

[a] the officer witnessed the offence; or
[b] a 3rd person gives the information and their name and address.

Q Outline police powers in relation to Injured Animals

A An animal for the purposes of Sll is, horse, mule, ass, bull, sheep, goat or pig.

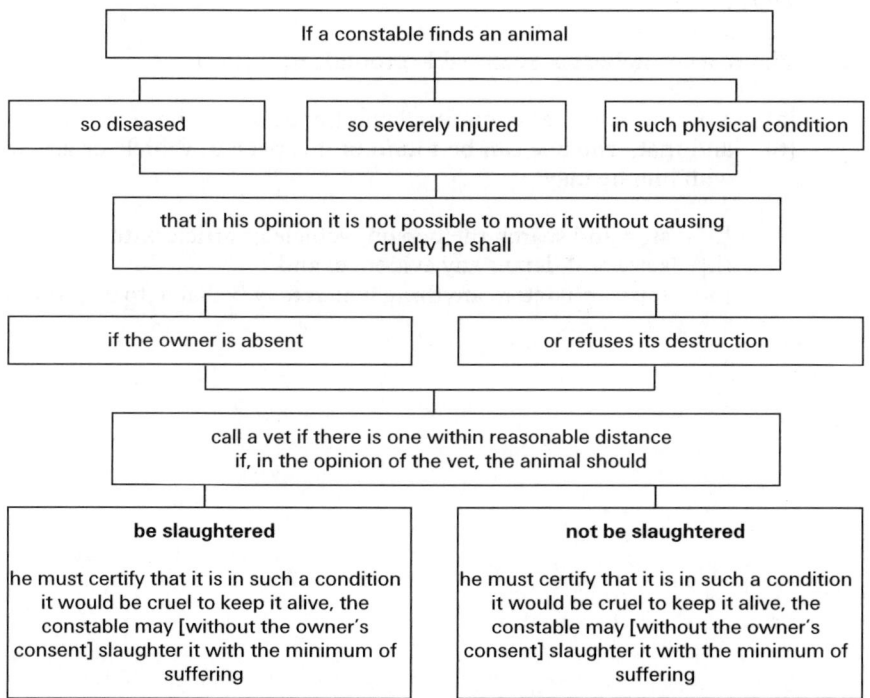

Costs. May be recovered by the police through the civil court.

ANIMALS

Q   Define the offence of Taking, Injuring or Killing Badgers

A   A person is guilty of an offence if he wilfully kills, injures or takes a badger [or attempts]. It is also an offence to dig for badgers or interfere with badger sets.

Defence. To prove his action was necessary for preventing serious damage to land, crops, poultry or property. However the defence does not apply if it is shown that he could have applied for a licence [or that it had been turned down.]

Q   Define the offence of Selling or Possessing Live Badgers

A   It is an offence to sell [or offer to sell] a live badger or possess a live badger.

Q   What are police powers in relation to The Badgers Act 1992?

A   Where a constable has reasonable grounds to suspect:

[a]   a person is, or has committed an offence under the act;
[b]   and that evidence can be found on his person, vehicle or article with him he may

   [i]   stop and search the person, vehicle or article with him
   [ii] seize and detain any evidence; and
   [iii] seize and detain anything which may be liable to forfeiture.

OFFENCES RELATED TO PREMISES

Q What is an Interim Possession Order?

A An order made by a court to start proceedings for the recovery of premises occupied by trespassers.

CRIMINAL JUSTICE AND PUBLIC ORDER ACT 1994.

Q Outline the Interim Possession Order Trespass Offence

Q When an interim possession order has been made and served then a person commits an offence if he:

[a] is present on the premises during the currency of the order unless:

[i] he leaves **within 24 hours** of its service and does not return; or
[ii] the order is void by reason of not being fixed to the premises;

[b] having been in occupation when the order was served he re-enters as a trespasser after the order expired but **within 1 year** of it being served.

Arrest. A constable in uniform may arrest.

Q Define the offence of Making False Statement to Obtain Interim Possession Order

A

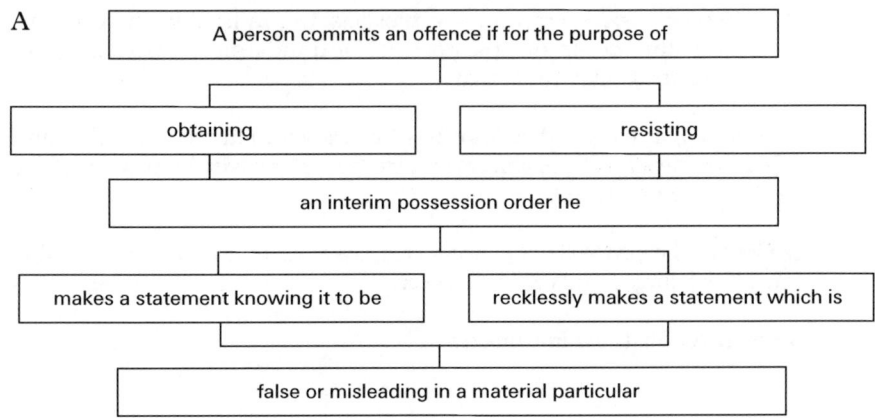

OFFENCES RELATED TO PREMISES

Q Outline the offence of Aggravated Trespass

A

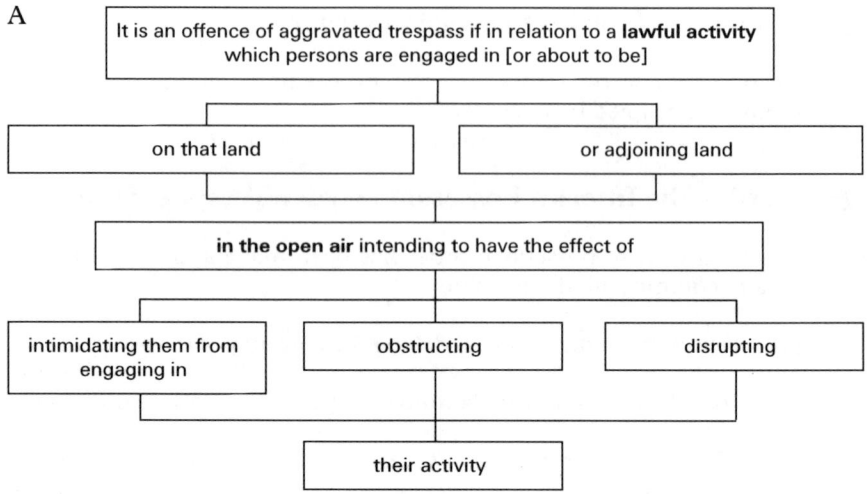

Arrest. A constable in uniform.

Q Define police powers in relation to Aggravated Trespass

A   The senior police officer present **at the scene** may direct persons to leave land if he believes:

[a] he is or is intending to commit the offence of aggravated trespass; or

[b] **two or more persons are trespassing** in land in the open air with the common purpose of intimidating, obstructing or disrupting a lawful activity.

Offence. Knowing a direction has been given, fails to leave the land ASAP, or having left, re-enters as a trespasser **within 3 months** of the direction being given.

Defence. To prove he was not a trespasser or that he had reasonable cause for failing to leave, or re-enter.

Arrest. A constable in uniform.

OFFENCES RELATED TO PREMISES

Q   **Outline the police powers of two or more people Trespassing for Residence**

A   The senior police officer present **at the scene may direct persons to leave land if he believes:**

[a]   **two or more persons are trespassing** on land; and
[b]   that their common purpose is to **reside there;** and
[c]   they have been **asked to leave** [or steps have been taken by occupier]; and

that any of those persons have:

[a]   caused damage to land or property; or
[b]   have used threatening, abusive or insulting words or behaviour towards the occupier, his family or employee; or
[c]   they have 6 **or more vehicles** on the land.

he may direct them to leave the land together with their vehicles and property.

Trespasser? Where persons were not trespassers at the outset but have subsequently become trespassers the police officer must believe that they have caused damage, used threatening etc words or behaviour or have 6 or more vehicles since becoming trespassers.

Arrest. A constable in uniform.

OFFENCES RELATED TO PREMISES

Q Outline police powers in relation to Raves

A

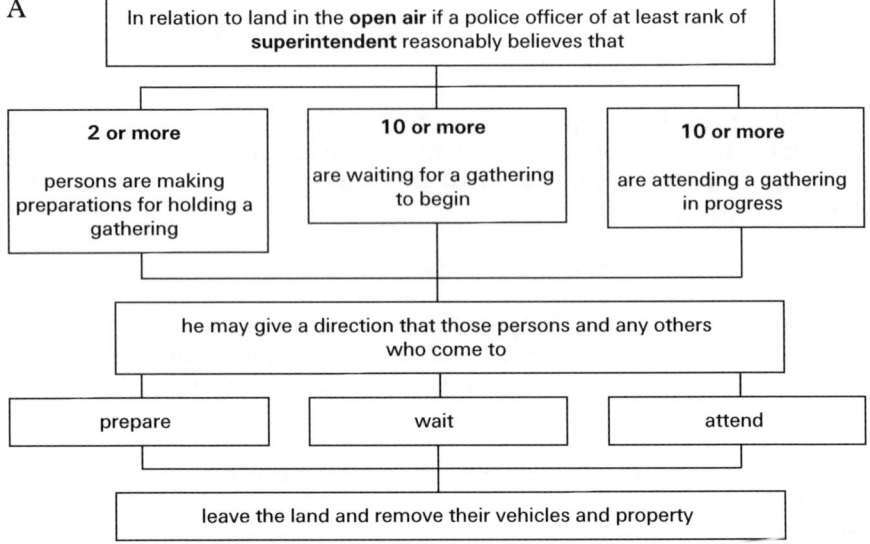

Who can give the direction at the scene? Any constable.

Q What is meant by a gathering?

A [a] on land in the open air;
   [b] of 100 persons or more;
   [c] trespassing or not;
   [d] at which amplified music is played during the night; and by reason of its loudness, duration and time it is played;
   [e] is likely to causes serious distress to the inhabitants of the locality.

The gathering continues during intermissions, and **music** includes sounds of a succession of repetitive beats.

Arrest. If a person knows a direction has been given:

   [i] fails to leave the land ASAP. or;
   [ii] having left, re-enters **within 7 days**
        he may be arrested by a constable in uniform.

OFFENCES RELATED TO PREMISES

Defence. For the accused to show he had a reasonable excuse for not leaving the land.

Exempt. The occupier, his family, employees etc or anyone whose home is on the land.

Q   **Define the powers of the Local Authority in relation to Residing in Vehicles on land**

A   If it appears to a Local Authority that persons are residing **in a vehicle** on any land:

[a] forming part of a highway;
[b] other unoccupied land; or
[c] occupied land without the consent of the occupier,
the authority may give a direction to leave and remove their vehicles and property.

Arrest. If a person knowing that a direction has been given:

[i] fails to leave the land ASAP; or
[ii] having left, re-enters the land **within 3 months,**
he may be arrested by a constable in uniform.

Defence. To prove that his failure to leave/re-entry was due to illness, mechanical breakdown, or other immediate emergency.

Removal order. The local authority can apply to a magistrates' court for a removal order if people ignore the direction. The local authority can enforce the order.

Notice. 24 hours notice must be given to the owner of the land and the residents of their intention to enforce the order.

Q   **Define the offence of Depriving Residential Occupier - [unlawful eviction]**

A   A person shall be guilty of an offence who:

Unlawfully deprives the residential occupier of premises, or occupation of them or part [or attempts] unless he proves that he believed and had reasonable cause to believe that the residential occupier had ceased to reside there.

S 1[2] PROTECTION FROM EVICTION ACT 1977

OFFENCES RELATED TO PREMISES

Q **Define the offence of Harassment of Residential Occupiers**

A A person commits an offence if with intent to cause the residential occupier to:

[a] give up the occupation of the premises [or part]; or
[b] refrain from exercising any right or from pursuing a remedy in respect of the premises,

does acts likely to interfere with the peace or comfort of the residential occupier or his household, or persistently withdraws or withholds services reasonably required for his occupation, **and in the case of a landlord or his agent,** he knows that his conduct is likely to cause the residential occupier to give up occupation or refrain from exercising any right to pursue any remedy.

Residential occupier. Means a person occupying the premises as a resident [under a contract or rule of law] giving him the right to remain in occupation, or restricting the right of any person to recover the premises.

Defence. To prove that he had reasonable grounds for doing the act.

Q **Define the offence of Using Violence to Enter Premises**

A It is an offence, without lawful authority, to use or threaten violence to secure entry to premises where **there is someone present** at the time who opposes the entry which the violence is intended to secure, and the person using the violence knows this is the case.

Defence. This section does not apply to a displaced residential occupier or an intended residential occupier.

Arrest. A constable in uniform.

S 6 CRIMINAL LAW ACT 1977

Q **Who is a Displaced Residential Occupier?**

A Any person who was occupying any premises as a resident immediately before being excluded from occupation by anyone who entered as a trespasser, **but not** a displaced trespasser.

Arrest. A constable in uniform.

OFFENCES RELATED TO PREMISES

Q   Outline the offence of Failing to Leave Premises

A   Any trespasser is guilty of an offence if he fails to leave the premises on being required

by [or on behalf of]:

[a]   a displaced residential occupier; or
[b]   a protected intended occupier.

Defence. To prove that he believed that the person requiring him to leave was not one of the two above.

Non-residential premises. This section does not apply to premises used **mainly** for non-residential premises, [e.g. factories, offices etc].

LICENSED PREMISES

Q   Define Intoxicating Liquor

A   It means any spirits, wine, beer, cider and any fermented, distilled or spirituous liquor.

Excluding
[a]   liquor less than 0.5 % proof; [at the time of sale]
[b]   flavouring essences;
[c]   liquor intended as medicine;
[d]   perfumes

At the time of sale. Where a shandy is poured in a pub and the beer is say 3.5 % but is reduced in strength to less than 0.5% when the lemonade is added, it is intoxicating liquor because it was over 0.5% at the time of sale.

Q   Define Licensed Premises and a Bar

A   **Licensed premises** means premises for which a justices' licence [or occasional licence] is in force.

Bar is any place exclusively or mainly used for both the **sale and consumption** of intoxicating liquor.

Q   What is an Occasional Permission?

A   A temporary licence for the sale of liquor by an organisation not operating for gain e.g. Parent Teachers Association, church committees etc.

Q   What is an Occasional Licence?

A   A temporary licence for the sale of liquor by **a licensee** other than at his premises, e.g. village hall, trade fair etc. Granted by a magistrates court and must **not exceed 3 weeks.**

If the applicant applies in person he must:

[a]   give at least **24 hours notice** to the police;
[b]   provide name and address;

LICENSED PREMISES

[c] provide details of the place and location;
[d] state the period and the hours the licence is to run.

A licence may be granted without a hearing. In order to apply, the applicant must submit to the Justices' clerk **two copies** in writing **within 1 month** of the event. 1 copy is sent to the police.

Note. There is no offence of sale outside permitted hours for an occasional licence nor is there an offence of children under 14 being on the premises. However evidence of children aged under 14 years being on the premises and 'sale after hours' could be used to object to further applications by the licensee.

Q What are Permitted Hours in Licensed Premises?

A

On-licences	
Weekdays	11 am - 11 pm
Sundays Good Friday	12 noon - 10.30pm
Christmas Day	12 noon - 3 pm 7 pm - 10.30 pm
Off-licences	
Weekdays Good Friday	8 am - 11 pm
Sundays	10 am - 10.30 pm
Christmas Day	12 noon - 3 pm 7 pm - 10.30 pm

Magistrates may modify the hours to begin earlier than 11 am but not earlier than 10 am

Q What is meant by Vicarious Liability?

A Where a licensee is himself in charge, he shall not be responsible for acts done by his employees without his knowledge [if the offence requires knowledge on his part.]

LICENSED PREMISES

However where the licensee **delegates all responsibility** to his employee [e.g. away on holiday] he is liable for acts done by his employee without his knowledge.

Q Outline the main exceptions to drinking after 11 pm

A

First 20 minutes	After permitted hours end
30 minutes	If drinking was ancillary to a meal
At any time	By residents
At any time	By friends of the resident entertained at resident's expense
After hours	Employees at the expense of the licensee or the person in charge of the business

Q What are offences relating to the terms of an Off-Licence?

A

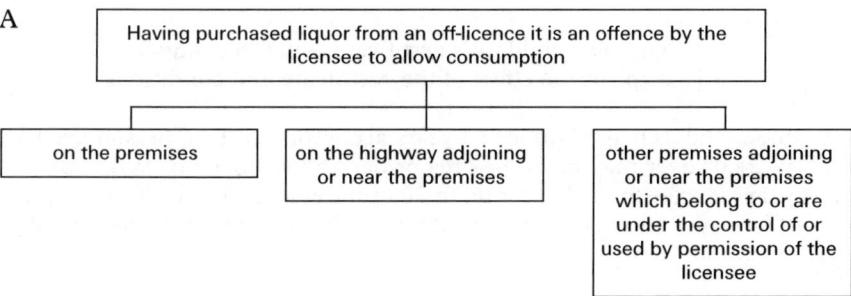

Q What is the offence of allowing under 14s in a bar?

A A licensee shall not allow persons aged under 14 years to be in a bar during permitted hours.

Defence. The person was **apparently** aged 14 years or he exercised due diligence to prevent it.

LICENSED PREMISES

Q   Which children aged under 14 years may be in a bar?

A

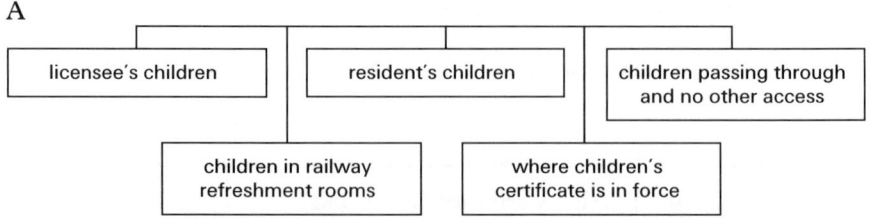

Q   What is a Children's Certificate?

A   A licensee may apply to the licensing justices for a certificate in relation to his premises which includes a bar. The justices may grant a certificate if it appears appropriate and they are satisfied that:

[a]   the area is a suitable environment for under 14 year olds; and
[b]   that meals and soft drinks will be available.

When granted the licensee must keep posted in a conspicuous place a certificate:

[i]   stating a children's certificate is in force; and
[ii]   explain the effect of the certificate and conditions

then, children aged under 14 years accompanied by a person aged 18 years or over may be in the area or bar and the person aged under 14 years may be in the bar for up to 30 minutes after the certificate expires if he or the adult is eating a meal bought before the certificate ceased to operate.

Offence. To fail to comply with the conditions of a children's certificate and where it is alleged that a person was under 14 and it appears to the court that he was aged under 14 years, he shall be deemed to be aged under 14 years unless the contrary is proven.

Defence. To prove that he took all reasonable precautions and exercised due diligence.

LICENSED PREMISES

Q **What is the offence of Providing Liquor to Under 18s?**

A The licensee/servant shall not sell liquor to a person aged under 18 years or knowingly allow him to consume in a bar, or knowingly allow the sale to a person aged under 18 years.

Defence. For the offence of selling it is a defence to prove that he exercised due diligence to avoid the offence; or that he believed he was aged 18 years or over. The licensee may claim the defence of due diligence for acts of his servants.

Buying aged under 18 years. It is an offence for a person aged under 18 years to buy [or attempt to] or consume liquor in a bar. No person shall buy [or attempt to] for a person aged under 18 years in a bar.

Q **Outline the offences of Delivery/Sending liquor for/to under 18s**

A [a] The licensee/servant shall not knowingly deliver, or allow any person to deliver to a person aged under 18 years liquor for consumption off the premises, unless it is made at the residence or workplace of the purchaser
[b] A person shall not knowingly send a person aged under 18 years to licensed premises or other premises for liquor for consumption off the premises.

No offence. Where the under 18 is a member of the licensee's family or employee and is acting as a messenger to deliver the liquor.

Q **Can an under 18 year old work behind a bar?**

A Yes, but only if he is a member of an Approved Training Scheme, and he complies with the conditions.

LICENSED PREMISES

Q **Outline the provisions of the Confiscation of Alcohol (Young Persons) Act 1997**

A

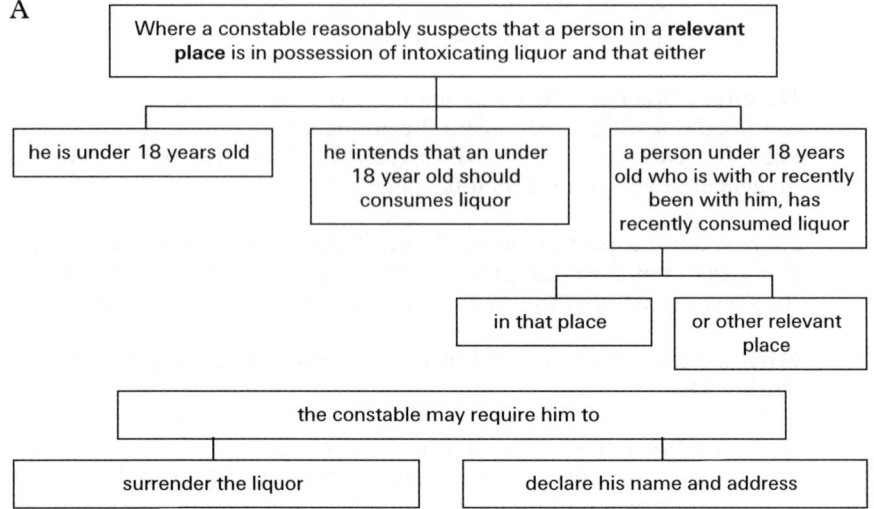

Relevant place. Means any public place [not licensed premises] or any place [other than a public place] to which he has **unlawfully gained access.**

Offence. Failure of the above is an offence.

Warning. Where a constable requires liquor/name and address? he must inform the person of his suspicions and that to fail is an offence.

Arrest. A constable may arrest any person failing the requirement.

Disposal of alcohol. The Constable may dispose of anything surrendered in a manner he considers appropriate.

LICENSED PREMISES

Q   Outline the drunkenness offence

Offence	Who is liable	Conditions	Arrest
Drunkenness	Licensee	permitting drunkenness, or any violent, quarrelsome or riotous behaviour on licensed premises	S 25 PACE Act
Selling to a drunk	Licensee		No
Procuring liquor for a drunk	any person	in licensed premises	No
Aiding a drunk	any person	to obtain or consume on licensed premises	No
Found drunk	Drunk	on a highway or public place or licensed premises	Yes

Q   What is the power to exclude drunks?

A   A Licensee may **refuse to admit, or expel** any person who is drunk, violent, quarrelsome or disorderly, or whose presence in the premises would subject him to a penalty.

Offence. To fail to leave the premises.

A constable. Is there to **help** *the licensee* to expel.

LICENSED PREMISES

Q What is the power of a constable to enter licensed premises?

A
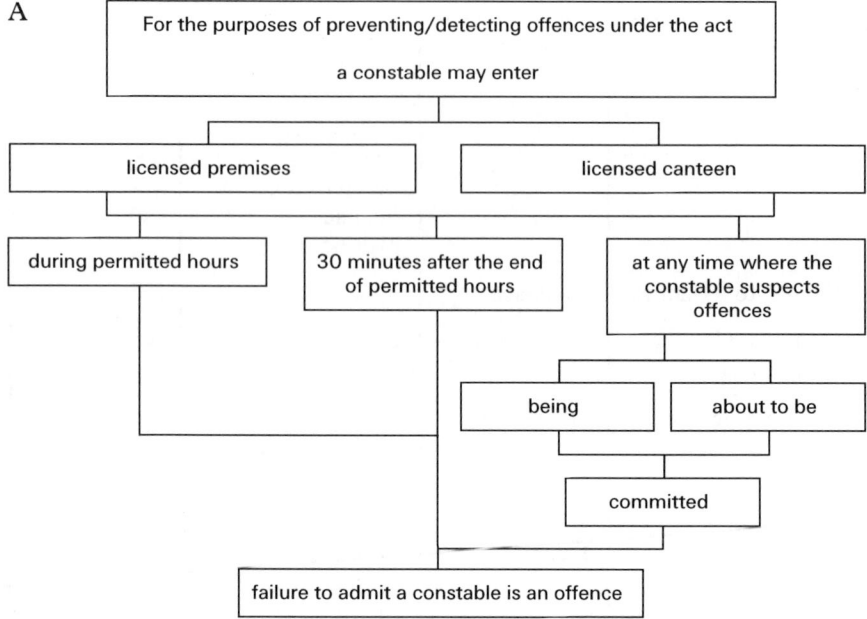

Q What if a Special Hours Certificate is in force?

A The power to enter is during the hours beginning at **11 pm** to **30 minutes after the** end of the hours **permitted in the certificate.**

Q What is an Exclusion Order?

A Under the Licensed Premises [Exclusion of Certain Persons] Act 1980, a court may order persons to be excluded from licensed premises for offences involving violence. The order may exclude persons for any period between **3 months** and **2 years.** The licensee may give express consent for the person to enter!

Offence. To enter the premises in breach of the order.

Power to expel. The licensee/servant may expel such a person and a constable shall, at the request of the licensee/agent **help to expel.**

LICENSED PREMISES

Q What are police powers of Entry and to Expel from Licensed Betting Offices?

A A constable may enter any licensed betting office to ascertain whether it is being run in accordance with the rules and a constable may, on the request of the licensee/servant, **help to expel** from a licensed betting office any person who is liable to be expelled, e.g. persons aged under 18 years, persons who are drunk, violent, quarrelsome or disorderly, or whose presence would subject the licensee to a penalty.

Q Outline police powers of Entry and Inspection of Gaming Machines

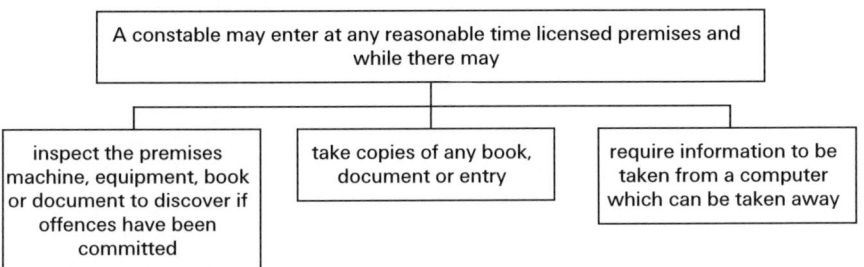

Offence. It is an offence if the licensee/servant:

[a] fails to admit a constable without reasonable excuse;
[b] fails to permit him to inspect the premises/equipment, without reasonable excuse;
[c] fails to produce any book or document which the constable wishes to inspect or copy, without reasonable excuse; or
[d] fails to obtain a computer printout if required, without reasonable excuse.

CIVIL DISPUTES

Q Under the Family Law Act 1996 what is a Non-Molestation order?

A

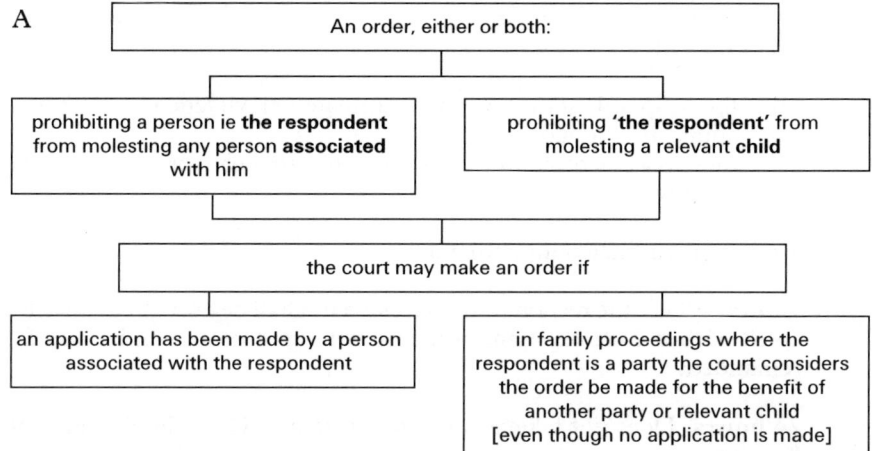

Associated. Means:

[a] they have been married to each other;
[b] they or cohabitees, or former cohabitees;
[c] they live or have lived in the same household [but not as employee, tenant, lodger or boarder];
[d] they are relatives;
[e] they have agreed to marry [whether or not the agreement is terminated]

In relation to a child they are both:

[i] parents; or
[ii] had parental responsibility.

Arrest. Where a court makes an order and it appears that the respondent has used or threatened **violence** against the applicant or relevant child it **shall attach a power of arrest** to one or more provisions of the order

CIVIL DISPUTES

unless satisfied the applicant or child will be adequately protected. A constable may arrest where he has reasonable cause to suspect a breach of the order.

Ex parte. The ability to attach a power of arrest ex parte [in the absence of the other person] exists only if:

[a] the respondent has used or threatened violence against the applicant or child; or
[b] there is a risk of significant harm to the applicant or relevant child if a power of

arrest is not attached immediately.

Court. Where the respondent is arrested he shall be brought before the court **within 24 hours;** and if the matter is not dealt with he may be remanded.

24 hours. Does not take account of Christmas Day, Good Friday or Sundays.

Q   What is a Magistrates Court Order in relation to Domestic Proceedings?

A

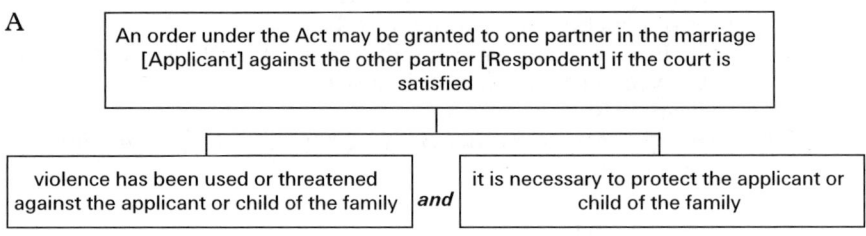

The Order. May contain one or more of the following requirements:

[a] that the respondent shall not use or threaten violence against the person of:

   [i] the applicant; or
   [ii] child of the family;

CIVIL DISPUTES

[b] and any of the following:

[i] he shall leave the matrimonial home;
[ii] prohibiting him from entering the matrimonial home;
[iii] he shall allow the applicant to enter the matrimonial home;
[iv] he shall not incite or assist another to use or threaten violence against the applicant or child of the family.

Arrest. The magistrates may attach a power of arrest if satisfied that the respondent has **physically injured** the applicant or a child of the family and considers **he is likely to do so again.**

A constable may arrest if he believes him to be in breach of the order by:

[a] his use of violence towards the applicant or child; or
[b] his entry into the matrimonial home.

Court. He shall be brought before a court **within** 24 **hours** and if the matter is not dealt with he may be remanded.

24 hours. No account shall be taken of Christmas Day, Good Friday or Sundays.

Q   What is meant by Peaceful Picketing?

A
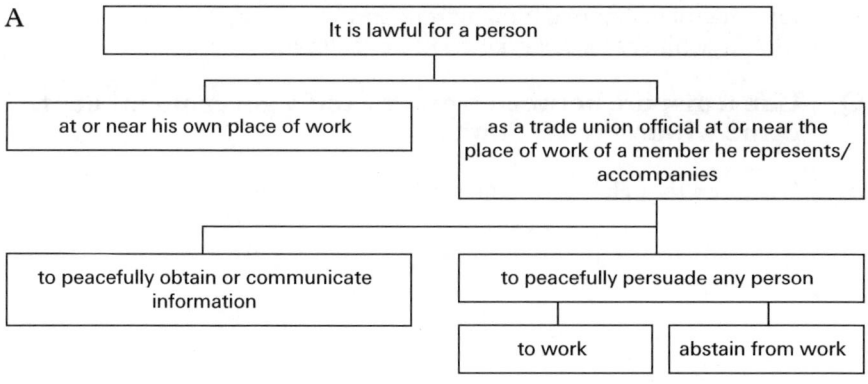

CIVIL DISPUTES

What if he works elsewhere? If he works:

[a]   other than at any one place; or
[b]   it is impracticable to picket there,
      then his place of work shall be deemed to be any premises of his employer from which he works or is administered.

What if he no longer works? If his last employment was terminated in connection with a trade dispute, or given rise to a trade dispute, his place of work shall be deemed to be **his last place of work.**

What if the workplace has moved? A person's place of work does not include new premises of an employer who has moved since dismissing the pickets.

Q   **What is meant by a Trade Dispute?**

A   A dispute between employers and workers relating mainly to:

[a]   terms and conditions of employment, including physical conditions;
[b]   engagement [or not] suspension/termination of employment/duties of 1 or more;
[c]   allocation of work;
[d]   discipline;
[e]   membership of a trade union; and
[f]   machinery for negotiation or consultation.

Q   **Can a dispute between workers and a government dept. come within the section?**

A   Yes, even though it is not the workers 'employer'.

CIVIL DISPUTES

Q Outline the offence of Intimidation in relation to Labour Relations

A

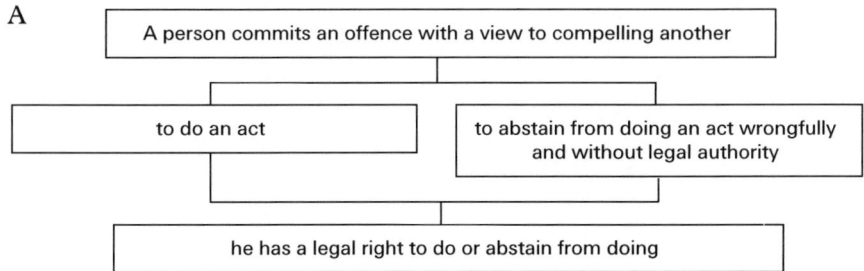

- [a] uses violence or intimidates him, his wife or children or damages his property;
- [b] persistently follows him;
- [c] hides his tools or property or deprives him of their use;
- [d] watches or besets his house or work business or where he is [or the approaches];
- [e] **three or more** follow him in a disorderly manner in any street or road.

Arrest. A constable found committing.

Seamen. This offence does not apply to seamen!

OFFENCES INVOLVING INFORMATION

Q **What is the offence of Unauthorised Access to Computers?**

A A person is guilty of an offence if:

[a] he **causes a computer to perform any func**tion intending to gain access to any program or data; and
[b] he knows that the access is **unauthorised.**

The intent. Need not be directed at:

[i] any particular program or data;
[ii] a program or data of a particular kind, or
[iii] a program or data held in any particular computer.

Secures access. Means by causing the computer to perform a function, he:

[a] alters or erases the program or date;
[b] copies or moves to a different storage;
[c] uses it; or
[d] has it printed from the computer which holds it.

Q **Outline the offence of Unauthorised Access with Intent**

A

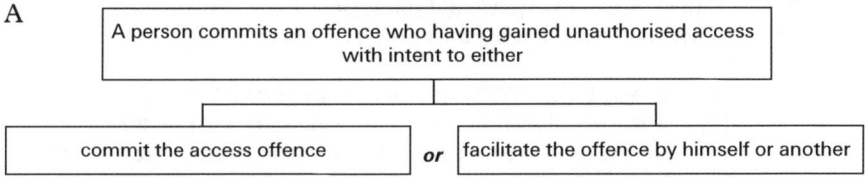

Arrest. Arrestable offence.

Q **Outline the offence of unauthorised Modification of Computer Material**

A A person commits an offence if:

[a] he does any act which causes unauthorised modification of the contents of any computer; with intent to impair its operation,

OFFENCES INVOLVING INFORMATION

        prevent or hinder access, or impair the operation of a program; and
[b]   he knows that it is unauthorised.

Arrest. Arrestable offence.

Virus implantation. Is an offence under this section,

Q   **Under the Data Protection Act 1998 what is the meaning of Data?**

A   Data means information recorded in a form in which it can be processed by equipment operating automatically or in response to instruction given for that purpose or is recorded as part of a relevant filing system.

Relevant filing system. Means any set of information relating to **individuals** to the extent that, although not processed by equipment operating automatically, the set is structured in a way that information relating to a **particular individual** is readily accessible.

Q   **Outline the offence of Obtaining, Disclosure and Sale of Personal Data**

A   1.   A person must not knowingly or recklessly, without the consent of the data controller

    [a]   obtain or disclose personal data; or
    [b]   procure the disclosure for another, unless:

        [i]   it was for preventing or detecting crime; or
        [ii]   authorised by an enactment, rule of law, or order of a court.
        [iii]   he believed he had a right in law to obtain, disclose etc;
        [iv]   he believed he would have had the consent of the data controller;
        [v]   it was justified as being in the public interest.

    [c]   it is an offence **to offer for sale personal data** unlawfully obtained.

Part 2 - Crime

CRIME INTRODUCTION

Define intent

A   A court or jury in deciding whether a person has committed an offence :

  [a] shall **not be bound to infer that he intended or foresaw** a result of his actions by reason only of its being a natural and probable consequence; but
  [b] shall decide whether **he did intend or foresee** that result by reference to all the evidence, drawing such inferences as appear proper.

Q   **Define recklessness**

A   A failure to consider an **obvious** risk or that he **foresaw harm but took the risk**

Q   **Give an example of transferred malice**

A   'A' throws a rock at 'B' intending him injury, but misses and causes injury to 'C'.

Q   **What is meant by actus rea and mens rea?**

A   Actus rea is the physical act of the crime and mens rea is the guilty knowledge, e.g. intent.

Q   **Distinguish between a principal and an accessory**

A   The principal is one who has met all the requirements of an offence whilst an accessory is a person who aids, abets, counsels or procures. An aider and abetter is guilty as a principal.

Q   **When can an omission amount to an offence?**

A   When the 'offender' has a **duty of care** to act in favour of the 'victim' e.g. where a police officer voluntarily fails to intervene to prevent an assault.

CRIME — INTRODUCTION

Q Define incitement

A It is an offence unlawfully to incite another to commit an offence. The offence need not be committed, incitement to commit is the offence.

Q Define Statutory Conspiracy

A It is an offence for any agreement between 2 or more persons to pursue a course of conduct, which, if carried out either:

[a] will involve committing an offence; or
[b] would do so, but in the event it is impossible to commit.

Arrest. Only if the substantive offence is arrestable.

No conviction. If the other party to the agreement is a spouse, child under 10, the victim. However a husband and wife can both be convicted if they conspire with a third party.

Q Define conspiracy to defraud at Common Law

A It is an offence for any agreement by 2 or more persons by dishonesty to deprive a person of what is his or he is entitled to or to harm his proprietary rights

Q Define a criminal attempt

A If with intent to commit an offence, a person **does an act which is more than merely preparatory** to the commission of the offence he is guilty of attempt.

Impossible offences. Where the above definition fits, a person may be charged with an attempt even though the offence is impossible. [e.g. searching an empty purse for money]

CRIME — INTRODUCTION

Q **Define the offence of Interfering with Motor Vehicles**

A

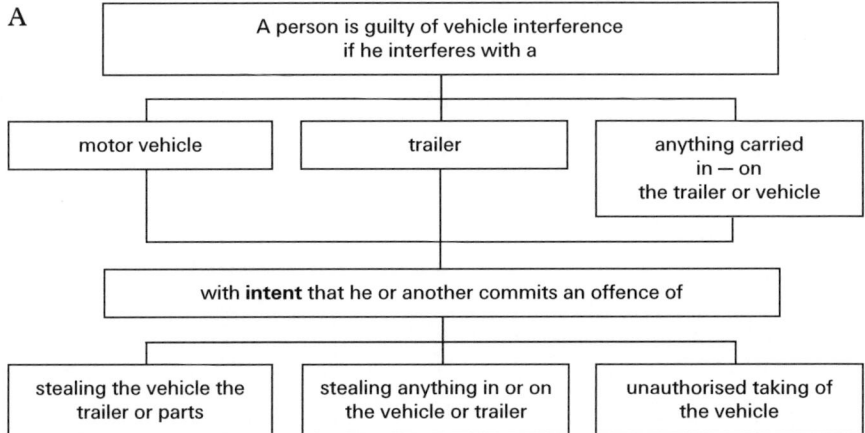

Which charge? Where it is shown that a person accused under this section intended that one of the offences should be committed, it is immaterial that it cannot be shown which one it was.

DEFENCES

Q   **Outline the general defences to crime**

A   **Automatism.** Involuntary action - e.g. a driver being attacked by a swarm of bees.

Intoxication. Voluntary intoxication is no defence, however if it is involuntary, i.e. brought about by a drink being 'spiked' the defence may be used.

Insanity. The test for insanity was established by the **McNaughten rules** i.e.

... to establish a defence on the ground of insanity, it must be clearly proved that, at the time of the committing of the act, the accused was labouring under such a **defect of reason, from disease of mind,** as not to know the nature and quality of the act he was doing, or if he did know it, that he did not know he was doing wrong.

Mistake. Mistake may be claimed where the mistake would negate mens rea.

Duress. Where a person is threatened with **death or serious injury :**

[a]   the threat must have caused the defendant to commit the crime;
[b]   he must have acted as would a reasonable person;
[c]   the threat or injury must be more or less immediate;
[d]   no defence to murder.

Duress of circumstances. Where a person commits an offence to avoid serious consequences, e.g. a disqualified driver driving a dying man to hospital, the court will decide the reasonableness of the offender's behaviour.

Defence of self, another, or property.

A person may use such force as is reasonable in the circumstances in the prevention of crime, or in effecting or assisting in the lawful arrest of offenders or suspected offenders or of persons unlawfully at large.

S 3[1] CRIMINAL LAW ACT 1967.

DEFENCES

A 'pre-emptive' strike may be justified in all the circumstances.

Infancy.

Irrebuttable. A child under 10 cannot commit crime [deli incapax];

Rebuttable. a child between 10 and 13 are presumed not to be capable of committing crime.

HOMOCIDE

Q Define murder

A   A person is guilty of murder who :

[a] being of sound memory and discretion;
[b] unlawfully kills;
[c] a reasonable creature in being;
[d] under the Queen's peace,
[e] with malice aforethought..

COMMON LAW

Arrest. Serious arrestable offence.

Mens rea. To kill or cause GBH.

Under the Queen's peace. Legitimises killing during the course of warfare.

The 3 year rule. Where the death occurs after 3 years from the time of the injury the consent of the Attorney-General is needed

LAW REFORM ACT 1996

Q Define the defences of Diminished Responsibility, Provocation and Suicide Pact

A   **Diminished responsibility.** Where a person is suffering from an **abnormality of mind** so as to substantially **impair his mental responsibility** he shall not be convicted of murder.

Provocation. Where a jury can find evidence that he was provoked to lose self-control the question whether it was enough to make **a reasonable man do as he did** shall be left to the jury and they shall take into account things said and done.

The test. The jury must consider how a reasonable person **sharing the defendant's characteristics** would have reacted to the provocation.

HOMOCIDE

Suicide pact. A common agreement between 2 or more persons, having for its object the death of them all, whether or not each take his own life, and must be done with the **settled intention of dying** in pursuance of the pact.

Where 'A' and 'B' form a suicide pact, 'B' kills himself and 'A' then changes his mind, the survivor is guilty of complicity. Where 'A' kills 'B' then changes his mind, he may be guilty of manslaughter.

Manslaughter. Where any of the above 3 defences are successful, a jury may bring in a verdict of manslaughter.

Q Define manslaughter

A   Manslaughter is the unlawful killing of another, by an unlawful act which was likely to cause bodily harm, or by gross negligence.

Distinguished from murder. On the grounds that there is no malice aforethought.

Unlawful act, The defendant must have the required mens rea for the act, e.g. assault.

Gross negligence. Such cases arise where there is a duty of care which is breached, i.e. medical staff, train drivers, machine operators.

Arrest. Serious arrestable offence.

Q Define the offence of Aiding Suicide

A   A person who aids, abets, counsels or procures the suicide of another, or attempts, commits an offence.

Alternative verdict. This offence is an alternative verdict on a charge murder or manslaughter.

Arrest. Arrestable offence.

Q   Define Solicitation of Murder

A   Whosoever shall solicit, encourage, persuade or endeavour to persuade, or propose to any person, to murder another shall be guilty of an offence.

'Contract killings' This would appear to be an appropriate charge prior to the killing. The offence is complete even if the person encouraged was an undercover police officer.

MISUSE OF DRUGS

Q Give examples of Class A, B and C drugs

A **Class A,** include the most dangerous drugs, heroin, morphine, opiates, cocaine, LSD;

Class B, includes cannabis, cannabis resin and some amphetamines;

Class C, include many commonly abused prescription drugs, e.g. diazepam.

Q What does Cannabis not include?

A [a] cannabis resin;
[b] the mature stalk [or fibre from it]; and
[c] seed from the plant.

What class ? Both cannabis and cannabis resin are Class B drugs.

Q Define the offence of possession

A It is an offence to unlawfully possess a controlled drug.

Arrest. Arrestable offence.

Q Define the 2 statutory defences to POSSESSION of a controlled drug

A [a] **to prevent an offence being committed:**

[i] knowing or suspecting it to be a controlled drug;
[ii] took possession **to prevent another person committing an offence;** and
[iii] as soon as possible took steps to **destroy the drug;** or
[iv] **to deliver to lawful custody.**

[b] **to deliver to lawful custody:**

[i] knowing or suspecting it to be a controlled drug;
[ii] he took possession **to deliver it to a person lawfully entitled** to receive the drug; and

MISUSE OF DRUGS

[iii] as soon as he took possession he took all steps reasonable **to deliver it to such a person.**

S 5 MISUSE OF DRUGS ACT 1971

Q Define the GENERAL DEFENCE under S 28 of the Misuse of Drugs Act 1971

A In relation to unlawful production, unlawful supply, unlawful possession, possession with intent to supply, unlawful cultivation of cannabis and offences connected with opium, it will be a defence to prove :

Lack of knowledge of fact:

[a] he did not know or suspect, [nor had reason to suspect]
[b] the existence of a fact alleged by the prosecution which it must prove.

Who is protected? An innocent messenger.

Lack of knowledge of Controlled Drug:

Where it is necessary for the prosecution to prove it was a particular controlled drug and it has been proved that it was that drug it will be a defence to prove :

[a] he thought the substance was **something other than a controlled drug,** and had no reason to believe it to be a controlled drug; or
[b] he thought it was a controlled drug **which he could lawfully possess,**

but he shall not escape conviction by only proving :

[i] he did not suspect or believe [nor have reason to]
[ii] that the substance was **the particular drug** in question.

Who is protected ? A person mistakenly believing a white substance [heroin] to be salt, or it was a drug prescribed for him by his doctor. **But not** that he thought it was one drug when in fact it was another.

MISUSE OF DRUGS

Q **Define the offence of Producing a Controlled Drug**

A It is an offence to:

[a] unlawfully produce a controlled drug; or
[b] to be concerned in the production of the drug.

Arrest. Arrestable offence.

Q **Define the offence of Supplying Controlled Drugs**

A It is an offence to:

[a] supply or **offer to supply** a controlled drug to another;
[b] to be concerned in the supply; or
[c] to be concerned in the making of an offer to supply.

Arrest. Arrestable offence.

Offer to supply. The offence is complete once the **offer** is made.

Q **Define the offence of Possession with Intent to Supply**

A It is an offence to possess [lawfully or not] a controlled drug with intent to supply.

Arrest. Arrestable offence.

Intent. A person in lawful possession, e.g. doctor, who intends to unlawfully supply is guilty of this offence.

Q **Define the offence of Cannabis Cultivation**

A It is an offence to unlawfully cultivate cannabis.

Arrest. Arrestable offence.

Cultivate. Includes watering, feeding.

MISUSE OF DRUGS

Q Define the offence of Supplying Articles for Administering or Preparing Drugs

A   A person commits an offence who supplies or offers to supply:

[a] any article which may be used or adapted [on its own or in conjunction with other articles] in the **administration** by a person of a controlled drug to himself or another, believing the article to be used unlawfully;

[b] any article which may be used to **prepare** a controlled drug for administration by himself or another, believing the article is to be used unlawfully.

Unlawful. Any administration of a controlled drug will be unlawful **except,** when the

[i] administration to self or another is not an offence of unlawful supply;

[ii] administration to himself is not an offence of unlawful possession.

Q Outline the offence of Opium Misuse

A   It is an offence for a person to :

[a] smoke or use prepared opium; or
[b] to frequent a place used for opium smoking; or
[c] to possess

[i] any pipes or other utensils made or adapted for use in connection with the **smoking of opium:**

which have been used in that connection, either by him, or with his knowledge and permission, or which he intends to use or permit others to use in that connection;

[ii] any utensils which have been used by him or with his knowledge and permission for the preparation of **opium for smoking.**

Arrest. Arrestable offence.

MISUSE OF DRUGS

Q Outline the offence of Drugs Misuse by Occupiers

A

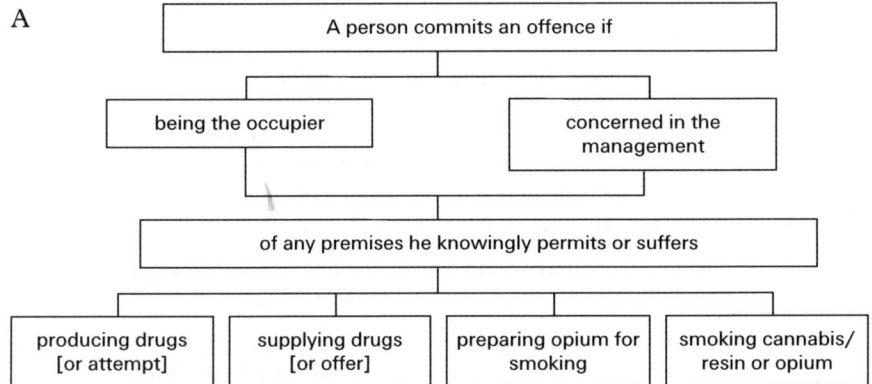

Arrest. Arrestable offence.

Management. The person planning, organising and actual use of the premises.

Permit/suffer. Turning a 'blind eye' to the activities will do.

Q Define the offence of Misuse of Drugs Outside the UK

A A person commits an offence if **in the UK** he assists or induces the commission in any place **outside the UK** of an offence under law in force in that other place.

Q Outline Police Powers of Entry etc

A

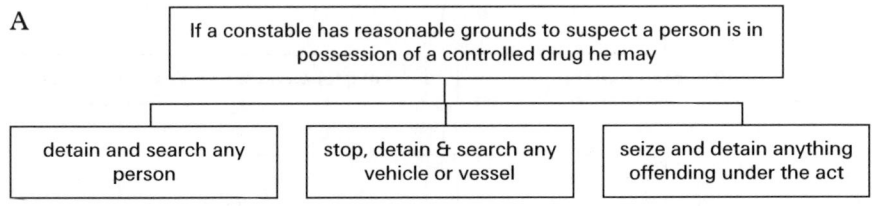

Vehicle/ vessel. Includes hovercraft.

S 23 MISUSE OF DRUGS ACT 1971

MISUSE OF DRUGS

Q   What are the grounds for the issue of a Warrant?

A   A magistrate may issue a warrant if satisfied on information on oath that there is reasonable grounds to suspect :

[a]   that any **controlled drug** is unlawfully in the possession of a person on the premises;
[b]   or that **a document** relating to an unlawful transaction or dealing is in possession of a person on the premises

Q   What are the powers under the Warrant?

A   [a]   at any time **within 1 month** from the date of the warrant;
[b]   enter, search the premises and persons; and

[i]   if there are grounds for suspecting that an offence has been committed in respect of **controlled drugs found;** or
[ii] there is reason to believe that **any document found** relates to an unlawful transaction,

seize and detain the drugs or document.

S 23 MISUSE OF DRUGS ACT, 1971

Obstruction. It is an offence to obstruct a constable.

Unlawful transaction.
The document is any document in relation to a transaction in the UK or, if carried out abroad would be an offence under the foreign law.

Q   What is the offence of Supply of Intoxicating Substances?

A

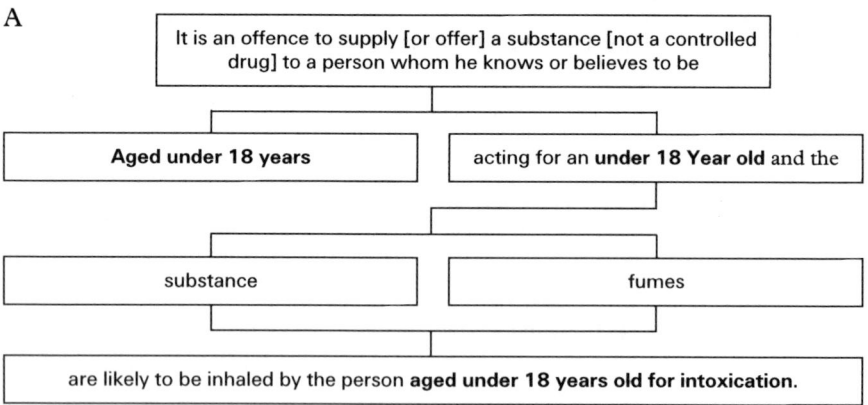

PREGNANCY AND CHILDBIRTH OFFENCES

Q Define Infanticide

A
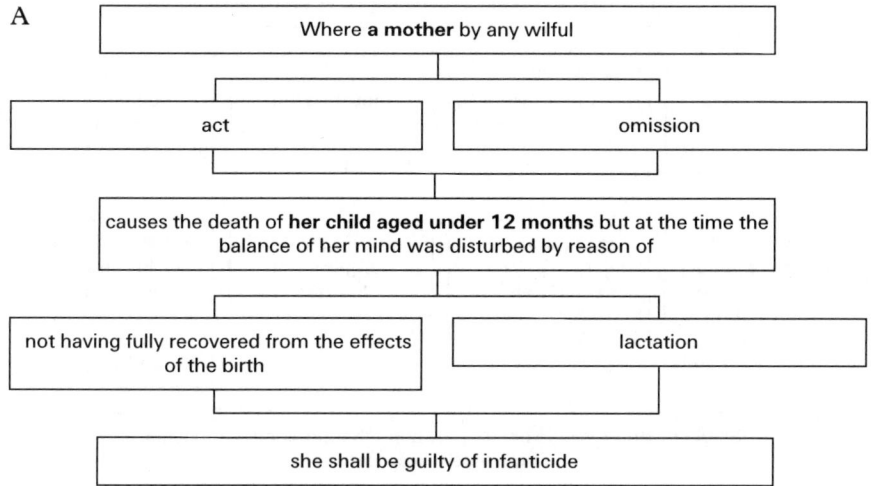

Lactation. The secretion of milk from the breasts.

Arrest. Arrestable offence.

S 1 INFANTICIDE ACT 1938

Q Define Concealment of Birth

A Where a woman gives birth to a child, any person who by any secret disposition of the dead body of the child, attempts to conceal its birth, commits an offence.

Other offences. Disposing of a body to prevent an inquest and preventing burial.

PREGNANCY AND CHILDBIRTH OFFENCES

Q   When is an Abortion Lawful?

A

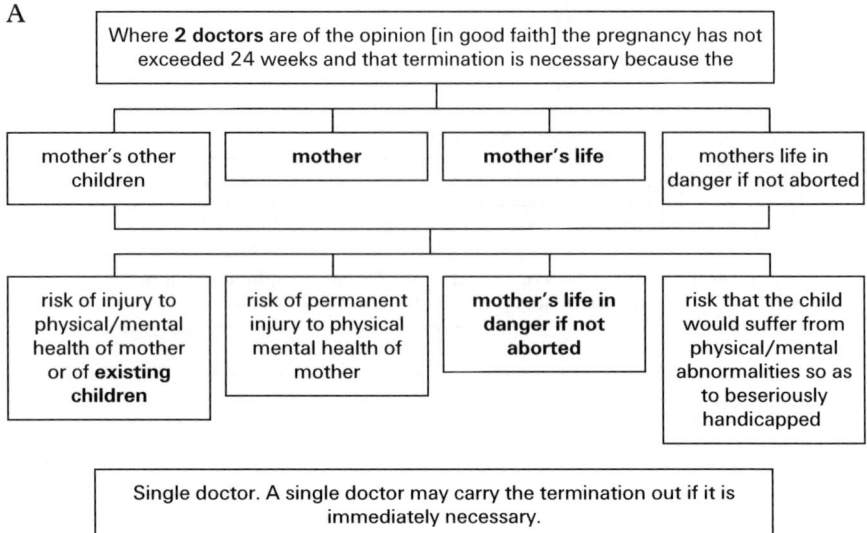

Q   Define Criminal Abortion

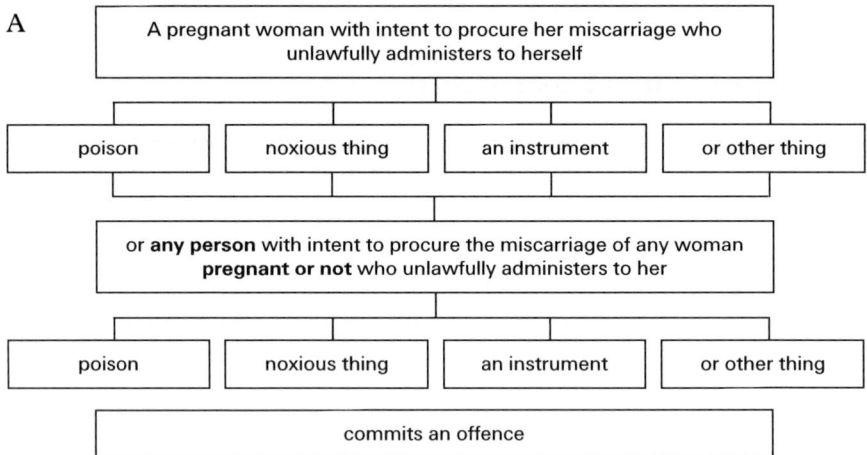

PREGNANCY AND CHILDBIRTH OFFENCES

Arrest. Arrestable offence.

What if the woman is not pregnant? For the offence to be complete the woman must be pregnant, otherwise it is a Criminal Attempt.

Q Define the offence of Procuring Drugs etc for Abortion

A   Any person who procures or supplies any poison, noxious thing, instrument or other thing, knowing it was for an unlawful abortion commits an offence.

Arrest. Arrestable offence.

S 59 Offences Against the Person Act 1861

Pregnant or not ? It is not necessary for the woman to be pregnant.

Q Define Child Destruction

A   The offence is committed by any person who:

[a] with intent to destroy the life of a child capable of being born alive;
[b] by any wilful act;
[c] causes the child to die before it has an existence independent of its mother.

Arrest. Arrestable offence.

S 1 Infant Life [Preservation] Act 1929

Capable of being born alive. Proof that the child was at least **28 weeks in gestation**

No offence. If done in good faith only to preserve the life of the mother.

OFFENCES AGAINST THE PERSON

Q **Define Common Assault and Battery**

A **Assault** is any act which, intentional or reckless, causes another **to apprehend** immediate and unlawful personal violence and **battery** is the actual **application of force.**

Q **What is a Certificate of Dismissal?**

A Where a defendant is acquitted of common assault, the magistrates must issue a certificate of dismissal which means that **a civil action cannot be brought** against him.

Q **Define Assault with Intent to Resist Arrest**

A It is an offence to assault any person with intent to resist or prevent the lawful apprehension of himself or another for any offence.

Who is protected? Police, store detectives, bailiffs etc.

Q **Define the offence of Assault on Police**

A A person commits an offence who assaults a constable in the execution of his duty or a **person assisting a constable** in the execution of his duty.

Q **Define the offence of Obstructing Police**

A Any person who resists or wilfully obstructs a constable in the execution of his duty or a **person assisting a constable** in the execution of his duty, commits an offence.

Obstruction. Involves some sort of wilful resistance.

Arrest. Only if the obstruction involves a breach of the peace.

OFFENCES AGAINST THE PERSON

Q Define ABH

A   A person commits an offence if he assaults another person so as to cause actual bodily harm.

ABH. Means any hurt or injury calculated to interfere with the health or comfort of the victim, it can include shock and mental 'injury'.

Arrest. Arrestable offence.

S 47 Offences Against the Person Act 1871

Q Define Unlawful Wounding Contrary to S 20

A

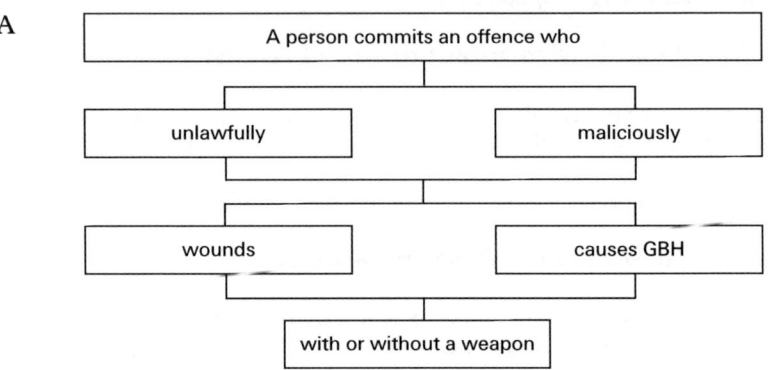

Arrest. Arrestable offence.

Wound. Is the breaking of the whole skin [internally or externally]

GBH. Means really serious harm including psychiatric harm.

Maliciously. Means that the defendant must realise that there is a risk of harm.

OFFENCES AGAINST THE PERSON

Q   Outline Wounding with Intent Contrary to S 18

A
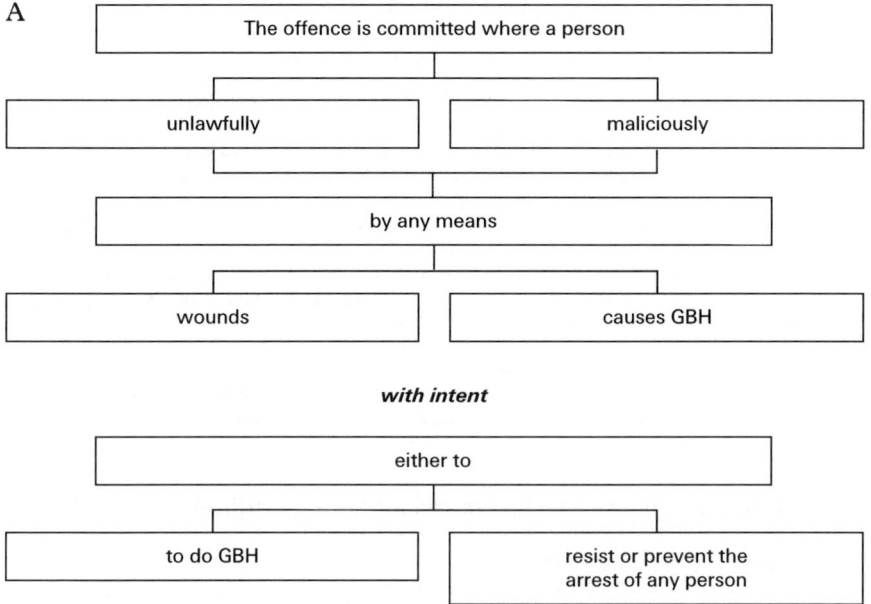

Arrest. Arrestable offence.

By any means. No actual contact is required, e.g. woman jumping from a train to escape a rapist.

Intent. There must be an intention to cause serious harm or to resist or prevent arrest.

OFFENCES AGAINST THE PERSON

Q Define Torture

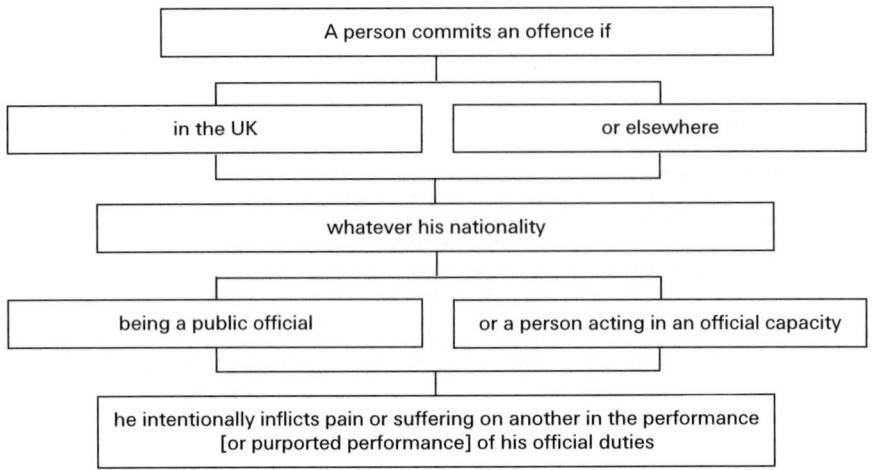

Defence. To prove he had lawful authority, justification or excuse.

Arrest. Arrestable offence.

AG. Consent of Attorney-General is needed to prosecute

Non public officials. Commit this offence if done with the consent or acquiescence of a public official and the public official was performing [purporting] his duties when he instigated the offence.

Pain and suffering. It is immaterial whether the pain or suffering is physical/mental or caused by an act or 0mission.

S 134 CRIMINAL JUSTICE ACT 1988

Q Define the offence of Poisoning

A It is an offence to unlawfully and maliciously administer [or cause to be] any poison, destructive or noxious thing to **endanger life** or cause **GBH**.

Arrest. Arrestable offence.

OFFENCES AGAINST THE PERSON

Q Define the offence of Poisoning with Intent

A It is an offence to unlawfully and maliciously administer [or cause to be] any poison, destructive or noxious thing **with intent to injure, aggrieve or annoy.**

Arrest. Arrestable offence.

S 24 OFFENCES AGAINST THE PERSON ACT 1861

Q Define the offence of False Imprisonment

A It is an offence at common law to falsely imprison any person.

Arrest. Arrestable offence.

Imprison. Keeping someone in a place unlawfully is imprisonment.

Q Define the offence of Kidnapping at common law

A It is an offence of kidnapping to take or carry away another without their consent and without lawful excuse.

Arrest. Serious arrestable offence.

OFFENCES AGAINST THE PERSON

Q Outline the offence of Hostage Taking

A
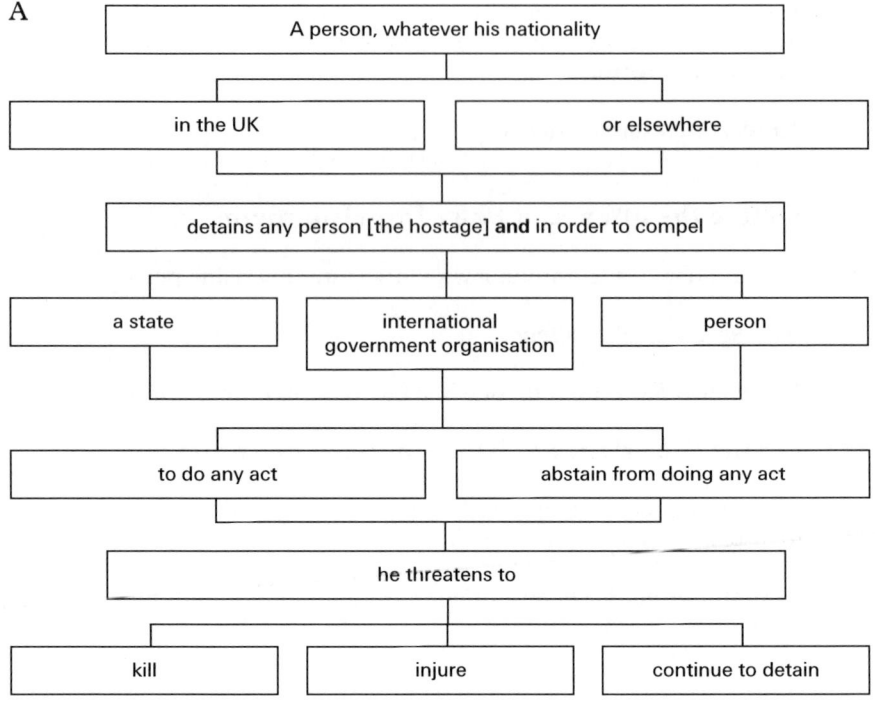

Arrest. Serious arrestable offence.

AG. Consent of the Attorney-General is required to prosecute.

S I Taking of Hostages Act 1982

OFFENCES AGAINST THE PERSON

Q Compare False Imprisonment, Kidnapping and Hostage Taking

False imprisonment	Kidnapping	Hostage taking
Detaining someone without lawful authority. The detention may be committed recklessly	Take someone away without lawful authority. The taking may be done recklessly	Detaining a person to compel a state, etc to do or not do something accompanied by threats

SEXUAL OFFENCES

Q   Why was the Sex Offenders Act 1977 introduced?

A   To monitor their movement and impose controls.

Q   To whom does the Act apply?

A   [a]   paedophiles;
    [b]   persons convicted of rape;

        [i]   rape;
        [ii]   intercourse with a girl aged under 13 years;
        [iii] intercourse with a girl aged between 13 and 16 years [if man was 20+];
        [iv]   sexual offences against a girl aged under 16 years, and, providing the victim is aged under 18 years:
        [v]   incest by a man;
        [vi]   buggery [if man was aged 20 years and over];
        [vii] indecent assault between men [if man was aged 20 years and over]; and
        [viii] assault with intent to commit buggery; and

    [c]   having been found not guilty by reason of insanity of such an offence;
    [d]   having been cautioned by the police for admitting such an offence;
        also other offences of:.
    [e]   indecency with a child;
    [f]   inciting a girl aged under 16 years to have incest;
    [g]   indecent photographs of children;

Q   What are the notification requirements?

A

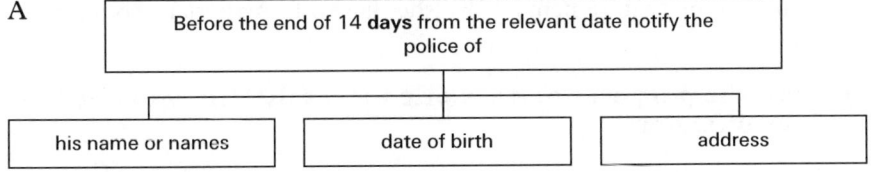

SEXUAL OFFENCES

Relevant date. From his conviction but does not include time spent in custody, outside UK or in hospital. Effectively it means 14 days from release from custody.

Q What if he has a change in circumstances?

A Within **14 days** of:

changing his name, address or residing in a different police area for the qualifying period

Qualifying period. Means 14 days or two or more times within any 12 month period which amount to 14 days.

Q What is the method of notification?

A By attending a police station in their area and giving oral notification to a constable or authorised person, or in writing.

Q Summarise the gist of the Act

A Where a person has been **convicted** of a relevant offence [paedophiles and serious sexual offenders], then within 14 **days** of release from custody, [hospital etc] they must report to the police, personally or in writing, stating name, date of birth and address, and if his circumstances change he must report again, within 14 **days** of the use of a new name or address. If he stays somewhere in the UK [say on holiday] for 14 **days** or **two or more times in any 12 months which amount to 14 days,** he must again notify the police in that area.

Q Outline the offence of Failing to Comply with Notification

A If a person, without reasonable cause, fails to comply with his notification requirement or furnishes false information, he commits an offence.

Q For the purposes of a sex offenders ORDER who else is a sex offender?

A A person who has committed an offence **in any part of the world** and which would amount to a sex offence [under the Act] **in the UK.**

SEXUAL OFFENCES

Q Who can apply for a Sex Offenders Order?

A The chief officer of police, where:

  [a] the person is a sex offender, and
  [b] he has acted in a way **which gives reasonable cause to believe** that an order is necessary,
  [c] to protect the public from serious harm.

Q What is the effect of a sex offenders order?

A It makes the offender:

  [a] subject to the notification rules, and
  [b] it may refrain him from doing any act [ie visiting schools].

Q How long does the order last?

A 5 years. The order can only be discharged with the consent of both parties.

Q Is there a power of arrest for breaching the order?

A Yes. Arrestable offence.

Q Define Rape

A

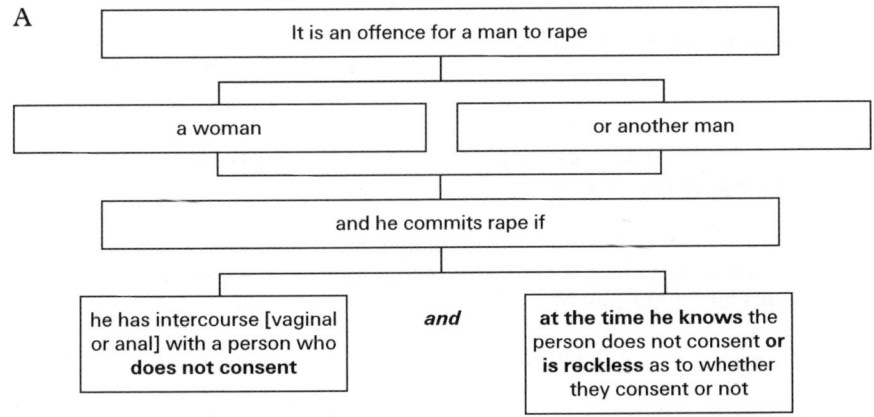

It is an offence for a man to rape

a woman | or another man

and he commits rape if

he has intercourse [vaginal or anal] with a person who **does not consent** | **and** | **at the time he knows** the person does not consent **or is reckless** as to whether they consent or not

149

SEXUAL OFFENCES

Arrest. Serious arrestable offence.

Impersonating husband. It is rape if he induces a married woman to have intercourse by impersonating her husband.

Consent. Cannot be obtained by force, fear or fraud.

Intercourse. Is complete upon proof of penetration only.

S 1 SEXUAL OFFENCES ACT 19%

Q   Define the offence of Procuration

A   It is an offence for a person to procure a woman by
 [a]   threats or intimidation; or
 [b]   false pretences or representations,
       to have sexual intercourse in **any part of the world.**

Q   Define Procuring Prostitution

A

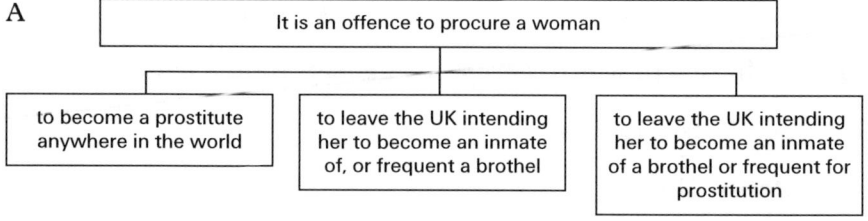

Arrest. Arrestable offence.

Ss22/23 SEXUAL OFFENCES ACT 1956

Q   Define the offence of Detaining a Woman for Unlawful Sexual Intercourse

A   It is an offence to detain a woman against her will on premises with the intention that she has unlawful sexual intercourse with a man or men, or to detain her in a brothel.

Arrest. Arrestable offence

Removal of clothes. A woman who 'steals' clothes to escape from the premises or a brothel shall not be liable to legal proceedings.

SEXUAL OFFENCES

Q Define the offence of Living on Immoral Earnings

A It is an offence for a man to knowingly live **wholly or partly** on the earnings of prostitution.

Arrest. Arrestable offence.

Living on. Means living with, or is habitually in the company of a prostitute, or exercises control, direction or influence over her movements showing he is aiding, abetting or compelling her prostitution.

What if the prostitute is a man? A man or woman living on the earnings of a prostitute is guilty of the same offence.

Q Define the offence of a Woman Exercising Control of a Prostitute

A It is an offence for a woman **for the purpose of gain** to exercise control, direction or influence over a prostitute in a way which shows she is aiding, abetting etc.

Arrest. Arrestable offence.

Q What is the offence of Keeping a Brothel?

A It is an offence for:

[a] **a person** to keep a brothel, or to manage, act or assist in its management;
[b] **a landlord** to let the whole or part of the premises as a brothel or where the premises is so used to wilfully allow it to continue;
[c] **a tenant, occupier or person in charge** of premises to knowingly permit them to be used as a brothel;
[d] a tenant or occupier of premises to knowingly permit it to be used for **habitual prostitution.**

Q Define the offence of Soliciting by a Common Prostitute

A It is an offence for a **common prostitute** to loiter or solicit in a street or public place for the purposes of prostitution.

Arrest. A constable finds committing.

SEXUAL OFFENCES

Cautioning. Before a prosecution is brought, it is usual for the woman to have been cautioned for the offence at least twice during the last 12 months.

Advertising services. Does not amount to solicitation as the woman needs to be present.

Q Define the offence of 'Kerb-crawling' by men

A

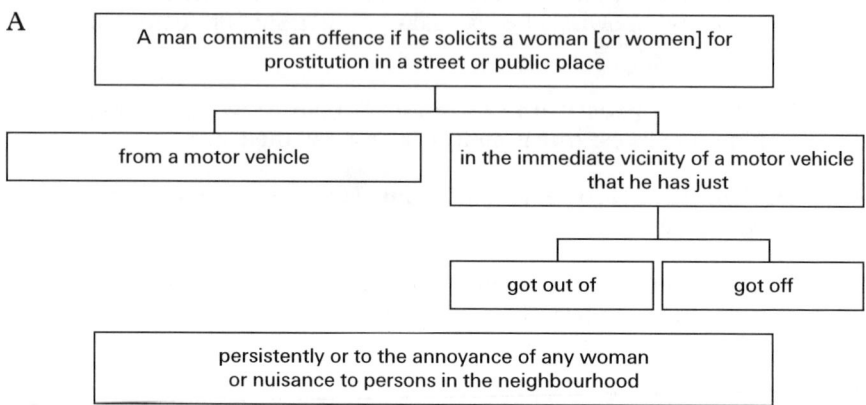

Q Define the offence of Importuning by Men

A   It is an offence for a man to **persistently** solicit or importune in a public place for immoral purposes.

Q Define Incest

A   **By a man,** it is an offence to have sexual intercourse with a woman he knows to be his mother, sister, daughter, granddaughter;

By a woman aged 16 or over to consent to sexual intercourse with a man she knows to be her grandfather, father, brother or son.

Arrest. Arrestable offence.

Ss 10 & 11 Sexual Offences Act 1956

SEXUAL OFFENCES

Q **Define the offence of a girl aged under 16 years of age being Incited to Incestuous Intercourse**

A It is an offence for a man to incite a girl **aged under 16 years of age** to have sexual intercourse with him whom he knows to be his granddaughter, daughter or sister [including half-sister].

Q **Define the offence of Buggery**

A

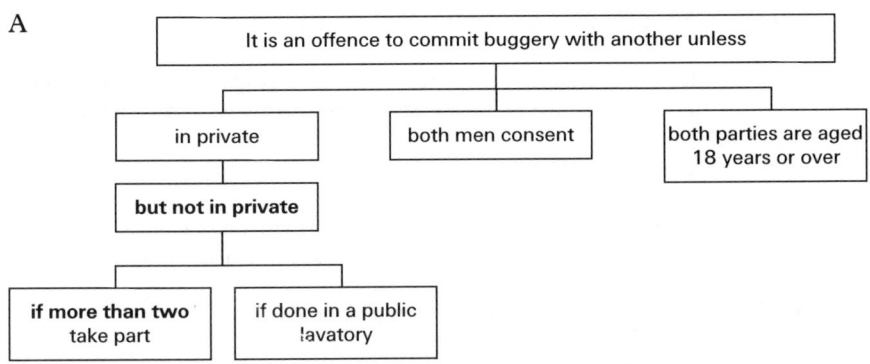

Arrest. Arrestable offence [if the 'victim' is aged under 16 years of age, Serious arrestable offence].

Buggery. Is anal intercourse with a male, female or animal and includes vaginal intercourse by a man with an animal or woman with a male animal.

Q **Define the offence of Assault with Intent to Commit Buggery**

A It is an offence for a person to assault another with intent to commit buggery.

Arrest. Arrestable offence.

SEXUAL OFFENCES

Q   Define the offence of Procuring Another to Commit Buggery

A   A man who procures another man to commit buggery with a third man commits an offence.

Note. The act between the two men may be no offence, the offence is in the procurement.

Q   Define the offence of Gross Indecency

A   It is an offence for a man to commit an act of gross indecency with another man or procure an act of gross indecency with a third man.

Arrest. Arrestable offence.

No offence. If done in private and both men are aged 18 years or over.

S 13 SEXUAL OFFENCES ACT 19.56

Q   Define the offence of Indecent Assault

A   It is an offence for a person to indecently assault a man or woman.

Arrest. Arrestable offence.

Consent. A boy or girl aged under 16 years of age cannot give consent.

SEXUAL OFFENCES

Q Define the offence of Administering Drugs for Unlawful Sexual Intercourse

A
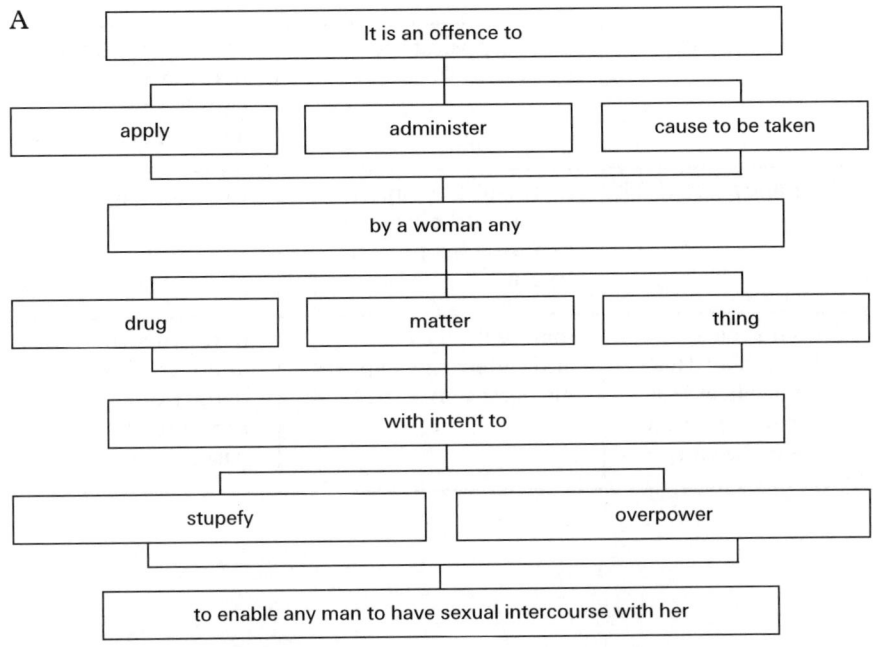

Date rape drugs. Are included in this offence.

S 4 Sexual Offences Act 1956

SEXUAL OFFENCES

Q Contrast the Indecent Exposure Offences

	Who, how and where	**Intent**
Common Law	man exposing the person	to outrage public decency or simulating a sexual act
Vagrancy Act 1824	man **w**illfully, **o**penly **l**ewdly and **o**bscenely exposing his person [**wolo**]	to insult a female
Town Police Clauses Act 1847 [not applicable in the Metropolitan Police District]	man willfully and indecently exposes his person in a street	to the obstruction, annoyance or danger or any resident or passengers

OFFENCES AGAINST CHILDREN AND VULNERABLE PERSONS

Q Outline the offence of Child Abduction [Person Connected with the Child]

A It is an offence for a person **connected with a child aged under 16 years of age** to take or send the child **outside the UK** without the appropriate consent.

Connected with: [a] parent;
[b] [where not married at the birth] father;
[c] guardian;
[d] person with a residence order; or
[e] has custody.

Appropriate consent means the consent of each of the following:

[a] mother;
[b] father [if he has parental responsibility];
[c] guardian;
[d] person with a resident order;
[e] person with custody; or
[f] leave of a court
[g] where a person has custody, leave of the court.

Arrest. Arrestable offence.

OFFENCES AGAINST CHILDREN AND VULNERABLE PERSONS

Defence.

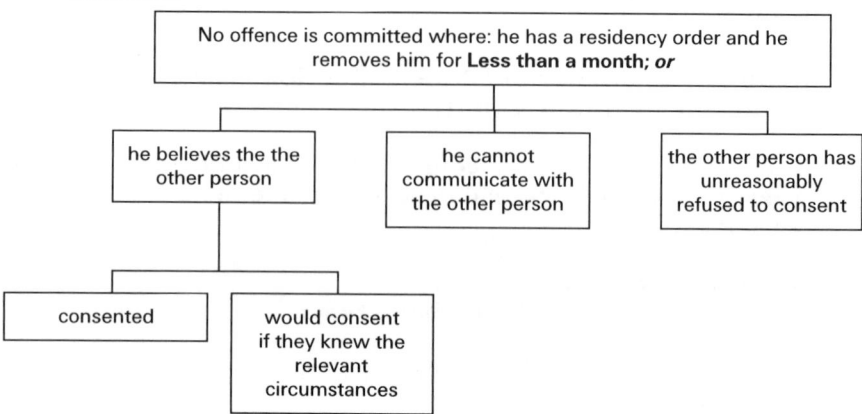

S 1 CHILD ABDUCTION ACT 1984

Q **Outline the offence of Child Abduction [Person NOT connected with the child]**

A It is an offence for a person **not connected with the child,** without lawful authority to take or detain a child **aged under 16 years of age so** as to remove him or keep him out of lawful control from a person entitled to lawful control.

Arrest. Arrestable offence.

Who commits the offence? Anyone who **is not:**

[a]   mother;
[b]   father [if married at the time of birth];
[c]   guardian, person with custody or residence order.

S 2 CHILD ABDUCTION ACT 1984

Defence. It shall be a defence to prove:

[a]   At the time he believed the child **had attained 16 years of age;**
[b]   [where the father and mother were not married at the time of his birth]

  [i]   he is the father; or
  [ii] he believed he was the father.

OFFENCES AGAINST CHILDREN AND VULNERABLE PERSONS

Q Give an example of when both S1 & 2 offences can be committed together

A 'A' and his wife are separated, and the wife has custody. 'A' hires 'B' to collect the child from school and deliver the child to the airport where 'A' takes the child to Belgium. Therefore 'A' commits the S1 [connected to] offence and 'B' commits the S2 [not connected to] offence.

Q Define the offence of Child Cruelty

A An offence is committed where a person has attained 16 **years of age** who has responsibility for a **child aged under 16 years of age,** who wilfully:

[a] assaults;
[b] ill-treats;
[c] neglects;
[d] abandons;
[e] exposes [causes or procures such treatment]

in a manner likely to cause **unnecessary suffering or injury to health.**

Arrest. Arrestable offence.

Q Define the offence of US1 with a girl aged under 13 years of age

A It is an offence for a man to have unlawful sexual intercourse with a girl aged under 13 years of age.

Arrest. Serious arrestable offence.

Q Define the offence of US1 with a girl aged under 16 years of age

A It is an offence for a man to have unlawful sexual intercourse with a girl aged under 16 years of age.

OFFENCES AGAINST CHILDREN AND VULNERABLE PERSONS

Defence.
[a] he believes her to be his wife;
[b] he is **under 24 years of age**

    [i] not previously **charged** with a like offence; and
    [ii] believes [with reasonable cause] the girl to be **aged 16 years or over.**

Q **Define the 2 offences of Permitting Girls to Use Premises**

A **Under 13 years of age,** it is an offence for a person who owns or occupies premises [assists/manages] to induce or knowingly suffer a girl **aged** occupies premises [assists/manages] to induce or knowingly suffer a girl **aged under 13 years** to resort to or be there for the purpose of having USI with men or a man.

Arrest. Arrestable offence.

Under 16 years of age. As above but no specific power of arrest.

Q **Define the offence of Encouraging Prostitution, etc of a Girl aged under 16 years of age**

A

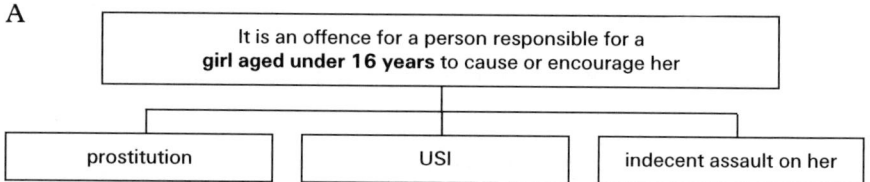

Q **Define Indecency with Children**

A A person commits an offence who commits an act of gross indecency **with or *toward*** a **child aged under 14 years of age,** or who incites such an act with him or another.

Arrest. Arrestable offence.

Note. No *contact* need be proved, masturbating in front of a child will suffice.

OFFENCES AGAINST CHILDREN AND VULNERABLE PERSONS

Q Outline the offence of Indecent Photographs of Children

A

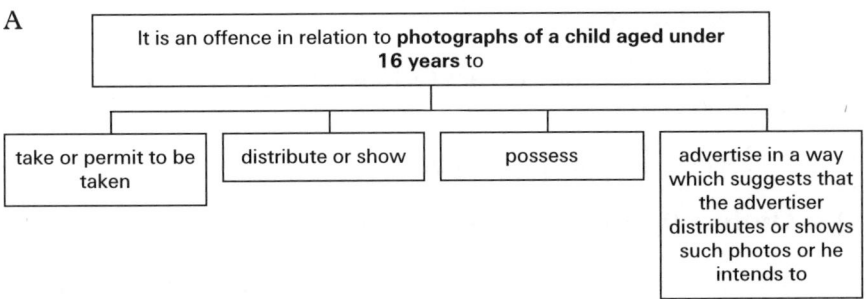

Arrest. Serious arrestable offence.

DPP. The consent of the DPP is required to prosecute.

Defence. In relation to * distribution/showing/possessing:

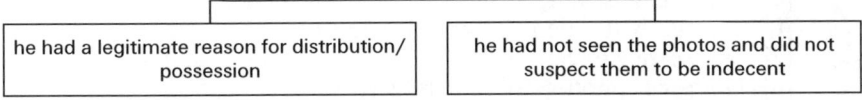

Note. A legitimate reason may be a training aid for police officers or social workers.

Q How does S 160 of the Criminal Justice Act 1988 reinforce the above offence?

A By making it an offence to possess only. It incorporates an extra defence e.g.
 [a] the photo was sent to him without request; and
 [b] he did not keep it for an unreasonable time.

Q Define the offence of Harmful Publications

A A person who prints, publishes, sell or hires **[people who trade in]** works likely to fall into the hands of a child or young person, portraying:

 [a] the commission of crimes; or
 [b] acts of violence or cruelty; or

OFFENCES AGAINST CHILDREN AND VULNERABLE PERSONS

[c] incidents of a repulsive or horrible nature,
in a way that the work would **tend to corrupt a child or young person,** commits an offence.

Q What was Pt II of the Sex Offenders Act 1997 enacted to outlaw?

A Sexual offences **outside the UK.**

Q Outline the provisions of the Act

A The offences outlined below which are committed **outside the UK** will be treated as if they have been committed in England or Wales and apply to **British Citizens or residents of the UK:**

[a] intercourse with a girl aged under 13 years;
[b] intercourse with a girl between 13 and 16 years of age;
[c] rape;
[d] buggery;
[e] indecent assault;
[f] assault with intent to commit buggery;
[g] indecency toward a child; and
[h] indecent photographs of children.

Q When is a child deemed to be under Police Protection?

A

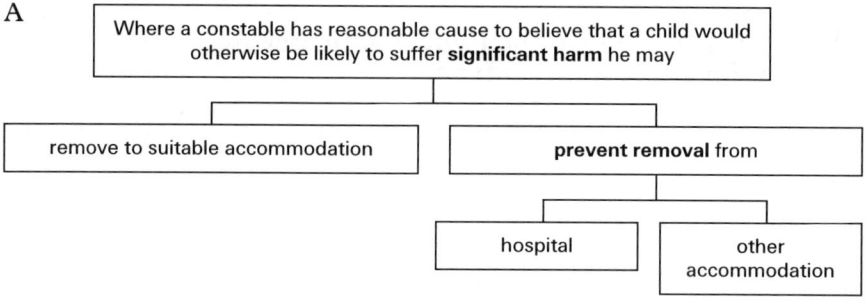

OFFENCES AGAINST CHILDREN AND VULNERABLE PERSONS

Q **What subsequent action must the constable take?**

A [a] inform local authority [where child found] of action taken/proposed/reasons;
[b] inform local authority [where child usually lives] of his whereabouts;
[c] inform the child of steps taken/proposed/reasons;
[d] discover how the child feels about this;
[e] tell parents or person with whom he was living of action taken/proposed/reasons
[f] if child removed from a place, arrange a refuge or local authority accommodation
[g] inform **designated officer.**

Q **What is the role of the Designated Officer?**

A [a] to enquire into the case, then **release the child unless** he considers that there is still reason to believe that the child would still suffer **significant harm** if released
[b] do what is reasonable for the child's welfare;
[c] allow such contact with the child as he believes is reasonable and in the child's interest [which may be no contact].
Contact may be by:

[i] the child's parents;
[ii] a person having parental responsibility;
[iii] the person the child was living with before police protection;
[iv] persons who have a right to contact; or
[v] someone acting on behalf of any of these.

Q **How old is a 'child' for the purposes of the Children Act 1989?**

A Under 18 years of age.

OFFENCES AGAINST CHILDREN AND VULNERABLE PERSONS

Q Outline the offences of Abduction of a Child in Care

A

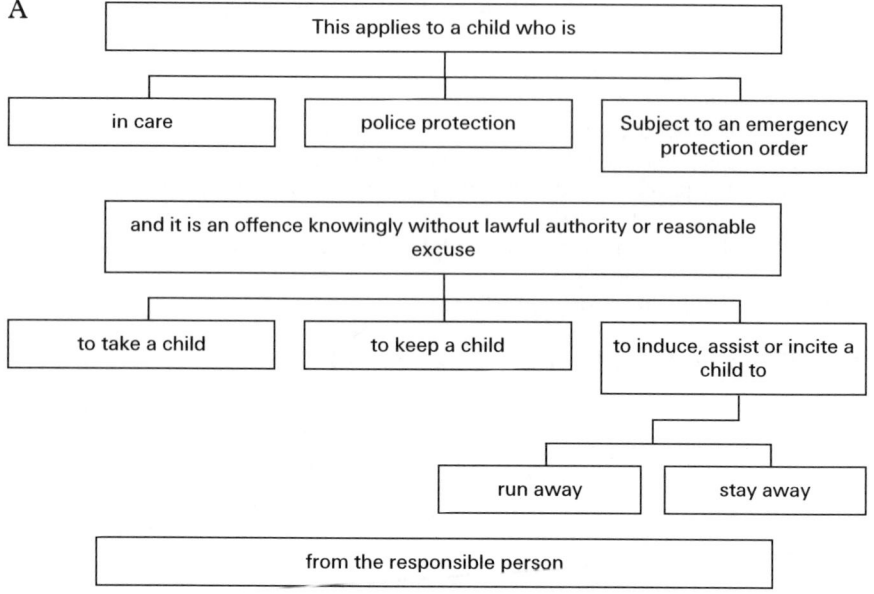

Arrest. S 25 PACE General arrest conditions.

S 49 CHILDREN ACT 1989

Q Define the offence of Sexual Intercourse with a Mental Defective

A   It is an offence for a man to have unlawful sexual intercourse with a woman who is a mental defective.

Defence. If he did not know and had no reason to suspect.

Q Define the offence of Procurement

A   It is an offence for a person to procure a woman who is a defective to have unlawful sexual intercourse, in any part of the world.

Defence. He did not know and had no reason to suspect.

OFFENCES AGAINST CHILDREN AND VULNERABLE PERSONS

Q **Define the offence of Allowing Defective to Use Premises**

A It is an offence for the owner/occupier of premises or who assists in the management or control to induce or knowingly suffer a woman defective to be on the premises for unlawful sexual intercourse with men or a man.

Defence. He did not know and had no reason to suspect.

Q **Outline the offence of Sexual Intercourse with a Mental Patient**

A

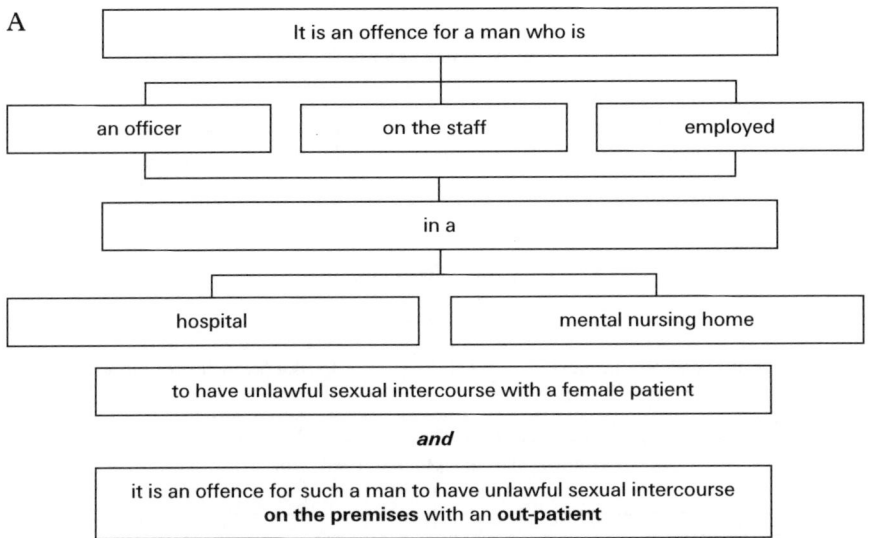

Where can the offence be committed	
In-patient	**Out-**patient
Anywhere, e.g. on an away day from the hospital	On the premises only

Defence. He did not know and had no reason to suspect.

S 128 MENTAL HEALTH ACT 1959

DPP. Consent of the DPP is required to prosecute.

OFFENCES AGAINST CHILDREN AND VULNERABLE PERSONS

Q Define the offence of Abducting a Mental Defective

A It is an offence to take a woman defective out of possession of her parent or guardian against her will, intending she have unlawful sexual intercourse with men or a man.

Defence. He did not know and had no reason to suspect.

Q Outline police powers to remove Mentally Disordered People from Public Places

A
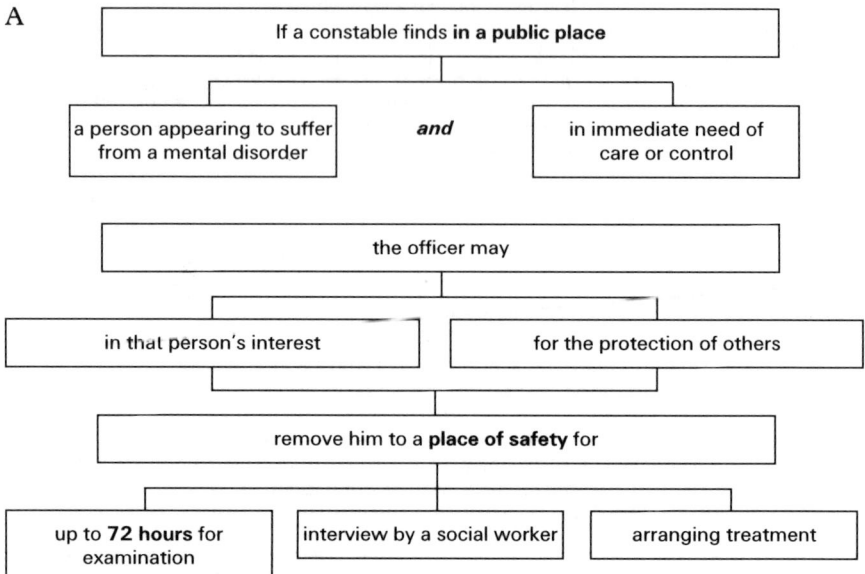

Place of safety. Is social services acc,ommodation, hospital, police station, mental nursing home or anywhere suitable where the occupier is willing to receive him.

OFFENCES AGAINST CHILDREN AND VULNERABLE PERSONS

Q What are the conditions of a Warrant to Search for Patients?

A Where a person suffering from a mental disorder has been, or is being, neglected or is unable to care for himself and is living alone, a warrant may be issued by a magistrate to a constable who may enter the premises and take him to a place of safety and **the officer *must be accompanied* by a social worker and doctor.**

Q How long do police powers last for the retaking of an Escaped Patient?

A A person taken to a place of safety by a constable, or under a warrant, who subsequently escapes cannot be retaken after **72 hours.**

When does the time begin?

At the place of safety	Escapes before arrival
time of arrival	time of escape

THEFT AND RELATED OFFENCES

Q Define Dishonesty

A

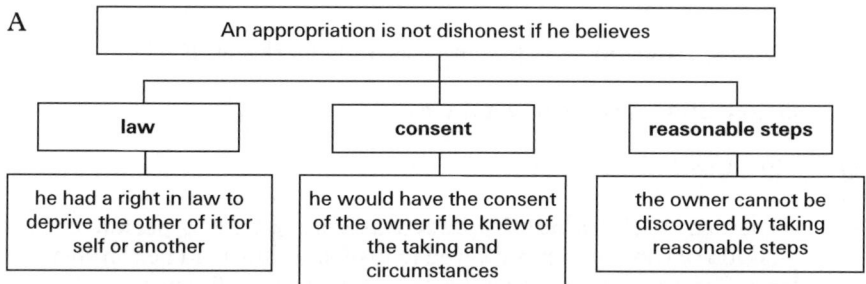

Willingness to pay. It may be regarded as dishonest notwithstanding he is willing to pay. [A stranger removing a pint of milk from your doorstep and leaving the money will probably be regarded as dishonest under this section, however, a person removing a pint from an unattended milk float and leaving the money probably will not].

S2 THEFT ACT 1968

Q Define what is and what is not an Appropriation

An appropriation **is**	An appropriation **is not**
any assumption of the rights of the owner, even if the property was come by innocently, a later assumption by keeping it or dealing with it as an owner.	where property is transferred **for value** to a person **acting in good faith,** who later assumes the rights of the owner. S 3 THEFT ACT 1968

THEFT AND RELATED OFFENCES

Q Define property

A It includes money and all other property, real or personal, including things in action and other intangible property.

Things in action. e.g. patents and trade marks, an IOU.

Other intangible property. Gas.

Q Can land be stolen?

A **Trustees & Personal Representatives.** Where a person is in a position of trust or is empowered to dispose of the land he can steal the land if he does something in breach of trust or confidence.

By persons who do not possess the land. He steals land if he **severs** the land.

By Tenants. He steals land by taking fixtures [wall sockets etc] or structure let for use with the land.

Q When can Mushrooms etc, be stolen?

A

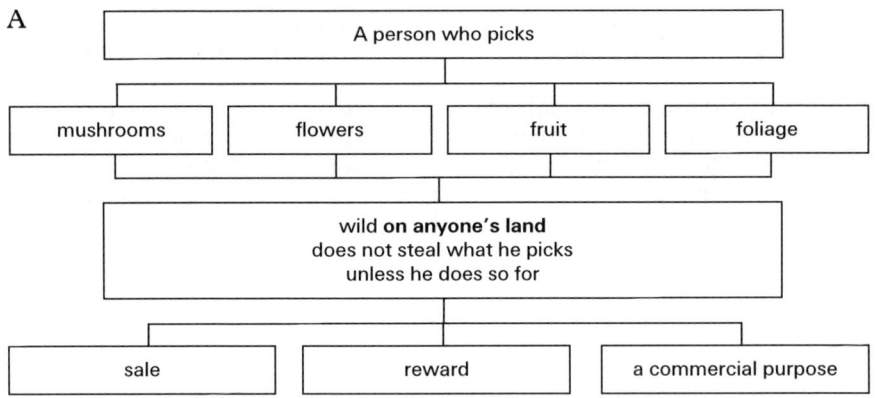

Digging up. Would amount to an offence as this section deals with **picking.**

THEFT AND RELATED OFFENCES

Q When can Wild Creatures be stolen?

A
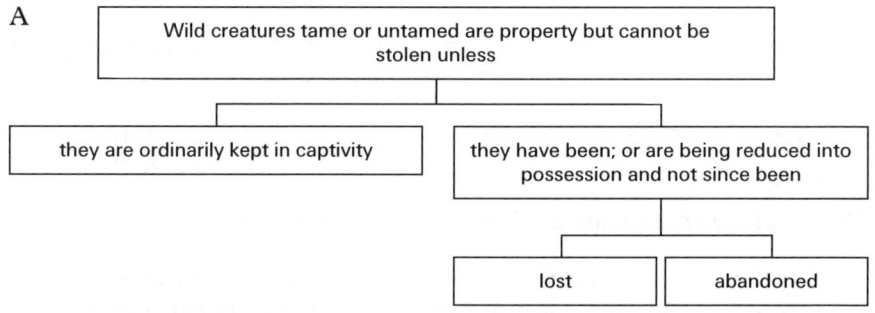

IE. Ordinarily kept in captivity means that a zoo creature can be stolen, and reduction into possession means that a person who has, for example, snared a rabbit is its new owner. If however he forgets where the snare is or simply abandons the snare [and rabbit], it then reverts to its wild state and cannot be stolen.

S 4 THEFT ACT 1968

Q Define Belonging to Another

A   Property belongs to a person having **possession** or **control** of it.

S 5 THEFT ACT 1968

Can you steal your own property? Yes, where another has possession or control, e.g. say a garage has completed an MOT on your vehicle and you sneak in and remove the vehicle then you are guilty of theft because the vehicle belonged to another.

Q What is the meaning of Obligations Regarding Another's Property?

A   Where a person receives property and is under an obligation to deal with it in a particular way the property shall be regarded as belonging [not him] to another.

e.g. Monies thrown into a fountain for charitable purposes being removed by the owner for himself, he would be guilty under this section.

S 5[3] THEFT ACT 1968

THEFT AND RELATED OFFENCES

Q   What is meant by an Obligation to Restore Another's Property?

A   Where a person gets property by another's mistake, an intention not to restore shall be regarded as an intention to deprive.

e.g. Money mistakenly credited to an account must be returned.

S 5[4] THEFT ACT 1968

Q   Define Intention to Permanently Deprive

A   [i] if he treats the property as his own to dispose of, regardless of the owner's rights, and a borrowing or lending' amounts to a permanent deprivation if done for a period or under circumstances that make it an outright taking. S 6[1] THEFT ACT 1968

e.g. Borrowing property and then 'lending' it to a total stranger in the 'hope' that he will return the goods!

[ii] where a person parts with property [of another] **under a condition for its return** which he may not be able to perform ... he commits an offence.

S 6[2] THEFT ACT 1968

e.g. Pawning another's property. The proof is in the parting with under a condition which he **may not** be able to perform.

Q   Define Robbery

A

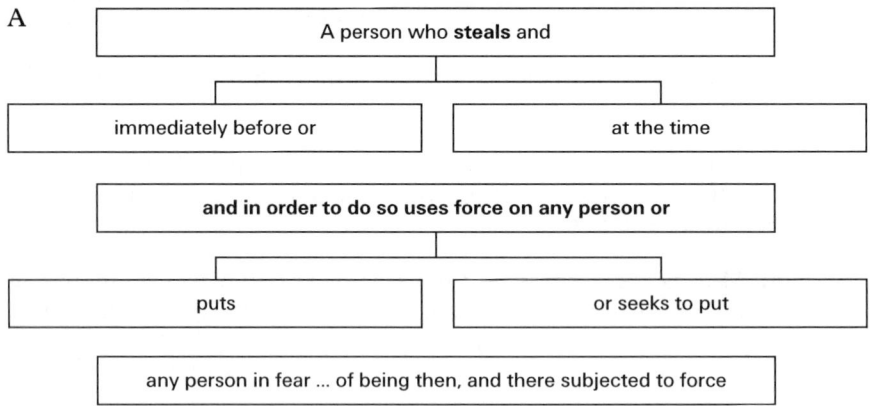

THEFT AND RELATED OFFENCES

Arrest. Arrestable offence.

Theft. No theft, no robbery.

S 8 Theft Act 1968

Q Define Burglary

A
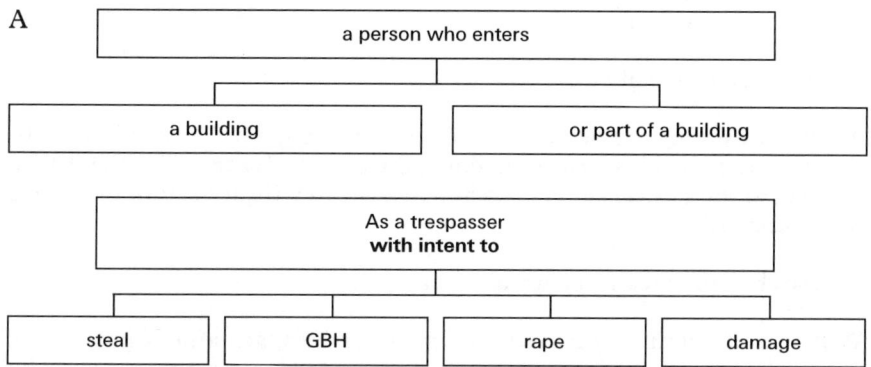

S 9 1[A]

OR

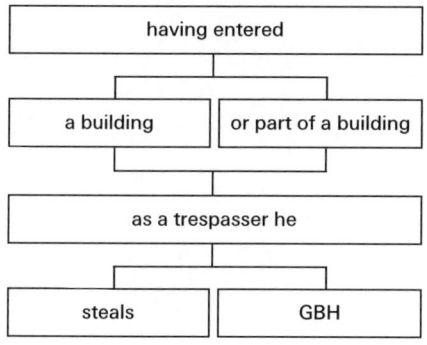

or attempts

S 9 1 [B] Theft Act 1968

Arrest. Arrestable offence.

Building. Includes inhabited vehicle and vessel [whether occupant there or not].

THEFT AND RELATED OFFENCES

Q   When does Burglary become Aggravated?

A   If he commits any burglary and **at the time** has with him any:

    W   weapon of offence;
    I   imitation firearm;
    F   firearm; or
    E   explosive.

S 10 THEFT ACT 1968

Arrest. Arrestable offence.

At the time. For the Set 9 1 [a] offence, entering **with intent** it must be shown that he had his **wife** with him at the **point of entry**. The Set 9 1 [b] offence, **having entered** requires him to have his **wife** at the time of stealing or causing GBH.

Has with him. Means readily at hand.

Weapon of offence. Includes an article for incapacitating a person and would therefore include rope, binding tape, sticking plaster etc [used for tying up victims].

THEFT AND RELATED OFFENCES

Q Outline the offence of Removal of Articles from Places Open to the Public

A

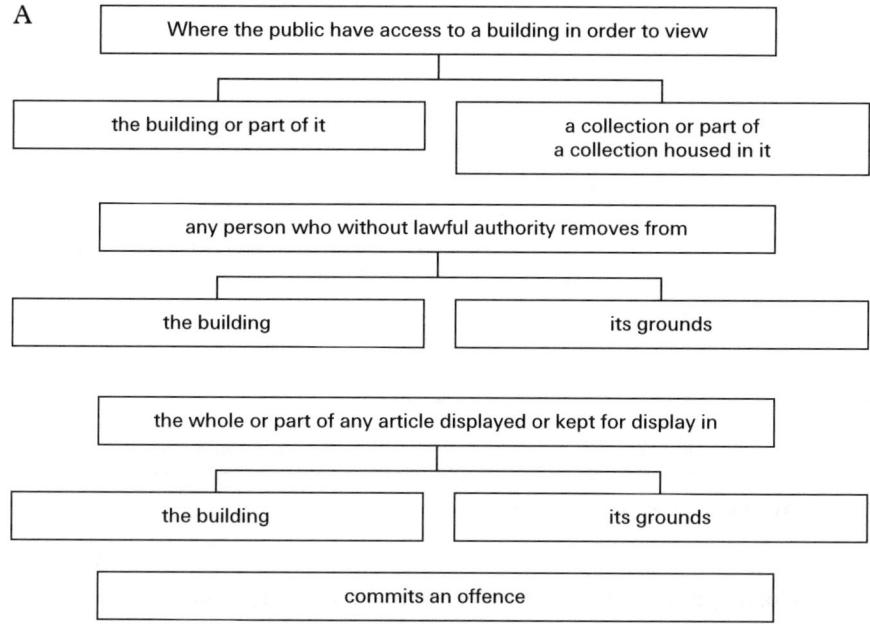

S 11 Theft Act 1968

Arrest. Arrestable offence.

Collection. Includes a temporary collection.

What is not protected. A collection for sale or commercial purpose.

Public access. Someone entering as a trespasser after the building has closed still commits this offence so long as the building was open to the public on that day.

Note. This offence was introduced to cover people who removed works of art from display so they could 'live' with the work and then return it!

THEFT AND RELATED OFFENCES

Q **Define the offence of Taking a Conveyance Without Authority**

A

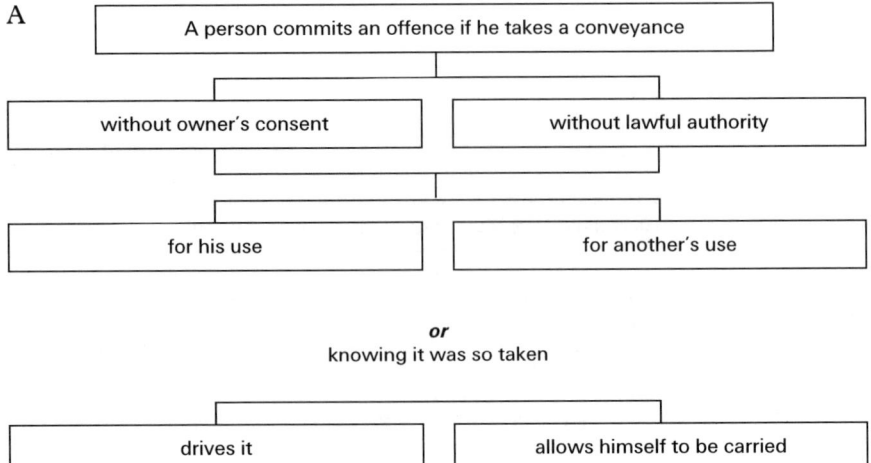

Arrest. Arrestable offence.

S 12 THEFT ACT 1968

Conveyance. Means any conveyance for use by land, water or air.

Pedestrian controlled vehicle. This section does not apply, e.g. Handcart.

THEFT AND RELATED OFFENCES

Q **When does this offence become Aggravated?**

A

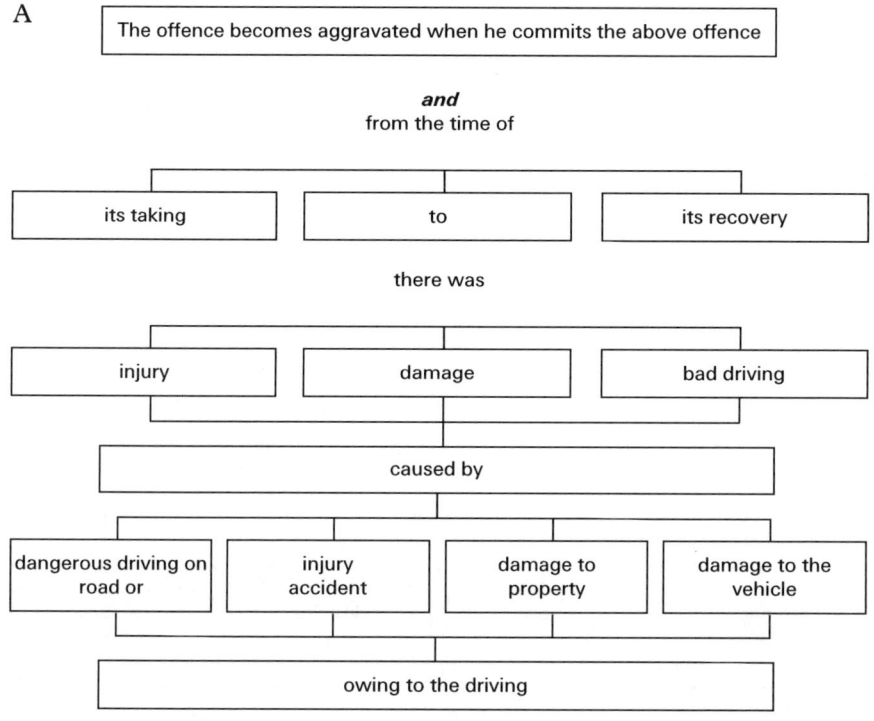

S 12A THEFT ACT 1968

Arrest. Arrestable offence.

Defence. The driving, accident or damage occurred:

[a] **before** the taking; or
[b] when the driving, accident or damage occurred, he was **not in or in the immediate vicinity** of the vehicle.

Q **Define Abstracting Electricity**

A A person who dishonestly uses without due authority, or dishonestly causes to be wasted or diverted any electricity, commits an offence.

Arrest. Arrestable offence.

THEFT AND RELATED OFFENCES

Q **Define Handling Stolen Goods**

A

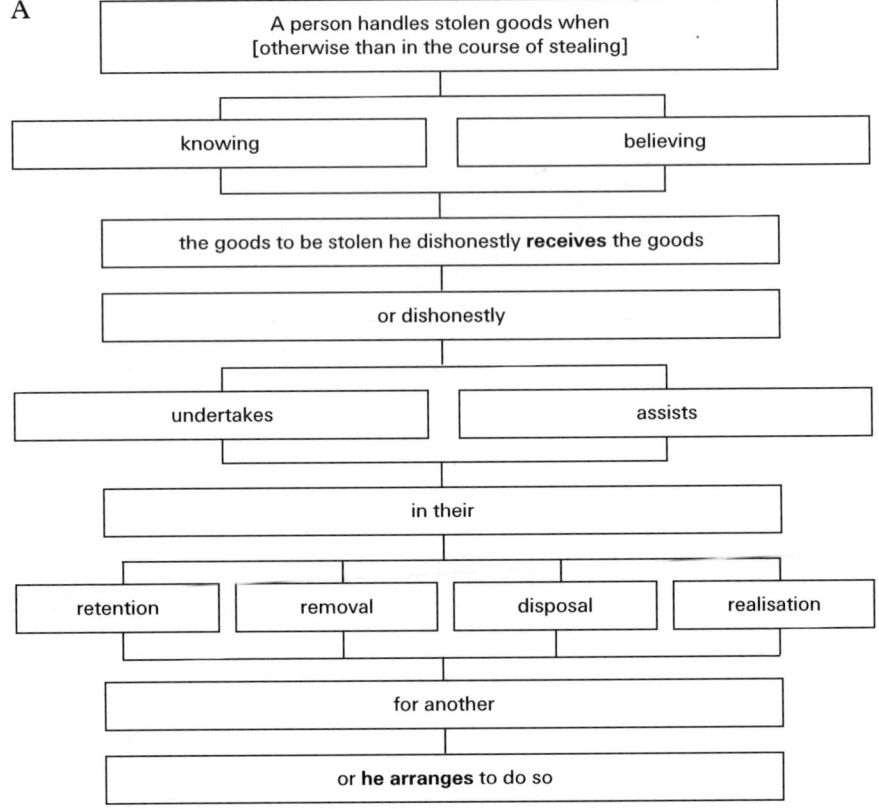

S 22 Theft Act 1968

Arrest. Arrestable offence.

Stolen goods:

[a] a person can be convicted of handling if the goods were stolen **anywhere in the world** so long as it is an offence in that other country;

[b] goods are classed as stolen if they are the original goods or now represent **the proceeds** of the goods;

[c] goods cease to be stolen when they are restored to lawful possession.

THEFT AND RELATED OFFENCES

Proof that goods were stolen:
In relation to the theft of anything in the course of transmission, a statutory declaration that a person despatched, received, or failed to receive any goods, or they were in a particular state or condition shall be evidence of the fact providing:

[a] oral evidence would be admissible; and
[b] **7 days notice** has been given to the person charged, and he has not, **within 3 days** of the trial given the prosecutor written notice requiring the attendance of the witness.

Q Define the offence of Advertising a Reward

A

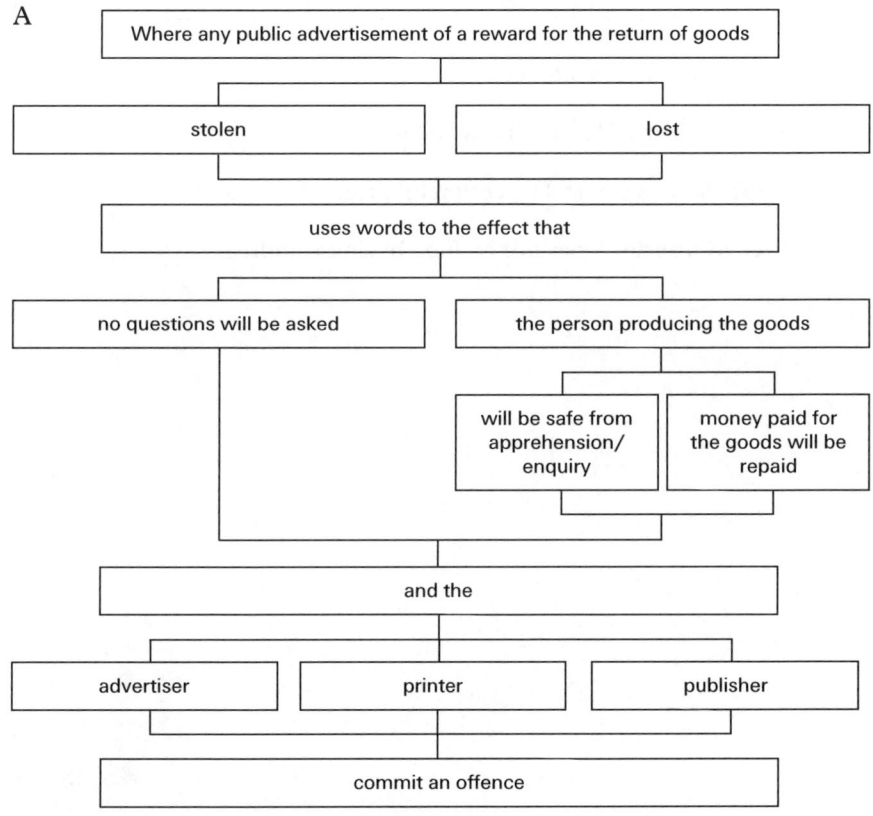

S 23 Theft Act 1968

THEFT AND RELATED OFFENCES

Q Define Going Equipped for Stealing

A

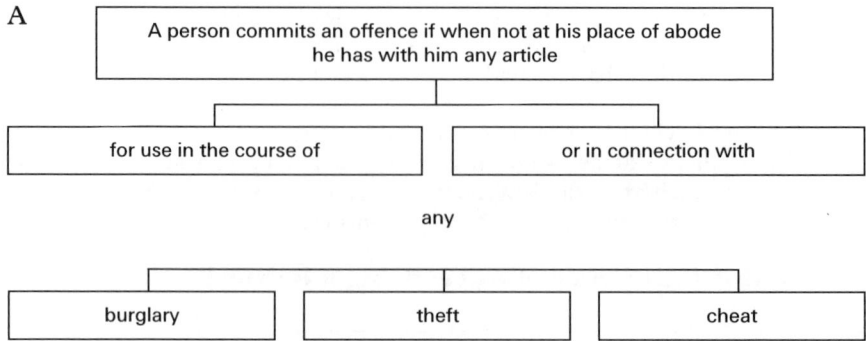

Arrest. Arrestable offence.

Has with him. Means readily to hand.

Cheat. Means a S 15 Deception offence.

Place of abode. Does not include business address.

DECEPTION

Q Define Deception

A

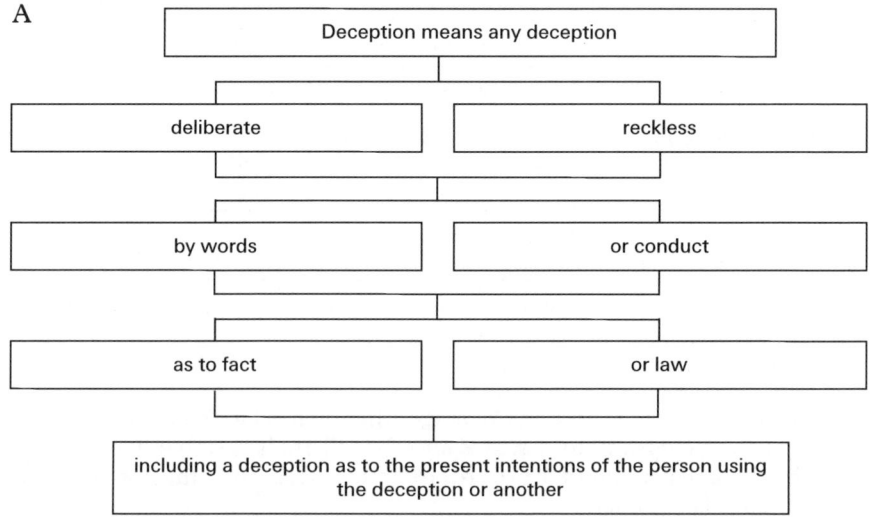

Words or conduct. The person must be deceived, otherwise it is an attempt.

Machines. A machine cannot be deceived.

Q Define Obtaining Property by Deception

A A person who by any deception dishonestly obtains property belonging to another, with intention of permanently depriving the other of it, commits an offence.

Arrest. Arrestable offence.

S 15 THEFT ACT 1968

Obtain. Means obtaining ownership, possession or control, for self of another, and also to enable another to retain.

DECEPTION

Q Outline the offence of Obtaining a Pecuniary Advantage

A

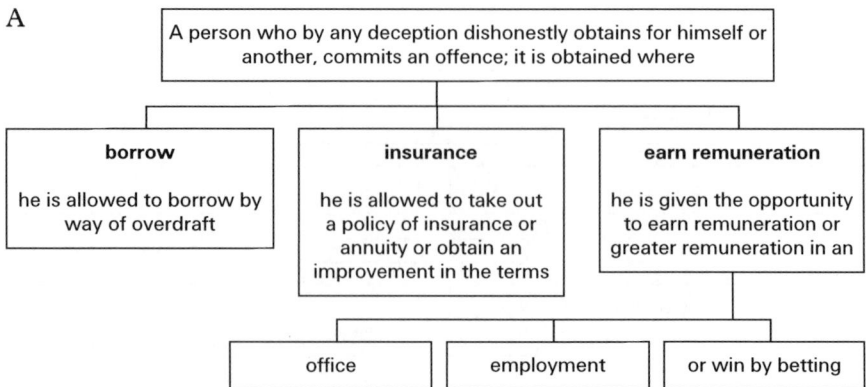

Arrest. Arrestable offence. S 16 THEFT ACT 1068

Borrow. 'x' tells his bank manager that he has landed a good job and needs an overdraft for a new wardrobe. There is no job in fact, but the bank manager allows the overdraft on the strength of the new job. The offence is complete.

Insurance. 'Y' deceives an insurer into issuing insurance in the belief that he holds a clean driving licence and has never been disqualified. His licence is in fact endorsed and he has been disqualified in the past. The offence is complete.

Opportunity to earn. 'Z' applies for a job requiring 2 'A' levels which he pretends to possess and is appointed to the job. The offence is complete.

Q Define the offence of Obtaining Services

A

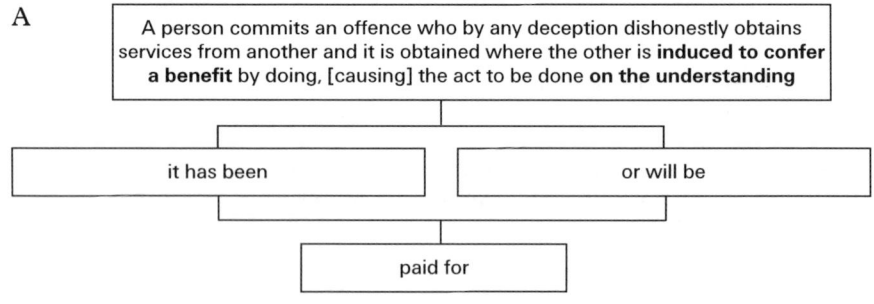

DECEPTION

Arrest. Arrestable offence.

Benefit. Includes a loan.

S1 THEFT ACT 1978

Q **Define the offence of Evading Liability**

A A person commits an offence where, by any deception:

[a] dishonestly secures the remission of the whole or part of any **existing liability to make payment;** or
[b] with intent to make permanent default of any **existing liability to make payment** [for self or another] he **dishonestly induces him to wait for payment;** or
[c] he dishonestly obtains **an exemption to make payment.**

Arrest. Arrestable offence.

S 2 THEFT ACT 1968

Liability. Means legal liability, therefore the payment for drugs, prostitution, or unlawful gaming, which is avoided, is not an offence.

Q **Define the offence of Making Off Without Payment**

A

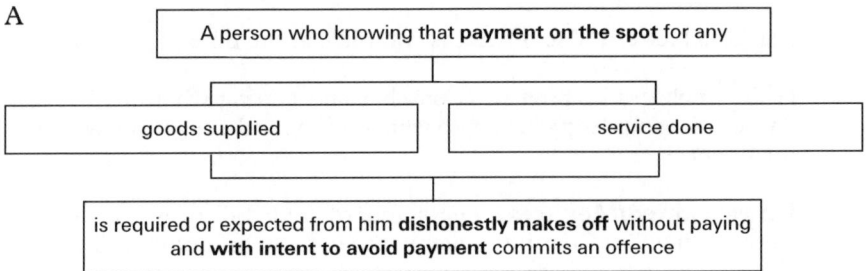

Arrest. Any person with cause to believe he is committing [attempting].

Contrary to law. This section does not apply to anything which is contrary to law, prostitution, drugs, unlawful gaming etc.

DECEPTION

Q   Define Blackmail

A

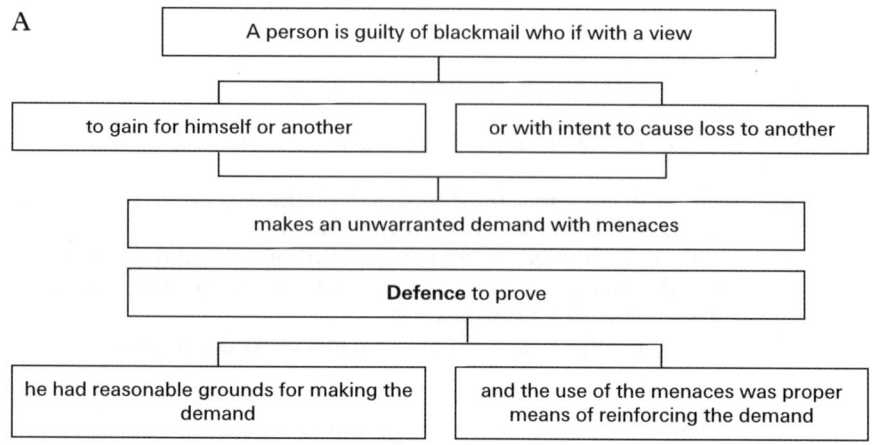

Arrest. Arrestable offence.

S 21 Theft Act 1968

Blackmail letters. The offence is complete at the time of posting.

Gain. Includes keeping what one has and getting what one has not; and **Loss.** Includes parting with what one has and not getting what one might get.

Unwarranted/Menaces. The standard 'red' bill of a last demand from say the Gas Board, threatening to cut you off unless you pay up, clearly is protected here.

Q   What did the Theft [Amendment] Act 1996 introduce?

A   An offence where, by any deception a person dishonestly obtains a **money transfer** for himself or another where one account is debited and the other credited [or vice versa]

Arrest. Arrestable offence.

S 15A Theft Act 1968

Account. Is one kept with a bank or a person carrying on a deposit taking business for the purposes of the Banking Act 1987.

DECEPTION

Q Define the offence of Retaining a Wrongful Credit

A A person is guilty of an offence if:

[a] a **wrongful credit** has been **paid into his account** [or in which he has an interest]
[b] **he** knows it is wrongful; and
[c] he dishonestly **fails to cancel.**

It is also an offence to receive a credit deriving from:

[a] theft;
[b] obtaining a money transfer;
[c] blackmail; or
[d] stolen goods

Arrest. Arrestable offence.

S 24A THEFT ACT 1968

Q Define the offence of False Accounting

A

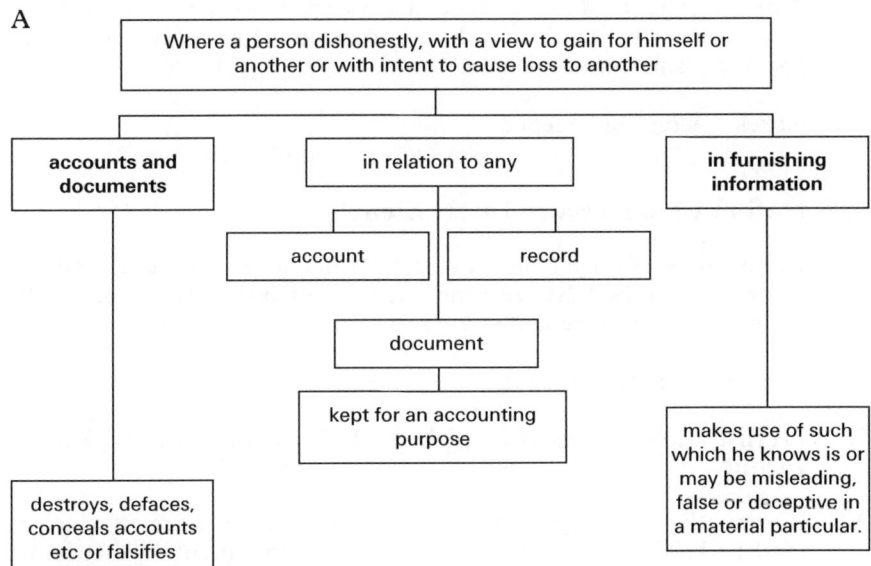

Arrest. Arrestable offence.

S 17 THEFT ACT 1968

DECEPTION

An act. Includes an omission

A person concurring. In making the account etc, is also guilty.

Q **Forgery, what is a False Instrument?**

A A document which tells a lie about itself.

Not false, if a constable makes out a claim for overtime he did not work and signs it, the claim is not a forgery because it does not purport to be something it is not.

False, if a constable makes out a claim for overtime and signs his supervisor's signature as having checked the claim to be correct, the document is a lie and therefore forged.

Bank notes, Cannot be forged, they are counterfeited.

Q **Define Making a False Instrument With Intent**

A A person is guilty of forgery if he makes a false instrument, with intent that he or another use it **to induce someone to accept it as genuine** and as a result someone is prejudiced.

Arrest. Arrestable offence.

S 1 FORGERY AND COUNTERFEITING ACT 1981

Q **Define Using a False Instrument**

A It is an offence for a person to use an instrument which is [and he knows or believes] to be false with the intention **of inducing someone to accept it as genuine** and as a result someone is prejudiced.

Arrest. Arrestable offence.

Q **Define the offence of Copying a False Instrument with Intent**

A It is an offence for a person to make a copy of an instrument which is [and he knows or believes] to be false with the intention that he or another shall use it **to induce someone to accept it as a copy of a genuine instrument,** resulting in someone being prejudiced.

Arrest. Arrestable offence.

DECEPTION

Q Define the offence of Using a Copy of a False Instrument with Intent

A It is an offence for a person to use a copy of an instrument which is [and he knows or believes] to be false with the intention of **inducing someone to accept it as a copy of a genuine instrument** resulting in someone being prejudiced.

Arrest. Arrestable offence.

Q Define An Instrument

A [a] any document;
[b] any Post Office stamp;
[c] any Inland Revenue stamp;
[d] any disc, tape, sound track or device on which information is stored or recorded by any means; and
[e] a mark used by the Post Office in lieu of a stamp.

Q Define Having Specific Instruments With Intent

A [a] It is an offence for a person to **have in his custody** or under his control an **instrument** which is false [or knows or believes] with the intention that he or another shall use it **to induce someone to accept it as genuine,** resulting in someone being prejudiced; and
[b] it is an offence for a person **to make** or have in his custody or control a **machine or implement, or paper or material** which is false [or knows or believes] with the intention that he or another shall make an instrument which is false and use it **to induce someone to accept it as genuine** resulting in someone being prejudiced.

Instruments are: Money orders, Postal orders, stamps, Inland Revenue stamps, Share certificates, passports and documents issued instead of passports, cheques, travellers' cheques, credit cards, copies of certificates of births, adoptions, marriages or deaths.

Q Define the offence of Acknowledging Bail in the Name of Another

A Any person, without lawful authority or excuse who acknowledges **bail** by a court or the police, in the name of another person, commits an offence.

DECEPTION

Q **What is meant by Counterfeiting?**

A [a] It is an offence for a person to make a counterfeit of a **currency note or protected coin** intending that he or another pass it as genuine ; and

    [b] it is an offence for a person to make a counterfeit **currency note or protected coin** without lawful authority or reasonable excuse.

Q **Define the offence of Passing or Tendering Counterfeit Coins and Notes**

A It is an offence for a person:

    [a] **to pass or tender** as genuine any thing which is [or he knows or believes] to be a counterfeit note or protected coin; or

    [b] to deliver to another any thing which is [or he knows or believes] to be counterfeit intending that **that person pass or tender it as genuine.**

CRIMINAL DAMAGE

Q Define simple Damage

A
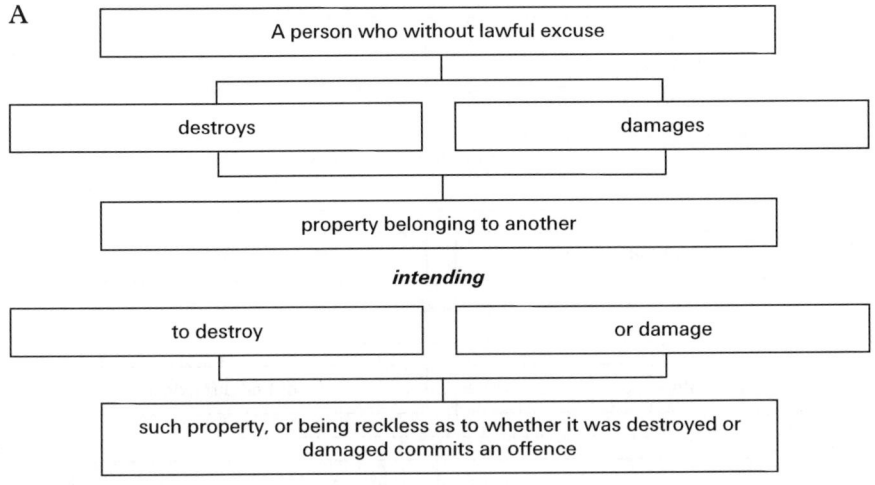

Arrest. Arrestable offence.

S 1 Criminal Damage Act 1971

Arson. Where the damage or destruction is caused by fire it shall be arson.

CRIMINAL DAMAGE

Q   Define the offence of Endangering Life

A

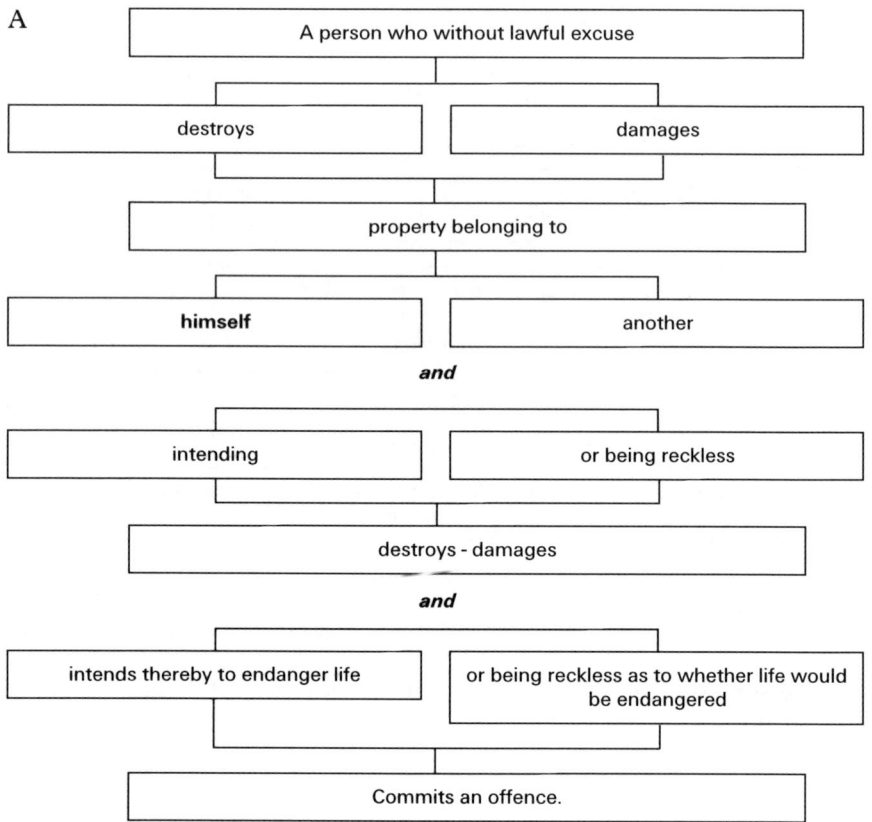

Arrest. Arrestable offence.

S 1[2] CRIMINAL DAMAGE ACT 1971

Lawful excuse. This defence does not apply to endangering life.

CRIMINAL DAMAGE

Q Define the offence of Threatening Damage

A

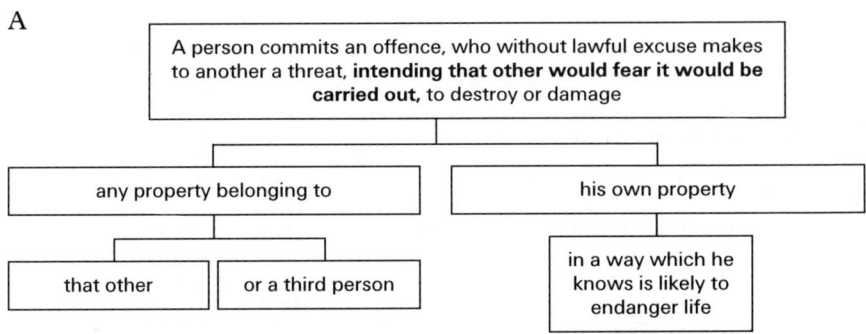

Arrest. Arrestable offence.

SEC 2 CRIMINAL DAMAGE ACT 1971

Q Define the offence of Having Articles with Intent to damage

A

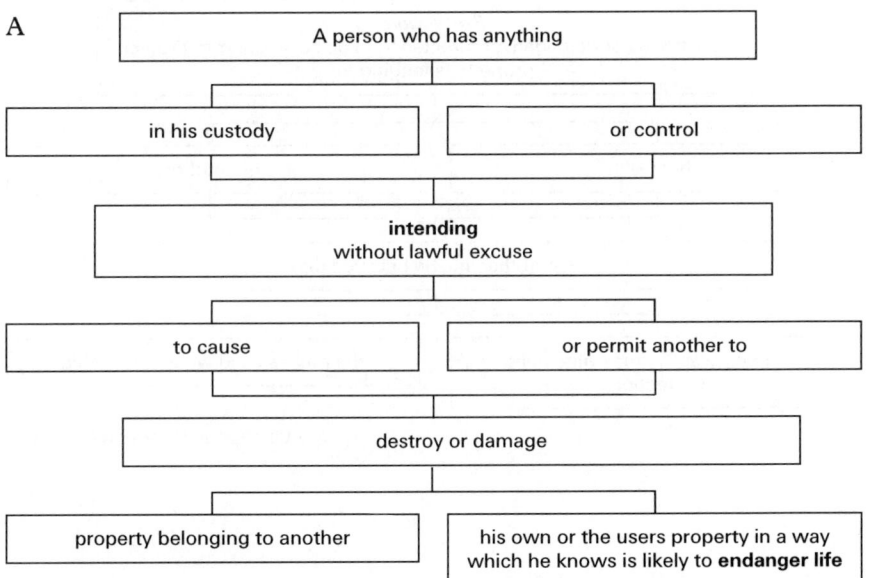

CRIMINAL DAMAGE

Arrest. Arrestable offence.

S 2 Criminal Damage Act 1971

Possession. This offence would ideally apply to a graffiti 'artist' going equipped to cause damage to other people's property.

Q Define Lawful Excuse

A

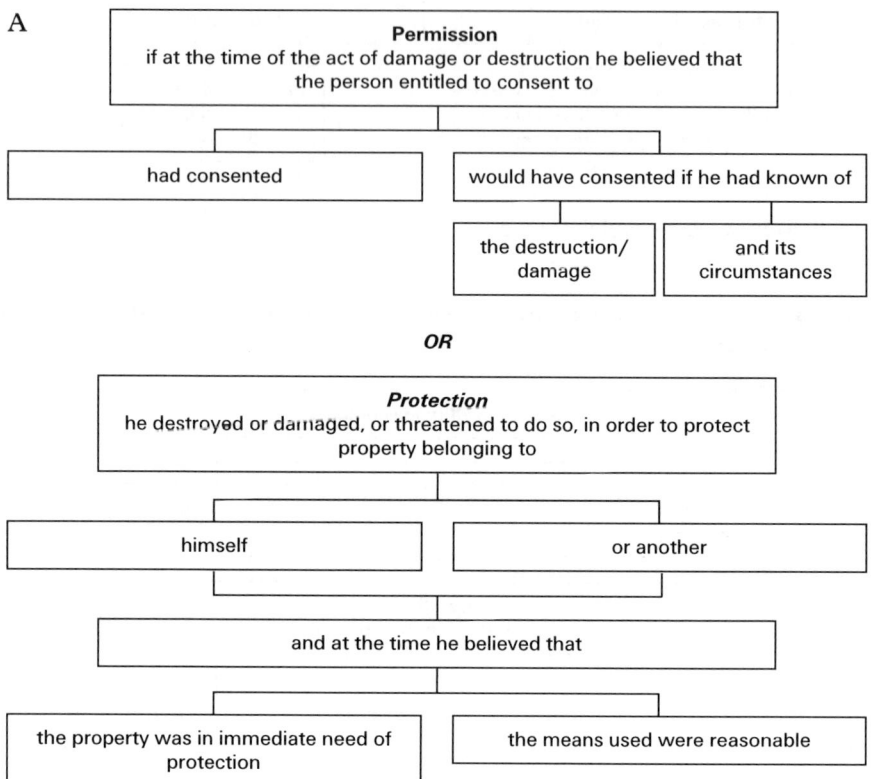

S 5 Criminal Damage Act 1971

CRIMINAL DAMAGE

Q Outline the Contamination/Interference with Goods offence

A

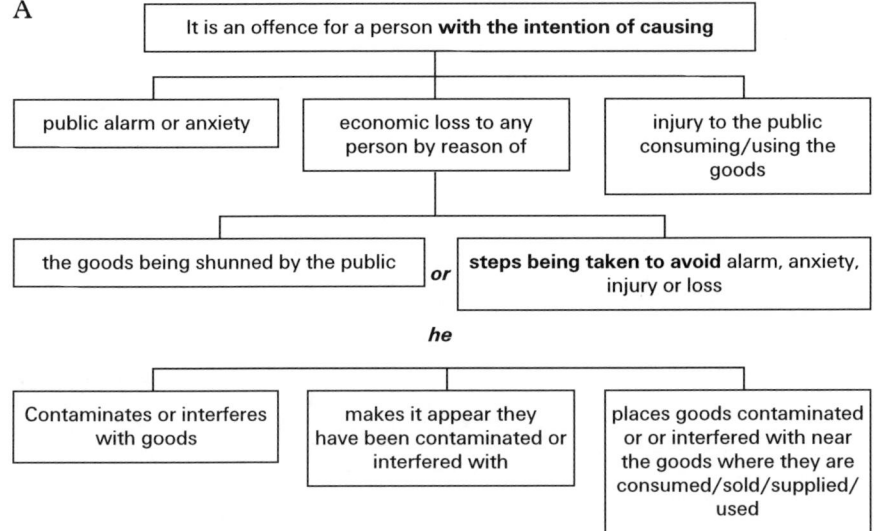

Arrest. Arrestable offence.

S 38 PUBLIC ORDER ACT 1986

OFFENCE AGAINST THE ADMINISTRATION OF JUSTICE & PUBLIC INTEREST

Q Define Perjury

A If any person **lawfully sworn** as a witness or interpreter in a judicial proceeding wilfully makes a statement material in that proceeding, which he knows to be false or does not believe to be true, he commits an offence.

Arrest. Arrestable offence.

S1 PERJURY ACT 1911

Q Define the offence of Aiding and Abetting Perjury

A Every person who aids, abets, counsels, or procures another to commit an offence of perjury, or incites the offence, commits an offence.

Q Define offences Similar to Perjury

A 1. If any **child** gives unsworn evidence, which, if it had been given on oath, would have been guilty of perjury, he commits an offence.

2. If any person in a **written statement** tendered in criminal proceedings wilfully makes a statement which is material, and which he knows to be false or does not believe to be true, he commits an offence.

3. If any person being required or authorised by law to make any statement on oath and being lawfully sworn **[otherwise than in judicial proceedings]** wilfully makes a statement which is material for that purpose and which he knows to be false or does not believe to be true, he commits an offence.

Q Define the offence of Perverting the Course of Justice

A It is an offence at common law to do an act tending and intended to pervert the course of public justice.

Arrest. Arrestable offence.

OFFENCE AGAINST THE ADMINISTRATION OF JUSTICE & PUBLIC INTEREST

Q Outline the offence of Intimidating Witnesses

A [a] A person who does to another:

  [i] an act which **intimidates,** and is intended to intimidate, that other person;
  [ii] knowing or believing that the person is assisting in the investigation of an offence is a witness, or juror; and
  [iii] intending thereby to cause the investigation to be **obstructed, perverted or interfered with** commits an offence.

  [b] a person who does or threatens to do to another:

  [i] an act which **harms him,** or is intended to harm him;
  [ii] knowing or believing that that person, or another, **has assisted in** an investigation into an offence or has **given evidence** or acted as a **juror;** and does or threatens the act because of what he knows or believes, commits an offence.

  Arrest. Arrestable offence.

  S 51 CRIMINAL JUSTICE AND PUBLIC ORDER ACT 1994.

Q Define the offence of Assisting Offenders

A Where a person has committed an **arrestable offence,** any other person who, knowing or believing him to be guilty of the offence, or some other arrestable offence, without lawful authority or reasonable excuse, **does any act with intent to impede** his arrest or prosecution, commits an offence.

  Arrest. Arrestable offence.   S 4 CRIMINAL LAW ACT 1967

Q Define the offence of Concealing Arrestable Offences

A Where a person has committed an **arrestable offence,** any other person, knowing or believing the offence or some other arrestable offence has been committed and **he has information which might be material** in securing the prosecution or conviction of an offender, **accepts** or agrees to accept **for not disclosing that information any consideration** [but not making good loss or injury caused by the offence/compensation] commits an offence.

  DPP. DPP's permission is required to prosecute.

OFFENCE AGAINST THE ADMINISTRATION OF JUSTICE & PUBLIC INTEREST

Q Define the offence of Escaping

A It is an offence at common law to escape from legal custody.
Arrest. Arrestable offence.

Assisting escape. A person who aids a prisoner to escape or who conveys anything **inside or outside a prison** with a view to its coming into the possession of the prisoner commits an offence.

Q Define the offence of Harbouring Offenders

A Any person who **knowingly harbours** an escapee or person unlawfully at large or **gives assistance with intent to prevent, hinder or interfere** with his arrest commits an offence.

Arrest. Arrestable offence.

S 22 Criminal Justice Act 1961

Q Outline the offence of Wasting Police Time

A
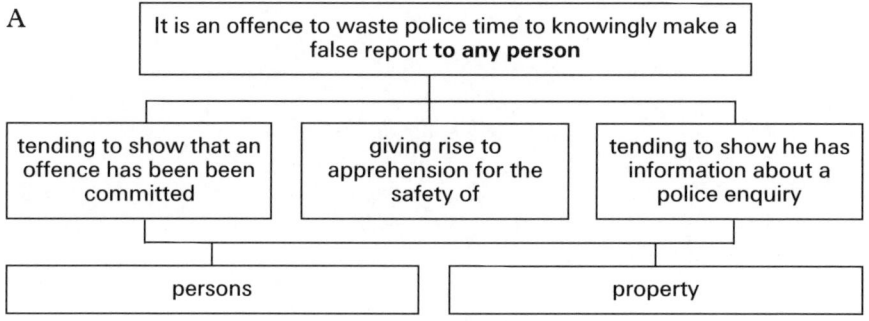

DPP. Consent of DPP is required to prosecute.

S 5 Criminal Law Act 1967

Q Define the offence of Corruption

A Any person who corruptly solicits, receives, or agrees to receive for himself or another any gift, loan, fee, reward **as an inducement to or reward for** doing or not doing anything in which he, a public body, is concerned commits an offence.

OFFENCE AGAINST THE ADMINISTRATION OF JUSTICE & PUBLIC INTEREST

Arrest. Arrestable offence.

S 1 PUBLIC BODIES CORRUPT PRACTICES ACT 1880

Agents. An agent of the public body [official] is also guilty.

AG. The consent of the Attorney-General is required to prosecute.

Part 3 - Road Traffic

STANDARDS OF DRIVING

Q Define the offence of Causing Death by Dangerous Driving

A

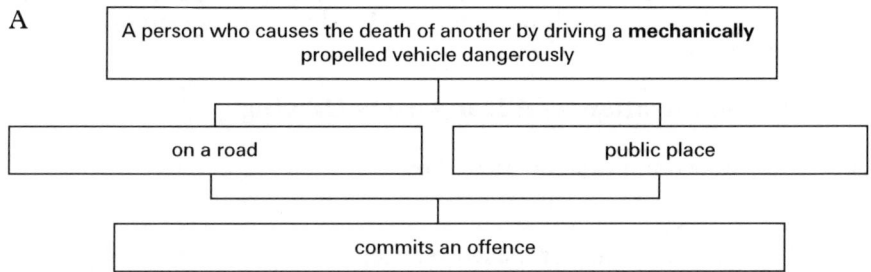

Arrest. Arrestable offence.

S 1 RTA 1988

Death. The driving must be 'a' cause, not the sole or substantial cause.

Driving. Must control both **direction and movement** of the vehicle. Pushing a car whilst steering is not driving. Straddling a motorcycle and pushing it along using feet is driving. It is also driving to 'free-wheel' down a hill in a car.

Mechanically propelled. A wider term than 'motor vehicle' and includes dumper trucks, fork lifts, cranes, trials and quad bikes. It must derive its power from an engine which may be powered by internal combustion, steam or battery.

Not Mechanically propelled. Pedestrian controlled vehicles, horse drawn vehicles, pedal cycles.

Road. Means any highway or road to which the public have access. Vehicles 'half on-half-off' a road, are on the road.

Not a road. If only a restricted section of the public has access [say, members of a club] it is not a road. Equally, it is not a road if members

STANDARDS OF DRIVING

of the public have to overcome physical barriers or defy prohibitions to gain access.

Public place. Includes driving off-road, in places to which the public have access and includes bridleways and footpaths. If the public have access, it is a public place.

How wide is the offence? A man free-wheeling, [controlling the brakes and steering wheel], down a multi-storey car park in a dumper truck, whose driving is dangerous and results in the death of another, can be guilty of this offence.

Q Define the offence of Dangerous Driving

A A person commits an offence who:

[a] drives;
[b] a mechanically propelled vehicle;
[c] dangerously;
[d] on a road or public place   S2RTA1988

Q What is the test of Dangerous Driving?

A

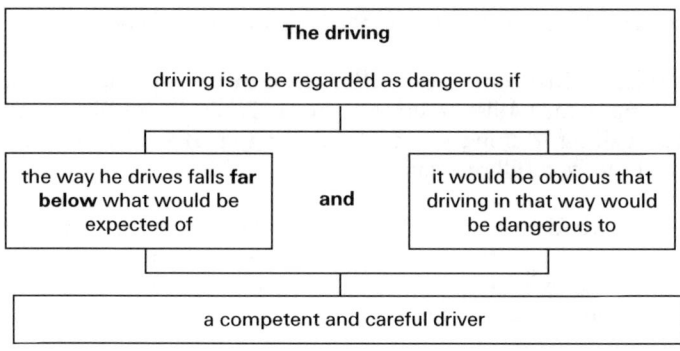

STANDARDS OF DRIVING

State of the vehicle. Regard may be given to anything attached to, carried on and the 'how' it is attached or carried.

Q Define Careless and Inconsiderate Driving

A
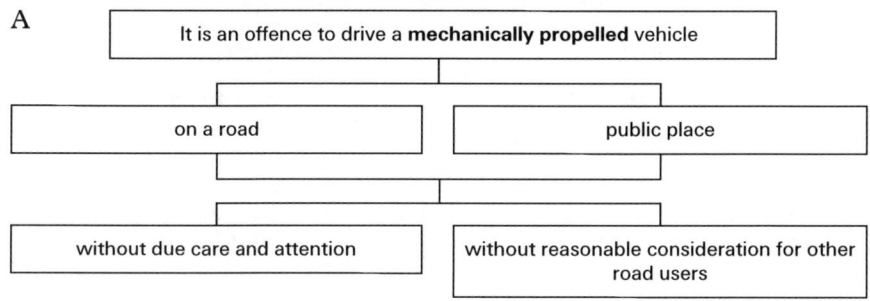

S3RTA 1988

Inconsiderate driving. e.g. driving through a puddle and splashing a bus queue.

Q Define the defence to bad driving of Automatism

A Automatism occurs when a driver's movements are beyond his control or his movements are brought about involuntarily. e.g. a driver being attacked by a swarm of bees or losing control as a result of a coma. The defence is not available to a person who knows that he is subject to a condition which will result in his losing control, e.g. a diabetic who begins to feel the effects of a hypoglycaemic episode but continues to drive.

STANDARDS OF DRIVING

Q Outline the offence of Causing Death by Careless Driving whilst Under the Influence

A

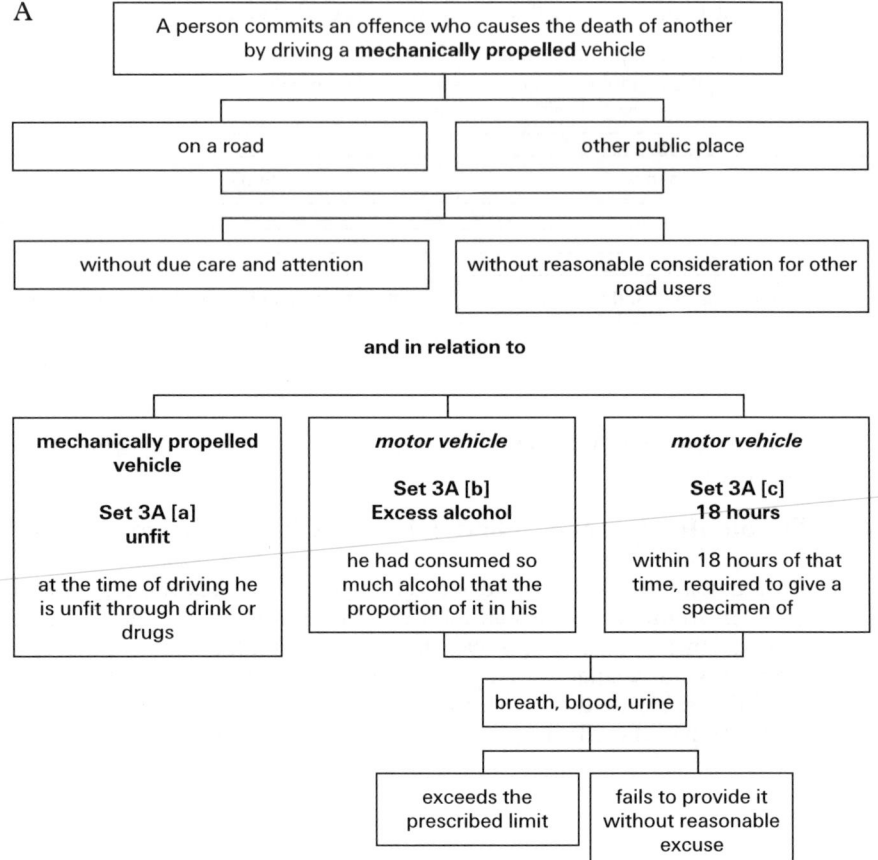

Arrest. Arrestable offence.

S 3A RTA 1988

Power of entry. Unfit - power of entry always. Excess alcohol - injury accident.

Set 3A [a]. Relates to a mechanically propelled vehicle. Power of arrest and entry.

STANDARDS OF DRIVING

Set 3A [b] & [c]. Relates to a **motor vehicle** [intended or adapted for use on a road] and the '18 hours' requirement under [c] relates only to police station procedures.

Q   Which offences are subject to NIP?

Section	Offence
S 2 RTA 1988	Dangerous driving
S 3	Careless and inconsiderate driving
S 22	Leaving vehicle in dangerous position
S 28	Dangerous cycling
S 35	Failure to comply with traffic directions
S 36	Failure to comply with traffic signs
S 16 RT Regulation Act 1984	Speeding [temporary restrictions]
S 17 RT Regulation Act 1984	Speeding [special roads]
S 88 & 89 RTRA 1984	Speeding

NOTICE OF INTENDED PROSECUTION

Q When is an NIP required?

A
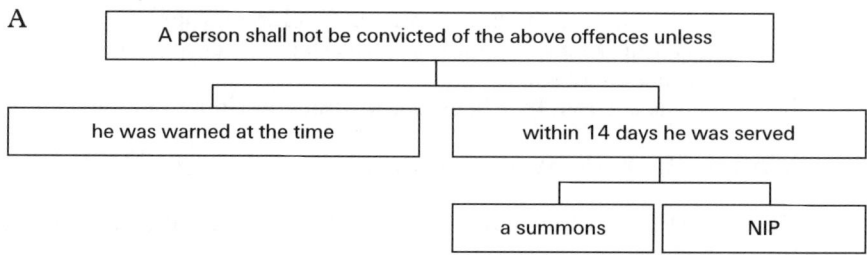

Q How is a Notice of Service proved?

A
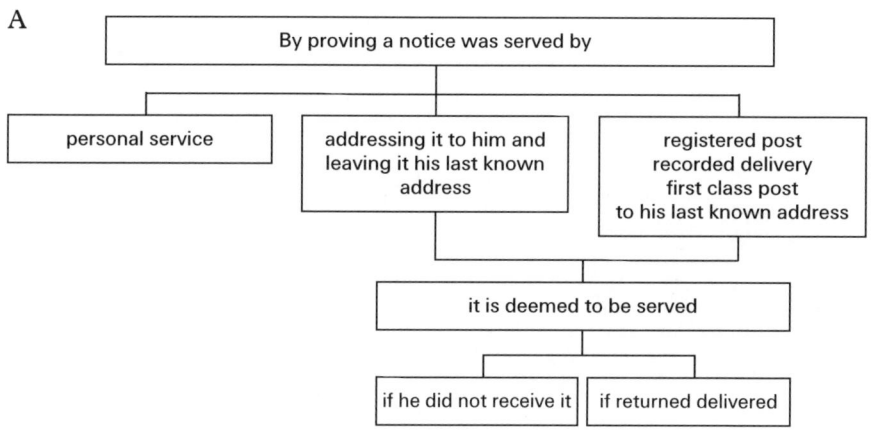

Q When is an NIP not required?

A   [a] At the time, or immediately after, **an accident** occurred owing to the presence of the vehicle concerned on a road;
      [b] when a **fixed penalty** has been issued.

Note. Where the accident is so minor that the driver is unaware of its occurrence then notices shall have to be served.

NOTICE OF INTENDED PROSECUTION

Q   What if you are unable to trace?

A   A lack of warning notice **will not be a bar to prosecution** where:

   [a]   neither the offender's name and address, nor that of the registered keeper, could be ascertained, despite reasonable diligence to do so; or

   [b]   that the accused **by his own conduct** contributed to the failure.

Q   What is the presumption in law in relation to NIPS?

A   They shall be deemed to have been served unless the contrary is proved by the defence.

ACCIDENTS

Q **Define an Accident**

A

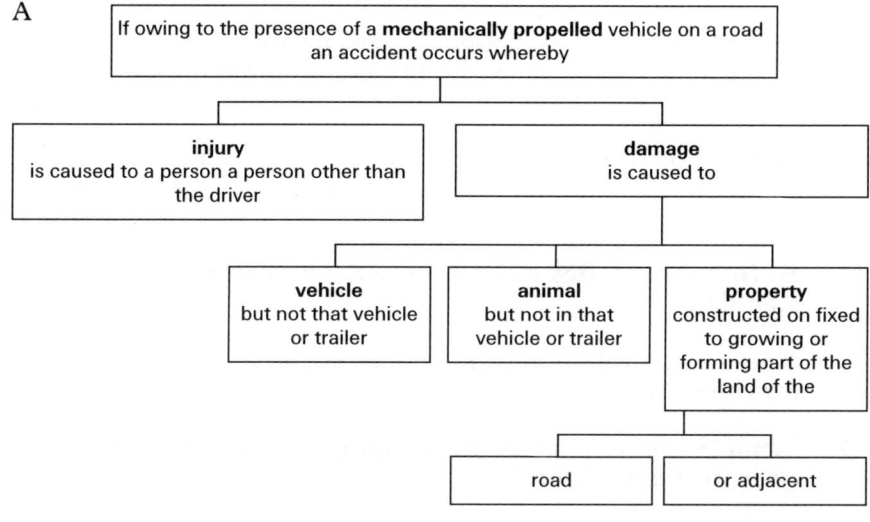

S 170 RTA 1988

Animal. Means horse, cattle, ass, mule, sheep, pig, goat or dog.

Q **What are the driver's Duties and Responsibilities?**

A   The driver shall:

   [a]   stop; and
   [b]   if required to do so by any person having reasonable grounds for doing so, give
      [i]   his name and address; and
      [ii] the name and address of the owner; and
      [iii] the identification mark of the vehicle.
         otherwise he commits an offence.

Q **What about Injury Accidents?**

A   The driver shall produce his insurance to:

   [a]   a constable; or
   [b]   to any person having reasonable grounds.

ACCIDENTS

Q   What is a Driver's Duty to Report an Accident?

A   Where the driver does not give his name and address he must report:

   [a]   to a police officer; or
   [b]   at a police station [personally]; and it must be done
         [i]   as soon as reasonably practicable; and in any case
         [ii]   within 24 hours.

24 hours. This does not give the driver 24 hours to report the accident, it must be done as soon as is reasonably practicable **and in any case** within 24 hours.

Q   Define the offence of Failing to Stop or Report an Accident

A   A person who fails to stop or report an accident commits an offence. [two offences].

Q   What is the defence to not producing Insurance at the time of the Accident?

A   To produce at a police station specified by him at the time of the accident within **7 days.**

Q   Define the offence of Giving False Details

A   In the case of an allegation of dangerous or careless driving or cycling, the driver/rider **who refuses,** or **gives a false name and address,** to any person with reasonable grounds for requiring it, commits an offence.

DRINK DRIVING

Q Outline the offence of being UNFIT to drive through drink or drugs

A
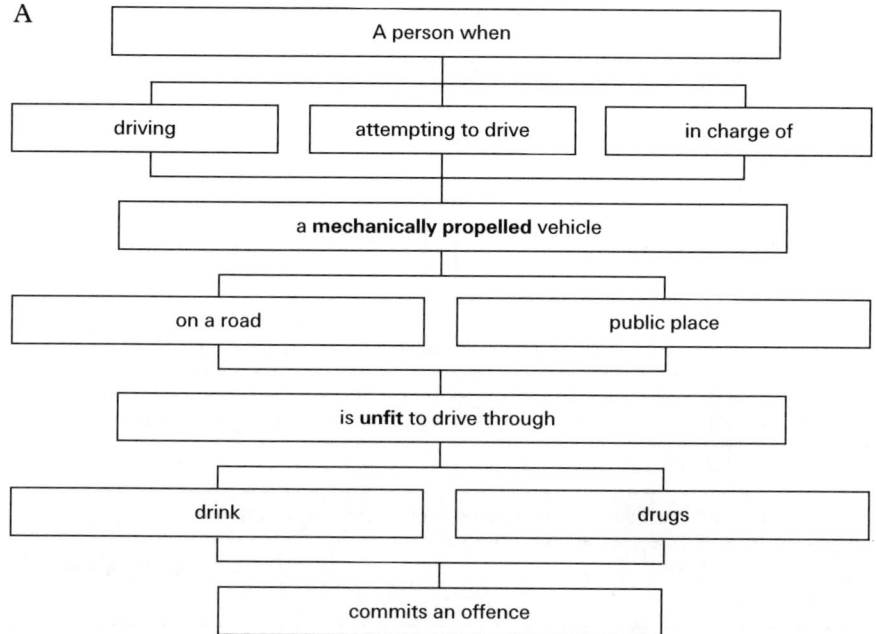

Police Powers. If a constable suspects that a person **is or has been** committing this offence he may arrest, **and may enter [if need be by force],** the place where he is or the constable suspects him to be.

S4 RTA 1988

Does the constable need to be in uniform. No.

Unfit. Means his ability to drive is for the time being impaired.

When is a driver not in charge? When he can prove that there was no likelihood of his driving so long as he remained unfit.

What if the driver is injured? The court may disregard any injury to the driver or damage to the vehicle.

Drugs. Means any intoxicant not alcohol.

DRINK DRIVING

Q Outline the offence of being **OVER PRESCRIBED LIMIT**

A

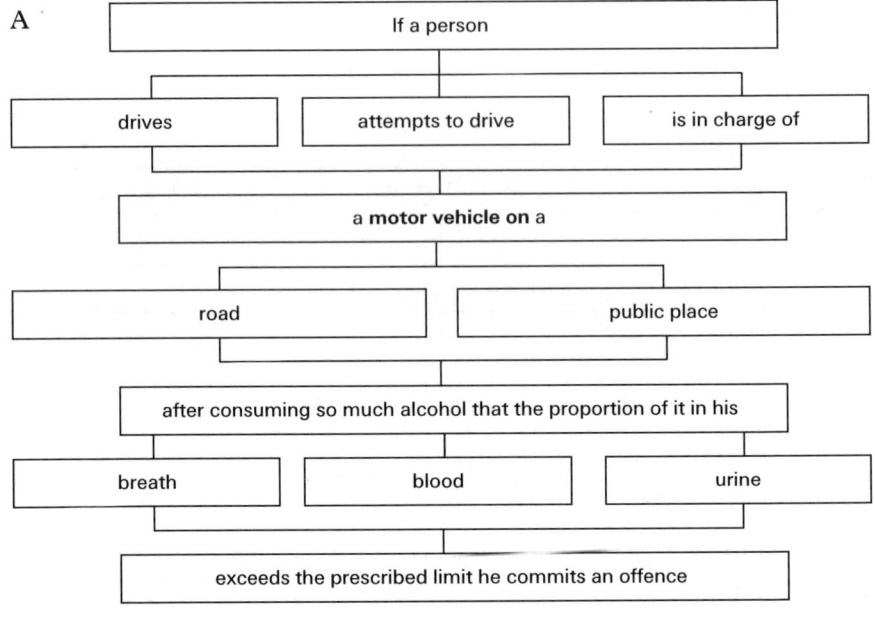

S 5 RTA 1988

Prescribed limits are		
35 microgrammes of alcohol	in 100 millilitres	of breath
80 milligrammes of alcohol	in 100 millilitres	of blood
107 milligrammes of alcohol	in 100 millilitres	of urine

Defence. For the driver to prove that there was no likelihood of his driving whilst he remained over the prescribed limit.

What if the driver is injured. The court may disregard any injury to the driver and damage to the vehicle.

DRINK DRIVING

Q Outline the requirement to Provide Samples of Breath

A
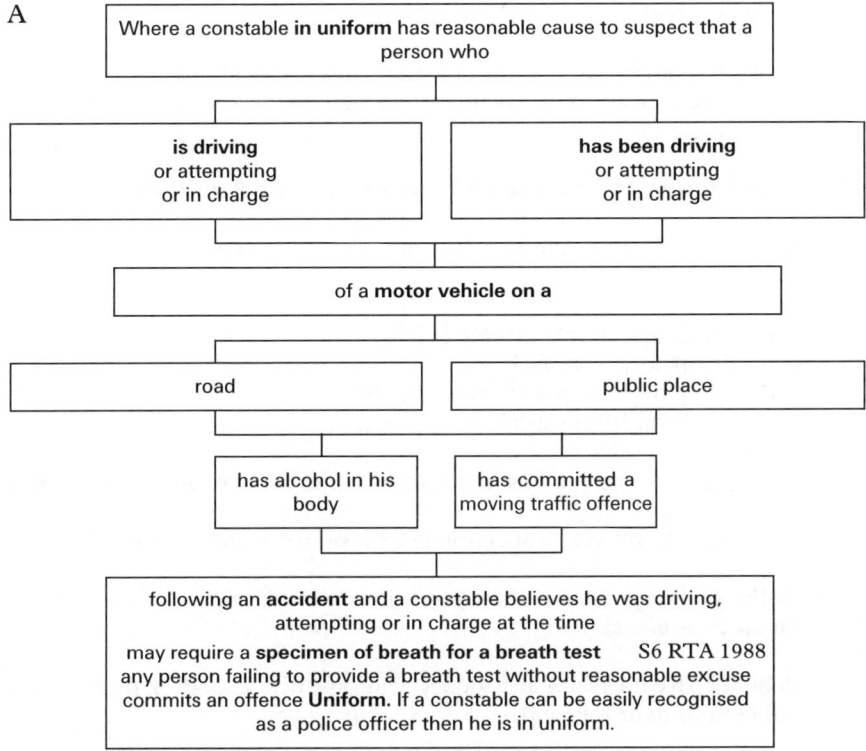

Q Where must the specimen he provided?

A [a] at or near where the requirement was made; or
[b] following an accident, if the constable thinks fit, at a police station.

Q Define the offence of Failing to Provide a Breath Test

A A person who, without reasonable excuse, fails to provide a specimen of breath commits an offence.

Arrest for being over the limit? Yes.

DRINK DRIVING

Arrest for failing to provide? No! - report for summons, unless the constable has reasonable cause to believe that **he has alcohol in his body** in which case arrest.

Power of entry? Where the constable has reasonable cause to suspect that there was an injury accident, he may enter any place he is or he suspects him to be.

Q Outline the Provision of Specimens for Analysis

A   In the course of an investigation into whether a person has committed an offence of:

  [a] death by careless driving [s 3A];
  [b] drunk in charge [s 4]; or
  [c] being over the prescribed limit [s 5]
       a constable may ask him to provide:

   [i] two specimens of **breath** by means of an approved device; or
   [ii] to provide a specimen of **blood or urine** for analysis.

Failure. The provision of only one breath specimen is a failure. Failure includes a refusal.

Where? Breath test - at a police station only. Blood or urine - at a police station or hospital.

What if no one admits to driving? The requirement can be made of more than one person in respect of the same vehicle.

Q When can a driver choose to replace a breath test with a specimen of blood/urine?

A   If the breath test specimen contains **no more than 50 mg** of alcohol in 100 ml of blood then the driver can ask that it be replaced by blood or urine.

Option. If the driver chooses the option of blood/urine and subsequently fails or refuses he commits no offence - revert to the original breath specimen.

DRINK DRIVING

Q Can you make a request for Blood or Urine?

A It cannot be made at a police station unless:

[a] for medical reasons a breath test cannot be provided or should not be required;
[b] a breath test device is not available or it is not practicable to use;
[c] in relation to **causing death by careless driving s 3A or unfit s 4** a doctor has advised that his condition might be due to a drug.

Who decides, blood or urine? The constable, unless a doctor is of the opinion that blood cannot or should not be taken, then it shall be urine.

Doctors advice. May be given over the telephone if appropriate.

Urine. Two specimens within one hour, the first being discarded.

Blood. Shall be divided into two parts one being supplied to the defendant.

Q What is the policy on Prescribed Limits?

A

between 35 - 39 mg of alcohol in 100 ml of breath	caution
between 40 - 50 mg of alcohol in 100 ml of breath	driver's option
more than 50 mg of alcohol in 100 ml of breath	charge

Q Define the offence of failing to provide Evidential Samples

A A person who, without reasonable excuse, fails to provide a specimen when required to do so commits an offence.

Reasonable excuse. The driver's conditional agreement is a failure, e.g. "I'll do it when my brief arrives" or "you can take it out of my big toe" or "after I've made a complaint about the arresting officer". For a

DRINK DRIVING

reasonable excuse defence to succeed it usually involves medical reasons.

Q **Outline the Post Procedure Detention of Subjects**

A [a] the person may afterwards be detained at a police station until it appears to a constable that, were that person **then driving** he would not be committing an offence;
[b] he shall not be detained if there is **no likelihood of his driving** whilst he exceeds the prescribed limit;
[c] in the case of drugs, a doctor's opinion should be sought concerning his fitness to be released.

Q **Outline the Hospital Procedure**

A A breath test or blood/urine specimens cannot be taken from a patient in hospital unless the doctor in immediate charge of his case has been notified of the proposal and:

[a] if the requirement is made, it shall be for a provision at the hospital; but
[b] if the doctor objects the requirement may not be made. The doctor may object on the grounds that the patient's care and treatment will be adversely affected by ny one of:

[i] he requirement to provide a specimen; or
[ii] he provision of the specimen itself; or
[iii] he warning [i.e. failure to provide may lead to prosecution].

Patient. A person continues to be a patient until his treatment is finished

Q **Outline the Evidence for offences under Sections 3A, 4 and 5**

A Evidence of the proportion of alcohol or drug in breath, blood or urine **shall in all cases be taken into account** unless the accused proves:

[a] he consumed alcohol between ceasing to drive; and
[b] before providing a specimen and
[c] had he not done so he would have not exceeded the limit or been impaired.

DRINK DRIVING

Distinguish between Sections 4 and 5

	Unfit - S4	Over prescribed limit - S5
Driving	driving, attempting, in charge	driving, attempting, in charge
Vehicle	**mechanically propelled vehicle**	motor vehicle
Where	road or public place	road or public place
Uniform	**No**	**Yes**
Power to arrest or to require a breath test	a constable may arrest [see breath test powers below]	Breath test where a constable suspects: 1. has alcohol in his body or has committed a moving traffic offence 2. has had alcohol in his body and still has alcohol in his body 3. has committed a moving traffic offence
Offence	unfit through drink or drugs	breath, blood, urine, exceeds the prescribed limit
Arrest	is committing or has been committing	1. positive breath test 2. Failed breath test **and** the constable suspects alcohol in his body
Entry	Yes where he is or suspected to be	conditional 1. to require breath test 2. to arrest following an injury accident
Defence	no likelihood of him driving whilst he remained unfit	no likelihood of him driving whilst he remained over the limit

DRINK DRIVING

A constable [in uniform *or out of uniform*]

1. May arrest a person following a positive breath test or where he has failed to supply a breath test **and** the constable suspects he has alcohol in his body.
2. May **enter** [if need be by force] any place where he is or the constable suspects him to be to:

   [a] require him to provide a breath test following an **injury accident,** or
   [b] to arrest under S5 following an **injury accident**

INSURANCE

Q **Define the offence of No Insurance**

A It is an offence to use, [cause permit] a motor vehicle on a road without insurance.

Q **What is the defence to No Insurance?**

A [a] the vehicle did not belong to him and was not under contract of hire or loan;
[b] he was using the vehicle in the course of his employment; and
[c] that he neither knew nor had reason to believe that there was no insurance.

Q **What restrictions in a Policy of Insurance are Void?**

A Breach of the following restrictions does not make the policy void:

[a] the age or physical or mental condition of the driver;
[b] the condition of the vehicle;
[c] the number of persons carried;
[d] the weight or physical characteristics of the goods carried;
[e] the times or areas in which the vehicle is used;
[f] the horsepower or cc or value of the vehicle; ;
[g] carrying any particular apparatus; or
[h] carrying any particular means of identification of the vehicle.

Q **Outline police powers to Demand the Production of Insurance**

A [a] a person driving a motor vehicle **on a road** [not an invalid carriage];
[b] a person whom a constable [or vehicle examiner] reasonably believes to have been the driver when an **accident** occurred; or
[c] a person whom a constable [or vehicle examiner] reasonably believes to have **committed an offence** in relation to the use of the vehicle on a road,

INSURANCE

shall, on being required by a constable or vehicle examiner:

[i] give his name and address;
[ii] the name and address of the owner.

Not produced at time. In proceedings for an offence, it is a defence to prove that the insurance was produced within **7 days** at a police station specified by him, or it was produced as soon as was reasonably practicable, or it was not practicable to produce before the proceedings began.

TRAFFIC SAFETY MEASURES

Q Define the law relating to Seat Belts

A Where a person is aged 14 **years old** and over, it is an offence to:

[a] **drive** a motor vehicle; or
[b] ride as a **front seat passenger;** or
[c] ride in the **rear seat** of a motor car or passenger car without wearing an adult seat belt.

Aiding and abetting. There is no offence of aiding etc, individuals are guilty only.

Q Define the law in relation to under 14 years of age and Seat Belts

A [a] where a child aged under 14 years is in the front seat, he must wear a seat belt;
[b] he must wear a seat belt in the **rear seat** if it is fitted, except
   [i] **aged under 12 years** and is a **small child,** [under 150cm];
   [ii] no seat belt is fitted in the rear; and
   [iii] a seat in the front has a seat belt but it is unoccupied.

Who commits the offence. The driver, without reasonable excuse.

Q Define the law on Motor Cycle Helmets

A A motor cycle means a 2 wheeled motor cycle [with or without sidecar] and it is an offence to ride a motor cycle without protective headgear, except
[a] mowing machines;
[b] it is being pushed [not straddled]; or
[c] a Sikh wearing a turban.

S 16 RTA 1988

Q What is the law in relation to Passengers on Motor Cycles?

A [a] only one passenger may be carried;
[b] sitting astride, on a secure seat, behind the driver.

Who commits the offence? The driver.

TRAFFIC SAFETY MEASURES

Q **Who is exempt from Speed Restrictions?**

A The under-mentioned are exempt if the observance of the speed limit would be **likely to hinder** its use on that occasion:

Fire Brigade, Ambulance Service, Police

Q **Define the Obstruction Offences**

A **Highway.** A person without lawful authority or excuse, who wilfully obstructs the highway commits an offence;

Arrest. S 25 PACE Act 1984.

Road. A person in charge of a motor vehicle or trailer who causes or permits it to cause an unnecessary obstruction of the road commits an offence.

Street. Any person in any street who, to the obstruction, annoyance, danger of residents or passengers, wilfully interrupts any public crossing, or causes any wilful obstruction in any public footpath commits an offence.

Q **Define the offence of Parking Heavy Vehicles on Verges**

A

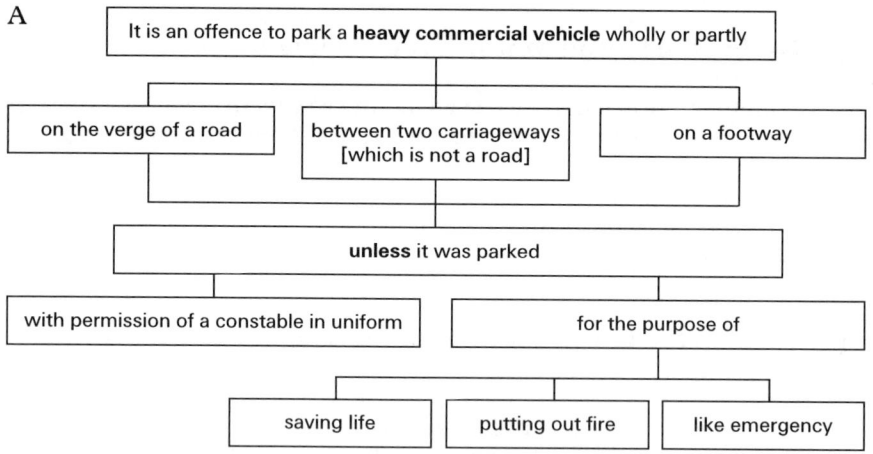

TRAFFIC SAFETY MEASURES

or

[a]	it was there for loading or unloading; and
[b]	it could not otherwise have been loaded, etc; and
[c]	it was never unattended.

Heavy commercial vehicle. Means its operating weight exceeds 7.5 tonnes.

Q Define the offence of **Leaving a Vehicle in a Dangerous Position**

A A person in charge of a vehicle/trailer, who causes or permits it to remain at rest in a road in such a position or in such condition or in such circumstances as to involve a **danger of injury** to other road users commits an offence.

Moving vehicle. This offence applies [e.g. failing to set handbrake].

Q Define the offence of **Wrongful Use of Disabled Person's Badge**

A A person who fails to comply with, or contravenes the order in relation to, parking commits an offence if at the time:

[a] a disabled badge sticker was displayed; and
[b] he was using the sticker in circumstances when the disabled person would have available a person's benefit.

Removal of badge. On third conviction or grounds for, it may be removed.

Q What is the law of **Removal and Immobilisation of Parked Vehicles?**

A Where a vehicle is permitted to remain at rest on a road:

[a] in contravention of a prohibition or restriction; or
[b] in a position or under circumstances as to obstruct or cause danger;
[c] or any **land in the open air** so as to appear to have been **abandoned/broken down**

TRAFFIC SAFETY MEASURES

then it may be moved from that road to another position on that road or another road.

Q Outline the offence of Causing Danger to Road Users

A   It is an offence if, intentionally and without lawful authority or reasonable cause:

[a] causes anything to be on or over a road; or
[b] interferes with a motor vehicle, trailer or cycle; or
[c] interferes with traffic equipment,

in circumstances that it would be obvious to a reasonable person **it would be dangerous.**

Traffic equipment. Means anything placed on or near a road by the highway authority, a traffic sign lawfully placed on or near a road by any person and any fence, barrier or light lawfully placed on or near a road, or by a constable or anyone acting under his instructions.

Arrest. Arrestable offence.

S 22A RTA 1988

Dangerous. Refers to danger either of injury to a person on or near a road or serious damage to property on or near a road and regard will be given to the circumstances which he could be expected to be aware, but also circumstances within the accused's knowledge.

TRAFFIC SAFETY MEASURES

Q Define the offence of Tampering with and Getting onto Vehicles

A
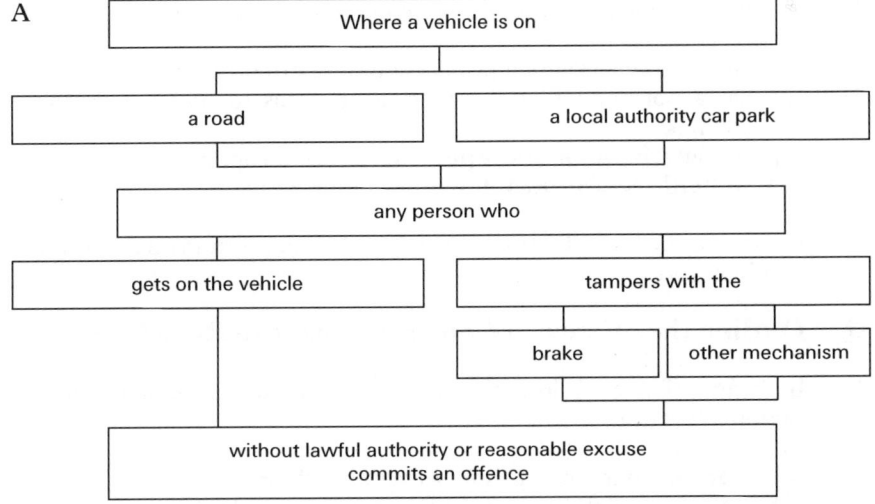

S 25 RTA 1988

Q Define the offence of Holding/Getting on to a Vehicle in Motion

A   If, for the purposes of being carried, a person without lawfully authority or reasonable excuse, takes hold of, or gets on to a motor vehicle or trailer in motion on a road, or for the purposes of being drawn, he takes hold of, he commits an offence.

Q Define the offence of Wrongful Use of Disabled Person's Badge

A   A person who fails to comply with, or contravenes the order in relation to, parking commits an offence if at the time:

[a] a disabled badge sticker was displayed; and
[b] he was using the sticker in circumstances when the disabled person would have available a person's benefit.

Removal of badge. On third conviction or grounds for, it may be removed.

TRAFFIC SAFETY MEASURES

Q What is the law of Removal and Immobilisation of Parked Vehicles?

A Where a vehicle is permitted to remain at rest on a road:

  [a] in contravention of a prohibition or restriction; or
  [b] in a position or under circumstances as to obstruct or cause danger;
  [c] or any **land in the open air** so as to appear to have been **abandoned/broken down**

then it may be moved from that road to another position on that road or another road.

Q Outline the offence of Causing Danger to Road Users

A It is an offence if, intentionally and without lawful authority or reasonable cause:

  [a] causes anything to be on or over a road; or
  [b] interferes with a motor vehicle, trailer or cycle; or
  [c] interferes with traffic equipment,

in circumstances that it would be obvious to a reasonable person **it would be dangerous.**

Traffic equipment. Means anything placed on or near a road by the highway authority, a traffic sign lawfully placed on or near a road by any person and any fence, barrier or light lawfully placed on or near a road, or by a constable or anyone acting under his instructions.

Arrest. Arrestable offence.

S 22A RTA 1988

Dangerous. Refers to danger either of injury to a person on or near a road or serious damage to property on or near a road and regard will be given to the circumstances which he could be expected to be aware, but also circumstances within the accused's knowledge.

TRAFFIC SAFETY MEASURES

Q Define the offence of Tampering with and Getting onto Vehicles

A
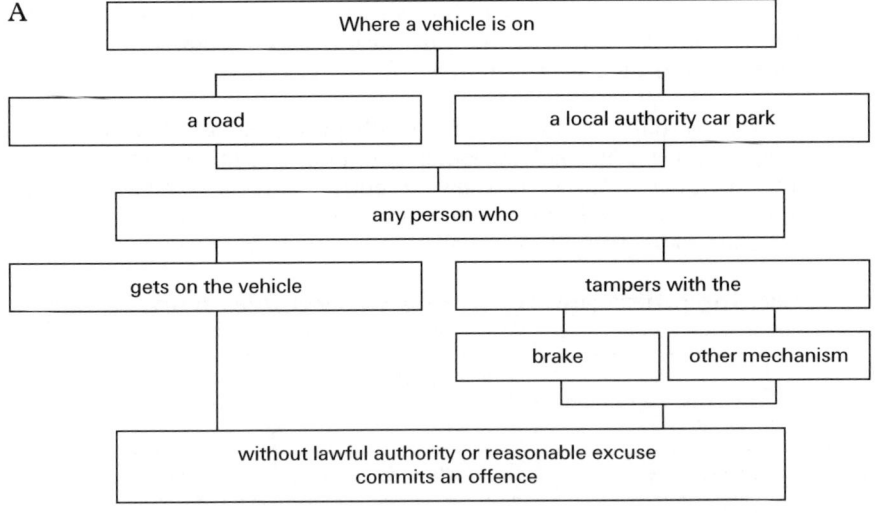

S 25 RTA 1988

Q Define the offence of Holding/Getting on to a Vehicle in Motion

A If, for the purposes of being carried, a person without lawfully authority or reasonable excuse, takes hold of, or gets on to a motor vehicle or trailer in motion on a road, or for the purposes of being drawn, he takes hold of, he commits an offence.

Q Define the offence of Abandoning Motor Vehicles

A A person is guilty of an offence who, without lawful authority:

[a] abandons **on any land in the open air,** or on a highway, a motor vehicle and anything which formed part of a motor vehicle and was removed whilst dismantling the vehicle on land; or

[b] abandons anything [not a motor vehicle] brought there for the purpose of abandoning it.

TRAFFIC SAFETY MEASURES

Q What is the duty of the local authority to Remove Abandoned Vehicles?

A Where it appears to a local authority that a motor vehicle is abandoned without lawful authority **on any land in the open air,** or on a highway, it is their duty to remove it.

Motor vehicle. Means a mechanically propelled vehicle intended or adapted for use on roads, whether or not it is in a fit state for such use, and includes trailers, chassis or body, with or without wheels, appearing to have formed part of the vehicle or trailer, and anything attached to the vehicle or trailer.

Q Outline police powers to Remove Vehicles from Roads

A

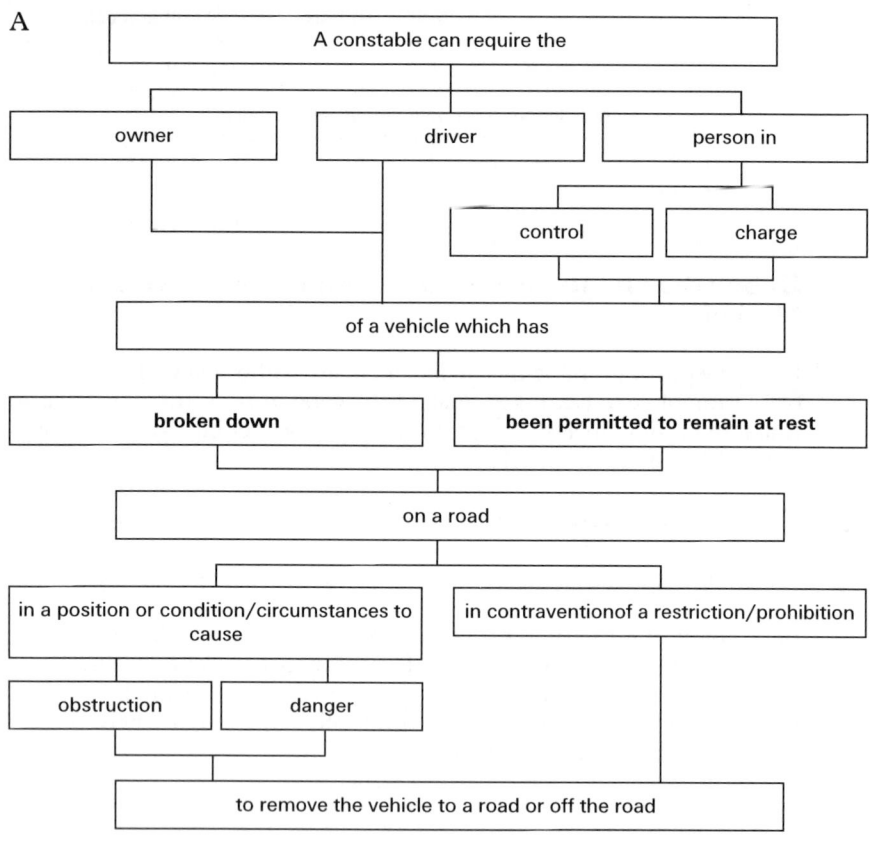

TRAFFIC SAFETY MEASURES

Q **Define the offence of Off-road Driving**

A It is an offence to drive a motor vehicle on:

[a] common or moorland, or any land; or
[b] footpath or bridleway,
except, it may be driven within **15 yards** of a road for parking.

No offence. If done for saving life, extinguishing fire, or like emergency.

Q **Outline the regulation on Builders' Skips**

A A skip can only be deposited with the permission of the Highway Authority.

Offences:

[a] placing on a highway without permission;
[b] not properly lit during the hours of darkness;
[c] it does not bear the owner's name and address **or** telephone number
[d] it is not removed as soon as possible after it has been filled;
[e] there is a failure to comply with a condition of the Highway Authority.

Who is liable? Both the owner of the skip and the offender.

Defence for owner. To prove that the offence arose due to the action or default of another **and** he had taken all reasonable precautions and exercised due diligence to prevent the offence.

Police powers. A constable **in uniform** may require the removal of the skip and failure to do so is an offence. The requirement must be made **in person**.

TRAFFIC SAFETY MEASURES

Q   Outline the law in relation to School Crossings

A

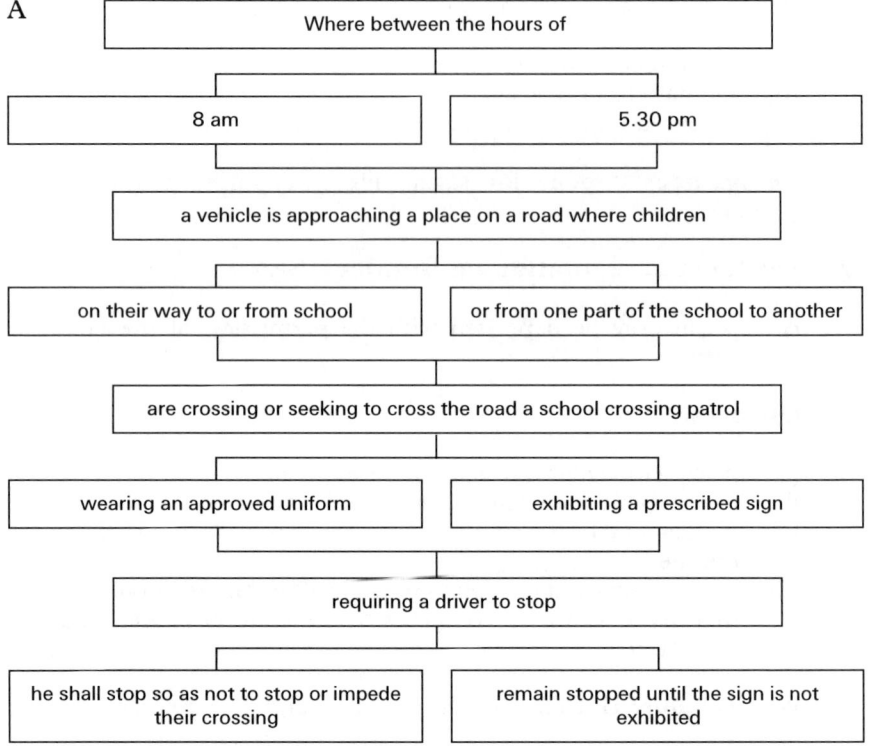

Offence. To fail to conform.

S 28 RT Regulation Act 1984

Presumptions. Unless the contrary is proven, it is presumed that he was in uniform, the prescribed sign was exhibited and that children were crossing or seeking to cross.

Traffic wardens. May exercise this function and they do not have to wear the uniform but they must exhibit the sign.

CONSTRUCTION AND USE

Q   Outline the law in relation to Maintaining BRAKES

A   Every part of every braking system and of the means of operation fitted to a vehicle shall be maintained in a good and efficient working order.

Can a constable check brakes? Yes, he may be able to give evidence that when the handbrake was applied he could push the vehicle along.

Q   Outline the law in relation to Defective TYRES

A   A tyre is defective when:

[a]   it is unsuitable for use;
[b]   it is under or over inflated;
[c]   it has a cut in excess of **25mm** or **10%** of its section [whichever is greater] and
      deep enough to reach the ply or cord;
[d]   it has any lump, bulge or tear caused by failure of the structure;
[e]   ply or cord is exposed;
[f]   the base of a groove in a tread is not visible; either:

   [i]   the tread does not have **1mm depth at least three-quarters of its breadth** of its tread round the entire outer circumference; or
   [ii] if the groove did not extend beyond three-quarters of the breadth of the tread any tread which does not have at least **1 mm;**

[g]   it is not maintained in a condition fit for its use; or
[h]   it has a defect which might cause damage to the road or to persons.

Q   Outline the law in relation to MIRRORS

A   With certain exceptions every passenger vehicle, goods vehicle or dual purpose vehicle first used on or after 1 June 1978, must be equipped with:

[a]   an interior rear view mirror; and
[b]   at least one exterior mirror fitted to the off-side.

CONSTRUCTION AND USE

If the interior rear view mirror is obscured the driver must have an exterior rear view mirror attached to the near-side of the vehicle.

Q Outline the law in relation to SILENCERS

A Every vehicle propelled by an internal combustion engine must be fitted with an exhaust system including a silencer and the exhaust gases from the engine must not escape without passing through the silencer.

Q Define the offence of QUITTING

A It is an offence to leave a motor vehicle unattended on a road unless **both** the engine has been stopped **and** the brake set.

Unattended. If there is a person with the vehicle, he must be licensed to drive it.

Q Outline the offence of DANGEROUS VEHICLE

A Every **motor vehicle,** trailer, parts and accessories must at all times be in such a condition that no danger is caused to any person in or on the vehicle or trailer or on a road. The number of **passengers** carried, or the manner of their carriage, is such that no danger is caused or likely to be caused to any person in or on the vehicle or trailer or on a road. The **load** carried by a motor vehicle or trailer must at all times be so secure and be in such a position, that neither danger nor nuisance is likely to be caused to any person or property by reason of the load or part of it falling or being blown from, or by reason of any other movement of the load or part.

Q Define the offence of Breach of Brake, Steering Gear, Tyres requirements

A A person commits an offence who:

[a] fails to comply with regulations as to brakes, steering gear or tyres; or
[b] uses on a road a motor vehicle or trailer [or causes or permits], which does not comply with the regulations.

CONSTRUCTION AND USE

Q Define the offence of Breach of Weight requirements

A A person commits an offence who:

[a] fails to comply with regulations in relation to weights applicable to:

[i] a goods vehicle; or
[ii] a motor vehicle or trailer adapted to carry **more than 8 passengers;** or

[b] uses on a road a vehicle [or causes or permits] which does not comply with the regulations.

Defence. It is a defence to prove that the vehicle was on its way to the nearest weighbridge to be weighed, or returning to reduce the weight to a relevant weight without causing an obstruction of the road.

Also. Where it does **not** exceed 5% it was not overweight at the time of loading and since then no one has added to the load.

Q Define the offence of No Test Certificate

A A person who uses on a road at any time, or causes or permits to be so used, a motor vehicle [to which the regulations apply] and to which no test certificate has been issued within 12 months, commits an offence.

Q What are police powers to demand the production of a Test Certificate?

A

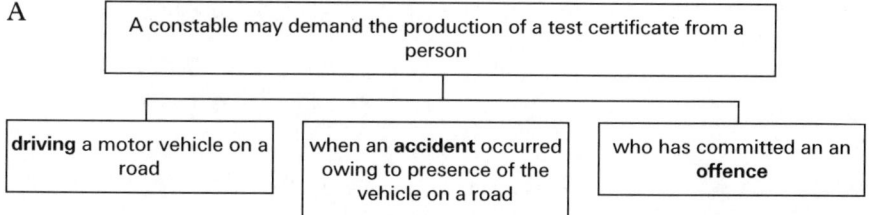

CONSTRUCTION AND USE

Defence. To fail to produce if he shows:

[a] he produced at a police station nominated by him at the time of the requirement within **7 days; or**
[b] it was produced there as soon as practicable; or
[c] it was not reasonable to produce it before the day proceedings commenced.

TRAFFIC SIGNS

Q Who can place a Traffic Sign on a road?

A A traffic sign may not be placed on or near a road unless such placing of the sign is authorised by:

[a] a traffic authority;
[b] a constable or other person authorised by the chief officer of police;
[c] any person in respect of a temporary obstruction.

Signs placed by the police. A constable or other person acting under the instructions of the chief officer of police, may place:

[a] on a road; or
[b] any structure on the road;

Traffic signs indicating, prohibitions, restrictions or requirements relating to traffic as may be necessary or expedient to mitigate congestion or obstruction of traffic, or danger to or from traffic, in consequence of extraordinary circumstances.

The 7 day rule. This power lasts for up to **7 days only.**

Signs placed by other persons. Any person is authorised to place the following for the purpose of warning traffic of a temporary obstruction on any part of the road, other than road works:

[a] a traffic cone;
[b] traffic pyramid;
[c] traffic triangle or warning lamp

as follows:

[i] cones and pyramids must number at least **4**;
[ii] cones and pyramids must be placed upright to guide traffic past an obstruction;
[iii] a warning lamp may be used in conjunction with a cone, pyramid or triangle. It must flash an intermittent amber light between 60 - 150 flashes per minute.

TRAFFIC SIGNS

[iv] traffic triangles shall be placed:

1. at least **45 metres away** from the obstruction; and
2. in a position to warn approaching traffic on the **same side of the road** as the obstruction.

Q **Define the offence of Failing to Comply with a Traffic Sign**

A It is an offence to fail to comply with:

[a] statutory restrictions or requirements;
[b] S 36 of the Road Traffic Offenders Act 1988; and
[c] other authorised signs.

S 36 signs [which are subject to NIP] include:

[a] stop;
[b] give way;
[c] keep left/right;
[d] no 'U' turn;
[e] no entry;
[f] stop board, manually operated;
[g] height restrictions;
[h] 'bus or cycle routes;
[j] red traffic light signals;
[k] green filter signals;
[l] double white line systems.

Q **Define the offence of Failing to Comply with a Sign**

A Where a traffic sign or the prescribed, colour, size etc, has lawfully been placed on or near a road, a person driving or propelling a vehicle who fails to comply with the indication given by the sign, commits an offence.

Lawfully placed. Signs shall be deemed to be lawfully placed unless the contrary is proved.

TRAFFIC SIGNS

Q **Define the offence of Failing to Comply with the Directions of a Constable**

A

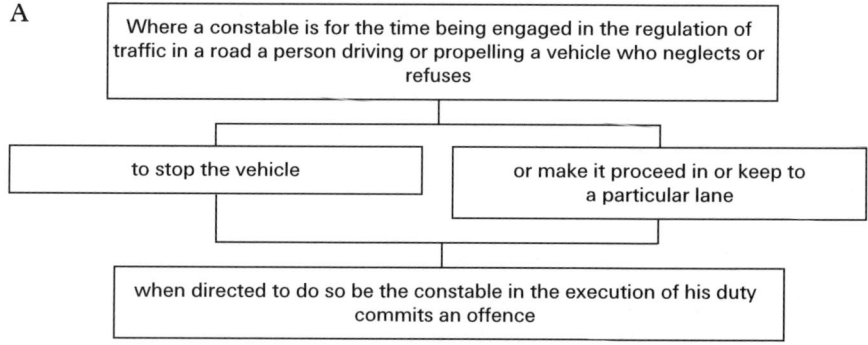

S 35 RTA 1988

Q **Define the offence of Failing to Stop when Required**

A   A person driving a mechanically propelled vehicle, or riding a cycle on a road must stop the vehicle on being required to do so by a constable in uniform, failure to comply is an offence.

Stop. Means bringing the vehicle to a halt long enough for the constable or traffic warden to exercise his powers.

Q **Define the offence of Pedestrians Failing to Comply**

A   Where a constable in uniform is for the time being engaged in the regulation of vehicular traffic in a road, a person on foot who proceeds across or along the carriageway in contravention of a direction to stop given by the constable in the execution of his duty is guilty of an offence.

Name and address. A person contravening this section may be required by a constable to give his name and address. Failure to due so is an offence.

Arrest. S 25 PACE Act 1984

DRIVER LICENSING

Q What are police powers in relation to Driving Licences?

A   Any person:

[a]   **driving** a motor vehicle on a road who
[b]   a constable or vehicle examiner has reasonable cause to believe has been the driver of a motor vehicle at the time when an **accident** occurred owing to its presence on a road; or
[c]   a person whom a constable or vehicle examiner has reasonable cause to believe **committed an offence** in relation to the use of the motor vehicle on a road ;
[d]   **supervisor** of a provisional licence holder driving a motor vehicle on a road:

must, on being required to do so by a constable or vehicle examiner:

[i]   give his name and address;
[ii] name and address of the owner; and

produce his licence to enable the constable or vehicle examiner to examine it and ascertain:

1. name and address of the holder;
2. date of issue; and
3. the authority by which issued.

S 164 RTA 1988

Defence. It is a defence for him to show that:

[a]   he produced the licence at a police station specified by him at the time the
      production was required **within 7 days;**
[b]   he produced them in person there as soon as was reasonably practicable; or
[c]   it was not reasonably practicable for him to produce them there before the day the proceedings were commenced.

In person. Driving licences must be produced in person by the holder.

DRIVER LICENSING

Q **What are the Grounds for Demanding Date of Birth?**

A The person fails to produce his licence forthwith; or
 [a] the driver number has been altered, removed or defaced; or
 [b] the person is a supervisor for a provisional licence holder and the constable has reason to suspect he is under 21; or
 [c] the constable has reason to suspect that the licence, was not granted to him, was granted in error or contains an alteration made with intent to deceive.

Q **Define the offence of Failing to Produce and State Date of Birth**

A A person required to produce his licence or state his date of birth or produce his certificate of completion of a training course for motor cyclist when required to do so commit and offence.

Q **Define the offence of Disqualified Driving**

A A person is guilty of an offence if, while disqualified for holding or obtaining a licence, he drives a motor vehicle on a road.

Arrest. A constable in uniform whom he has found committing and whom he has reasonable cause to suspect is disqualified.

Licence obtained by person disqualified. Has no effect.

Disqualified by reason of age. No power of arrest.

Q **Outline the law in relation to Provisional Licences**

A [a] a provisional licence shall not authorise a **person aged under 21 years:**

 [i] to ride a solo motor cycle unless it is a 'learner motor cycle', or it was first used before 1.1.1982 and does not exceed 125cc; or
 [ii] to ride a motor cycle with a sidecar unless its power to weight ratio is less than equal 0.16 kilowatts per kilogram

 [b] or authorise a person, to ride a motor cycle on a road unless he has successfully completed an approved training course, or is driving while undergoing training on such a course.

DRIVER LICENSING

How long does the licence last. Two years. No licence will then be issued for 1 year.

Q **What are the Conditions for a Provisional Licence Holder**

A **Supervision.** A provisional licence holder shall not drive a motor vehicle [not a motor cycle] otherwise than under the supervision of a qualified driver who is present with him in or on the vehicle, who is:

[a] **aged 21 years or over; and**
[b] **has held a full licence for at least 3 years.**

'L' & 'D' plates. Plates are required to be clearly visible to other road users within a reasonable distance from the back and front of the vehicle. In Wales there is an option to use 'D' plates. Where a learner is moving on the border between England and Wales he will be required to change to the appropriate plate on crossing the border!

Towing trailers. The licence holder must not draw a trailer.

Q **Define the offence of Supervisors Failing to Give Details**

A A person who:

[a] supervises the holder of a provisional licence who is driving a motor vehicle on a road; or
[b] whom a constable or vehicle examiner has reasonable cause to believe was supervising a provisional licence holder:

[i] when an **accident** occurred; or
[ii] when **an offence** was suspected by the holder,

the supervisor must on being required by a constable or vehicle examiner:

1. give his name and address; and
2. the name and address of the owner.

Q **What is the law in relation to Driving Instruction?**

A It is an offence to give driving lessons **for money** or money's worth unless the tutor is a registered approved instructor.

'Free' driving lessons. Offered by a person in the business of buying and selling cars will be deemed to be given for payment if the lessons are a condition of buying the vehicle.

S 123 RTA 1988

Q   How long can Foreign Nationals Drive in this Country?

A   12 months.

Q   Define the offence of Driving with Uncorrected Defective Eyesight

A   If a person drives a motor vehicle on a road with uncorrected defective eyesight he commits an offence.

Test. A constable having reasonable cause to suspect that a person driving a motor vehicle may be guilty of this offence may require him to submit to an eyesight test, refusal to do so is an offence.

Q   What is the law in relation to New Drivers?

A   A newly qualified driver is a new driver for **2 years** and if he sustains **six or more penalty points** the full entitlement to drive is lost until they pass a further test.

EXCISE AND REGISTRATION

Q   Define the offence of Keeping an Unlicensed Vehicle on a Road

A   If a person uses, or keeps, on a public road, a vehicle which is unlicensed, commits an offence. A vehicle is unlicensed if no licence or trade licence is in force.

Public roads. Is a road maintained at the public expense.

Parking. A vehicle parked on a road is 'kept' and needs to be licensed.

Failing to display licence. Is an offence in itself

Q   What is a Trade Licence [Trade Plates]?

A   Motor traders and vehicle testers may apply for trade licences which exempt them from the rates of duty. A motor trader is a person who:

[a]   manufactures;
[b]   repairs; or
[c]   deals in vehicles; or
[d]   anyone else carrying on a business of modifying or valeting vehicles.

The licence covers the use of vehicles:

[i]   temporarily in his possession in the course of his business as a motor trader
[ii]   kept and used solely for research and development in the course of his business as a manufacturer; and
[iii]   received from other manufacturers for testing on road in the course of his business as a manufacturer;
[iv]   vehicles submitted for testing in the course of his business.

Duration/display. 1 year, must be displayed back and front.

Offence. To use a vehicle [or greater number than permitted] on a road for a purpose other than that prescribed.

How many licences? Only one vehicle may be used on one licence at a time but he may hold more than one licence.

EXCISE AND REGISTRATION

Q What is the law in relation to Furnishing Information?

A **Vehicle used.** Where it is alleged that a vehicle has been used on a road:

[a] the keeper shall identify the driver or user; and
[b] any other person shall give information within his power which will lead to the identification of the driver.

Vehicle kept. Where it is alleged that the vehicle has been kept on a road:

[a] the keeper shall identify the keeper of the vehicle; and
[b] any other person shall give information within his power which may lead to the identification of the keeper.

It is an offence to fail to comply.

S 46 Veh Excise and Registration Act 1994

Defence. To show that he did not know, and could not have with reasonable diligence have ascertained, the identity of the person concerned.

Q Define the offence in relation to Registration Marks

A The driver, and if not driven the keeper, shall keep fixed on the vehicle a registration mark. The mark shall not be allowed to be obscured or rendered not easily distinguishable. Failure to comply is an offence.

GOODS VEHICLES AND PASSENGER VEHICLES

Q Define a Large Goods Vehicle

A A motor vehicle [not a medium-sized goods vehicle], constructed or adapted to carry or haul goods, having a maximum weight **over 7.5 tonnes.**

Q Define a Passenger Carrying Vehicle

A
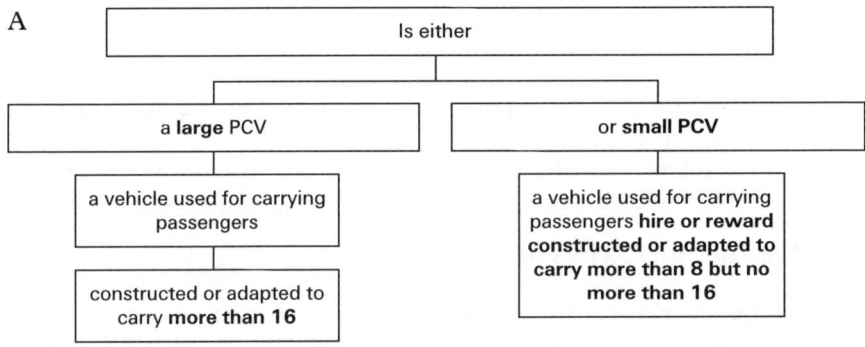

Disqualification. Where a person is disqualified by a court from driving, he may also have his LGV/PCV licence revoked for such a period as the licensing authority thinks fit. If the holder of a LGV licence is **aged under 21 years** and he accumulates **more than three penalty points** he must be disqualified from holding that licence:

[a] indefinitely or
[b] until he is 21.

Q What is an Operators' Licence?

A A licence issued to operators and users of goods vehicle who use the vehicle on a road for hire or reward or in connection with a trade or business. The licence authorises the operation of a number of goods vehicles.

GOODS VEHICLES AND PASSENGER VEHICLES

Q   Define the offence of Using a Vehicle without an Operators Licence

A   No person shall use a goods vehicle on a road for the carriage of goods:

   [a]   for hire or reward, or
   [b]   for or in connection with any trade or business.
   It is also an offence to contravene any condition of the licence.

Q   Define a Public Service Vehicle [PSV]

A   A motor vehicle [not a tramcar] which:

   [a]   being a vehicle adapted to carry **more than 8 passengers** for hire or reward; or
   [b]   a vehicle for carrying passengers for hire or reward **at separate fares** in the course of a business for carrying passengers.

Q   Define the 3 types of Carriage

A   **Stage carriage.** Are PSVs being used for local service carrying passengers on specified short journeys for hire or reward. e.g. each passenger is carried a stage at a time as with a local bus service;

   Express carriage. Are PSVs being used for carrying passenger for hire or reward at separate fares, other than local services. e.g. Bristol to London, stopping at Heathrow.

   Contract carriage. Are PSVs being used for carrying passengers for hire ore reward other than at separate fares. e.g. hiring a coach for a mystery tour or stag night.

   Operators' Licence. All PSVs must have an operators' licence.

Q   To which vehicle does Drivers' Hours apply?

A   [a]   **Passenger vehicles.** PSVs and other motor vehicles constructed or adapted to carry **more than 12 passengers;** and
   [b]   **Goods vehicles.** Articulated vehicles and vehicles constructed or adapted for the carriage of goods.

GOODS VEHICLES AND PASSENGER VEHICLES

Q What are the Driving Periods?

A

hours per day	9
can it be increased?	yes, to 10 twice per week
maximum continuous driving	4.5 hours
total hours driving in 1 week	56
total hours driving in a fortnight	90

Q What are the Rest Breaks?

A [a] at least **45 minutes** [unless he is beginning a rest period];
   [b] rest breaks may be replaced by a rest period of at least 15 minutes each totalling 45 minutes distributed within the continuous driving period or immediately after.

Can rest breaks be taken as part of a daily rest period? No

Q Outline Rest Periods

A [a] after 6 daily driving periods drivers must take a weekly rest period;
   [b] the weekly rest period may be postponed until the end of the 6th day if the total driving time over the 6 days does not exceed the maximum corresponding to 6 daily driving periods;
   [c] in the case of national and international carriage of passengers [not regular services i.e. coach tours] it is 12 and not 6 daily driving periods;
   [d] drivers must have a daily rest period of at least 11 consecutive hour in each period of 24 hours;
   [e] the rest period may be reduced to at least 9 consecutive hours not more than three times a week. This applies provided that an equivalent period is granted as compensation before the end of the following week;
   [f] where there is no reduction in hours, daily rest periods may be taken in two or three separate periods during a 24-hour period but one of these must be at least 8 consecutive hours;

GOODS VEHICLES AND PASSENGER VEHICLES

[g] where there is a reduction in hours, the minimum length of rest for that day must be increased to 12 hours;
[h] daily rest periods may be taken in a vehicle as long as it is fitted with a bunk and is stationary;
[j] during each period of 30 hours when a vehicle is manned by at least two drivers each shall have a rest period of not less than 8 consecutive hours;
[k] in the course of each week one of the rest periods shall be extended by way of weekly rest to a total of 45 consecutive hours;
[l] weekly rest may be reduced to 36 hours if it is taken at a vehicle base or driver base or to a minimum of 24 hours if taken elsewhere. If this is done there will be compensation by an equivalent rest taken en bloc before the end of the 31d week following the week in question;
[m] a weekly rest period which begins in one week and continues into the following week may be attached to either of these weeks.

Driver. Is any person who drives a vehicle, even for a short period, or who is in the vehicle in order to be available for driving if necessary.

Week Means the period between 00.00 hours on Monday and 24.00 hours on Sunday.

Day. Means successive periods of 24 hours beginning with the resumption of driving after the last weekly rest period.

Rest. Means any uninterrupted period of at least one hour during which the driver may freely dispose of his time, i.e. when the employer cannot direct the driver to work.

Q **What is a Tachograph?**

A   A combination of a speedometer, an odometer and a clock.

GOODS VEHICLES AND PASSENGER VEHICLES

Q What must a Tachograph Measure?

T	times of driving
A	any break in the journey
C	case housing being opened
H	hours of work/availability
O	overall distance travelled
S	speed

Q How long must an employer keep the Disk?

A 1 year.

Q What information must be entered on the Disk by the Driver?

A [a] name;
   [b] date and place where the sheet starts and ends;
   [c] registration number of the vehicle [and any other vehicle used during the driver's duties;
   [d] odometer reading at the start of the first and end of the last journey recorded;
   [e] the time any change of vehicle takes place.

What must the driver produce? Record sheets for the current week and last day of the previous week on which they drove. They must be returned to their employer within 21 days.

Q Outline the offences in relation to Tachographs

A It is an offence to use, cause or permit a vehicle to be used without tachograph equipment. It is an offence for an employed driver, without reasonable excuse to fail to return his record sheet to his employer within 21 days, or where he has 2 or more employers, to fail to inform each of them of the name and address of the other. It is an offence, with intent to deceive, force, alter or use any seal on the equipment and to contravene any of the requirements as to books, records and documents.

FIXED PENALTY SYSTEMS

Q What is a Fixed Penalty?

A A fixed penalty notice means a notice offering the opportunity of the discharge of any liability to conviction of the offence to which the notice relates by payment of a fixed penalty.

Q When can a fixed penalty NOT be issued?

A [a] where the penalty points would involve disqualification; or
[b] where the driver does not consent to surrendering his licence.

Q Outline the procedure where the driver is PRESENT

A

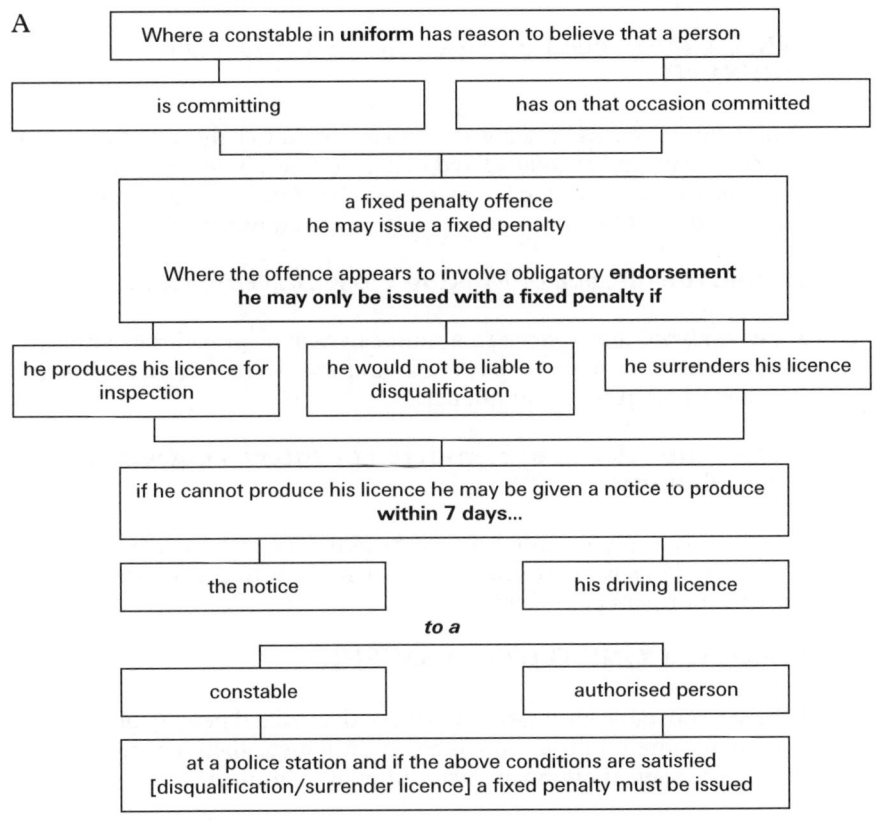

S 54 RT OFFENDERS ACT 1988

FIXED PENALTY SYSTEMS

Q What is the procedure if the person does not pay the penalty?

A If a person has not paid the fixed penalty, or given notice requiring a court hearing the police can register a sum equal to 1.5 times the amount of the penalty. Where this happens the justices' clerk will notify the person. Where a person receives such a notice he can serve a statutory declaration to the effect that either:

[a] he was not the person who was given the fixed penalty; or
[b] he has given notice requesting a court hearing.

He must serve this notice on the clerk **within 21 days** of receiving his notification.

Q What is the procedure when the driver is NOT PRESENT?

A Where on any occasion a constable has reason to believe in the case of any stationary vehicle that a fixed penalty offence is being or has on that occasion been committed he may issue a fixed penalty notice unless the offence appears to him to involve obligatory endorsement.

Q Define the offence of Making False Statements etc

A A person who, in response to a notice to owner, provides a statement which is false in a material particular and does so recklessly or knowing it to be false is guilty of an offence.

Q Define the offence of Removing or Interfering with a Fixed Penalty

A A person is guilty of an offence if he removes or interferes with any notice fixed to a vehicle, unless he does so by or under the authority of the driver or person in charge

Q What is a CONDITIONAL OFFER?

A Where a constable has reason to believe that a fixed penalty offence has been committed and no notice has been issued, then a notice can be sent to the alleged offender. A conditional offer must:

[a] outline the offence;

FIXED PENALTY SYSTEMS

[b] state the amount payable; and
[c] state that no proceedings will take place before **28 days.**

The conditional offer must indicate:

[a] **within 28 days** the alleged offender:

   [i]   makes payment; and
   [ii] where the offence involves obligatory endorsement, delivers his licence

[b] then if the clerk is satisfied that he is not liable to disqualification, the liability is discharged.

PEDAL CYCLES

Q Define an Electrically Assisted Pedal Cycle

A Do not exceed 40 kg kerbside weight [60 kg if a tandem] with an electric motor incapable of propulsion once the cycle has reached 15 mph.

How old do you have to be to ride? 14 .

Q What Braking System must a pedal cycle have?

A They must have at least 1 braking system unless they are fixed-wheeled or a cycle temporarily used in GB by a visitor. Cycles made on or after 1.8.1984 with a saddle height over 635 mm require:

[a] 2 braking systems with 1 on the front wheel and 1 on the rear if free-wheel;
[b] 1 system on the front if it is fixed-wheel.

Testing. A constable may test a pedal cycle to ensure conformity on a road or in the case of an **accident within 48 hours** on any premises where the owner of the premises consents.

Q Define the offence of Cycling whilst Unfit

A A person who, when riding a cycle on a road or other public place, is unfit through drink or drugs, commits an offence.

What is he's pushing the cycle? Offence of being in charge of any carriage when drunk.

S 12 Licensing Act 1872.

Q Define the offence of Cycle Racing on the Highway

A A person who promotes or takes part in a race or trial of speed on a public highway commits an offence, unless:

[a] it is authorised; and
[b] is conducted in accordance with the conditions imposed.

PEDAL CYCLES

Q   **Outline police powers in relation to Cycle Racing**

A   The chief officer of police may give direction with respect to movement of, or the route to be followed by traffic during any period, to prevent or mitigate:

   [a]   congestion or obstruction of traffic, or
   [b]   danger to or from traffic.

FORGERY AND FALSIFICATION OF DOCUMENTS

Q Define Forgery of Documents

A A person who, with intent to deceive:

[a] forges, alters or uses a document or thing, or
[b] lends, allows to be used by another a document or thing, or
[c] makes or has in his possession any document or thing so closely resembling a document or thing as to be calculated to deceive, commits an offence.

S 173 RTA 1988

Documents or things. Include, licences, test certificates, insurance, certificates of exemption to seat belts, haulage permits and goods vehicle plates.

Q Outline the offence of False Statements and Withholding Information

A [a] A person who knowingly makes a **false statement** for the purpose of:

[i] obtaining a licence;
[ii] preventing the grant of a licence;
[iii] procuring a provision or condition on a licence;
[iv] obtaining the grant of an international road haulage permit, or

[b] **in supplying information** or producing documents:

[i] makes a statement which he knows to be false or is reckless in so doing
[ii] makes use of a document he knows to be false or is reckless in so doing

[c] knowingly produces false evidence or statement in a declaration; or
[d] wilfully makes a false entry in a record required to be kept or with intent to deceive makes use of such an entry; or

FORGERY AND FALSIFICATION OF DOCUMENTS

[e] makes a false statement or withholds any information for the purpose of the issue:

[i] of insurance; or
[ii] any document issued under the Act commits an offence.

Issue of documents. It is also an offence to issue such documents.

Q Outline police powers in relation to False Documents/ Forgery

A If a constable has reasonable cause to believe that a document produced to him is a document in relation to which an offence has been committed he may seize the document

Q Define the offence of Forging/Altering Registration Documents

A A person is guilty of an offence if he forges, fraudulently alter, fraudulently uses, lends or allow to be used an registration document.

Q Define the offence of Forgery relating to PSVs

A A person who, with intent to deceive:

[a] forges or alters, or uses or lends to, or allow to be used; or
[b] makes or has in his possession any document or other thing so closely resembling a document or other thing as to be calculated to deceive,

commits an offence.

Which documents? Licences, certificates of fitness, certificate of type, operator's disc certificate of competence of any person.

Q Define the offence of Forgery relating to Goods Vehicles

A A person is guilty of an offence if, with intent to deceive, he forges, alters or uses a document or thing, lends to or allows to be used, or has in his possession a document or thing so closely resembling a document or other things as to be calculated to deceive.

FORGERY AND FALSIFICATION OF DOCUMENTS

Q **Define the offence of Misuse of Parking Documents and Apparatus**

A A person shall be guilty of an offence if, with intent to deceive:

    [a]   uses, lends or allows to be used:

        [i]   any parking device or apparatus designed to be used in connection with parking devices;
        [ii] any ticket issued by a parking meter, parking device or apparatus;
        [iii] any authorisation by a certificate or other means of identification; or
        [iv] any permit or token.

    [b]   makes or has in his possession anything so closely resembling any such thing as to be calculated to deceive.
    [c]   a person who knowingly makes a false statement for the purposes of procuring the grant or issue of any such authorisation commits an offence.

Part 4 - Evidence and Procedure

SUMMONSES AND WARRANTS

Q   Before a summons or warrant can be issued what must be Laid?

A   An information.

Q   What is an Information?

A   A written or verbal allegation made to a magistrate that a person has committed or is suspected of having committed an offence.

Q   What must the information Contain?

A
- [a] the name and address of the informant;
- [b] particulars of the offence suspected;
- [c] the law which has been contravened.

S 4 Magistrates' Courts Rules 1981

Q   What is a Summons?

A   A written order issued by a magistrate [or his clerk], ordering the person named to appear at a court at a time and date to answer an allegation of an offence.

Witness summons. Requires a witness to give evidence/produce exhibits.

Q   When can a summons be Issued?

A   A summons can be issued if:

- [a] the offence relates to the justices' area;
- [b] where the justices feel that the accused should be tried jointly with or in the same place as another who is charged with an offence and who is:

  - [i] in custody in their jurisdiction; or
  - [ii] is being proceeded against in their jurisdiction; or

SUMMONSES AND WARRANTS

[c] the accused resides in their area; or
[d] a court, by virtue of a statutory provision, has jurisdiction to try the alleged offence; or
[e] the offence was committed outside England and Wales and if the accused were before the court, they would have jurisdiction to try the offence.

Q Before issue, what must the Justices' Clerk ensure?

A [a] the information alleges an offence known to law;
[b] it was laid within the time limit;
[c] consents to bring the prosecution have been obtained; and
[d] there is jurisdiction to issue the summons.

When can a summons be refused? If it is frivolous or vexatious or amounts to an abuse of the process of the court.

Q What are the rules regarding Service of the Summons?

A The summons must bear the name and signature [rubber stamp] of the clerk and state:

[a] the substance of the information laid; and
[b] the time and place where the act used must attend.

Q How may a summons be Served?

A

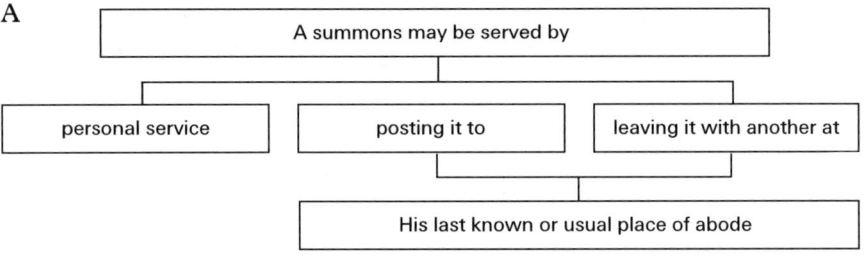

What if by posting/leaving he does not receive it? It is treated as served.

SUMMONSES AND WARRANTS

Q Can summonses be served in Scotland and Northern Ireland?

A Yes. S 39 Criminal Law Act 1977

Q Define the 5 types of Warrant

A **Arrest warrant.** Where a magistrate can issue a summons they may issue a warrant instead if:

[a] the information is in writing and on oath; and
[b] the offence is indictable or imprisonable, or
[c] the accused's address is insufficient to serve a summons.

Can the clerk issue a warrant? No.
Warrant to arrest a witness. Where a magistrate is satisfied that a person who could give material evidence would not voluntarily attend court he may issue a warrant.

Warrant to arrest in default. Issued for non-payment of fine etc.

Warrant to commit to prison. This warrant authorises a constable to take a person directly to prison [and obtain a receipt].

Warrant to distrain property. This warrant is issued to collect money in the form of goods to be seized and sold.

Q Which warrants do not need to be in the Possession of a constable to Execute?

A [a] to arrest for an offence;
[b] Army/An Force and Naval Discipline Act;
[c] distress;
[d] for the protection of a party to a marriage or child of the family;
[e] non-appearance of a defendant;
[f] committal; and
[g] witness arrest warrants.

What about a fine defaulter? The constable must possess the warrant.

What if the warrant is in a police car 'nearby'? The constable has possession.

What about entry? A constable may enter and search if he has reasonable grounds for believing the person is on the premises.

Q   Outline the law on the Execution of Warrants throughout the UK

Warrant issued in	Can be executed in	By
Scotland or Northern Ireland	England or Wales	a constable
England, Wales or Northern Ireland	Scotland	a constable
England, Wales or Scotland	Northern Ireland	RUC constable or reserve RUC

COURT PROCEDURE AND WITNESSES

Q Who is Competent and Compellable to give Evidence?

A All people are competent and all competent witnesses are compellable, except:

Q What is the law in relation to Accused Persons?

A **On behalf of the prosecution,** The accused is not competent to give evidence on behalf of the prosecution, therefore an accused person cannot give evidence against a co-accused until that person is no longer an accused person.

e.g.

[a] he is acquitted;
[b] he pleads guilty;
[c] there are to be separate trials;
[d] no evidence is offered.

On behalf of the defence. Every person charged with an offence shall be a competent witness for the defence at every stage of the proceedings, whether charged solely or jointly, but shall not be called except on his own application.

Q When is a Spouse competent and compellable to give Evidence?

A

Competent	Compellable
A spouse is competent to give evidence against any co-accused	
A spouse [other than when the husband and wife are jointly charged]	The spouse [unless jointly charged] when the offence charged: [a] involves **assault on,** or injury or a threat of injury to the other **spouse;**

COURT PROCEDURE AND WITNESSES

Competent	Compellable
	[b] involves **assault on,** or injury or a threat of injury to a person who is **under 16;** [c] is a **sexual offence** alleged to have been committed in respect of a person who is **under 16;** [d] aiding and abetting the above.

Q   Outline the position of Children as Witnesses in Criminal Proceedings

A   The evidence of any child **under 14** shall be unsworn. A deposition of a child's unsworn may be taken for criminal proceedings as though it had been given on oath.

Q   How is a Child's Age Determined?

A   By all the evidence available to the court at the time, usually by the production of a birth certificate.

Q   Outline the law in relation to Hostile Witnesses

A   A hostile witness is a witness who does not give evidence fairly or shows no regard for the truth **by the side calling him to give evidence.** In such cases the Judge may deem the witness to be hostile when the party calling him can:

   [a]   ask leading questions;
   [b]   contradict him with other evidence;
   [c]   prove that on another occasion he made a statement inconsistent with the present testimony.

Q   When can Live Television Links be used for giving evidence?

A   It may be used [other than for the accused] for witnesses who:

   [a]   are outside the UK; or
   [b]   a child; or

COURT PROCEDURE AND WITNESSES

in the case of trials on indictment, appeals to the Court of Appeal, proceedings in youth courts and appeals to the Crown Court arising from offences of:

[a] assault on, or injury or threat of injury, to a person;
[b] cruelty to a person under 16;
[c] certain sexual offences;
[d] offences under the Protection of Children Act 1978; and
[e] aiding and abetting the above.

S 32 CRIMINAL JUSTICE ACT 1988

Q When can pre-recorded Video Evidence be given?

A In trials on indictment and in proceedings in youth courts [and appeals]pre-recorded video evidence may be given [not by the accused] between an adult and a child. with the leave of the court.

Child. Is a person **aged under 14 years** [offences of violence or cruelty] and **aged under 17years** [sexual offences].

Q When can a witness Refresh his Memory?

A A witness may refresh his memory providing:

[a] the document was made or verified at the time of the incident, or shortly after, while the circumstances were fresh in his mind; and
[b] the document is produced in court for inspection; and
[c] where a witness cannot remember the events, the original document is used.

A witness may also refresh his memory by reading his own statement outside the court and before giving evidence.

Q What did R v Bass 1953 decide?

A Where 2 police officers have acted together they can refresh their memories from notes made in collaboration.

*'The officers' notes were almost identical. They were not made at the time **of** the interview. One officer made his notes after the appellant had been charged, and the other made his an hour later.... This court has observed that police officers nearly always deny that they have collaborated in the making of notes, and we cannot help wondering why they are the only class **of** society*

who do not collaborate in such a matter, It seems to us that **nothing could be more natural or proper when 2 persons have been present at an interview with a third person that they should afterwards make sure that they have a correct version of what was said. Collaboration would appear to be a better explanation of almost identical notes than the possession of a superhuman memory!**

Q **What is the rule regarding Privilege against Self-incrimination?**

A The rule is that no-one is bound to answer any question if the answer thereto would, in the opinion of the judge, have a tendency to expose him to any criminal charge, penalty or forfeiture which the judge regards is likely to occur, except:

S 31 Theft Act 1968. A person shall not be excused, by reason that to do so may incriminate him or his/her spouse of an offence under the Theft Act:

[a] from answering any questions for the **recovery of property,** for the execution of any trust or for an account of property; or
[b] from **complying with an order,** [but no statement made by him in proceedings under the Act shall be admissible against him or his/her spouse];
[c] where property has been stolen or obtained by fraud the title to the property shall not be effected by reason only of the conviction of the offender.

S 9 Criminal Damage Act 1971. A person shall not be excused, by reason that to do so may incriminate him or his/her spouse of an offence under the Criminal Damage Act:

[a] from answering any questions for the **recovery of property,** for the execution of any trust or for an account of property; or
[b] from **complying with an order,** [but no statement made by him in proceedings under the Act shall be admissible against him or his/her spouse].

S 98 Children Act 1989. In proceedings relating to care, supervision and protection of children no person shall be excused from:

[a] giving evidence on any matter; or
[b] answering any questions put to him in the course of his evidence; and

COURT PROCEDURE AND WITNESSES

a statement made shall not be admissible in evidence against him or his/her spouse.

S 1 Criminal Evidence Act 1898. Every person charged with an offence is a competent witness for the defence providing:

[a] he cannot be called to give evidence except at his own application;
[b] he can be asked any questions during cross-examination which might incriminate him;
[c] a defendant called as a witness cannot be asked any questions about his previous convictions or character unless:

  [i] where the proof of another offence is admissible to show that he is guilty of the offence charged [e.g. disqualified driving]; or
  [ii] where he puts his character in issue or challenges the character of witnesses; or
  [iii] he has given evidence against any other person charged.

Q **Under the Crime and Disorder Act 1998 summarise a Parenting Order?**

A The order requires a parent to:

[a] comply with the requirements of the order for **not more than 12 months**; and
[b] to attend counselling and guidance sessions specified by the responsible officer. This shall **not exceed 3 months** and **not more than 1 a week.**

The order shall not infringe on the parents:

[i] religious beliefs, or
[ii] his times of work, or
[iii] attendance at an educational establishment

Q **Who can the order be made against?**

A [a] 1 or both biological parents, and
[b] a guardian.

COURT PROCEDURE AND WITNESSES

Q Which court can discharge or vary the order?

A The original court making the order.

Q When SHALL an order be made?

A Where a person **under 16** is convicted of **an offence**.

Q Who is the Responsible Officer?

A [a] a probation officer;
[b] a social worker, or
[c] a member of a youth offending team.

Q What is the position if the terms of the order is breached?

A The parent who breaches the order without reasonable excuse commits an offence.

Q What is the purpose of a Child Safety Order?

A To prevent children **under 10** from turning to crime.

Q When can a Child Safety Order be made?

A If a magistrates' court, on the application of a local authority, is satisfied that a **child under 10**:

[a] has committed an offence;
[b] the Order is necessary to stop him committing offences;
[c] that the child has breached a curfew notice, and
[d] the child has caused harassment, alarm or distress, to someone other than a person in his own household.

Q What if the child breaches the Order?

A The court can:

[a] vary the order, or
[b] cancel the order and make a care order.

COURT PROCEDURE AND WITNESSES

Q What is a Child Curfew Scheme?

A Where the scheme is in force, a local authority may:

[a] ban children **under 10**,
[b] for up to **90 days**,
[c] from being in specified areas :

[i] **between 9 pm and 6 am**, and
[ii] without a responsible person **aged 18 or over**.

Q What if the child breaches the ban?

A A constable shall:

[a] inform the local authority asp, and
[b] take the child home [unless he is likely to suffer significant harm].

Q What are Police Powers to deal with Truants?

A Where the Act is in force, if a constable has reasonable cause to believe that a child he finds is:

[a] of school age, and
[b] is absent from school without authority,
the constable can remove him to:

[i] a designated place, or
[ii] back to his school.

PRIVILEGE AND PUBLIC POLICY

Q What is Legal Privilege?

A Communication between:

[a] legal adviser and client for the purpose of obtaining and giving legal advice; and
[b] legal adviser/client and 3rd parties, the dominant purpose of which was preparation for contemplated or pending litigation.

Q What is mean by Waiver of Privilege and By-passing the Privilege?

A **By-passing.** Where enquiries reveal **other sources** from which the privileged information can be proved, the privilege is not breached.

Waiving. The client himself can waive the privilege.

Q What is meant by Public Interest Immunity?

A Means that the exclusion of evidence on the grounds of public policy is claimed, usually because the evidence would harm the nation or the proper functioning of public service.

Q Who can raise the Immunity?

A [a] the relevant minister or Attorney-General intervening in a case;
[b] the party seeking to withhold the evidence or at the request of the government minister or department; or
[c] he judge in the case.

Q What is the effect of a successful claim to Immunity?

A [a] he may refuse to answer questions or disclose a document;
[b] the facts may be proved by other evidence; and
[c] no adverse inferences may be drawn against him.

PRIVILEGE AND PUBLIC POLICY

Q **What are the Types of Public Immunity?**

A   Those recognised by the courts are:

  [a]   national security and diplomatic relations;
  [b]   the proper functioning of the public service;
  [c]   police communications;
  [d]   informers and information for the detection of crime;
  [e]   judges and jurors; and
  [f]   sources of information contained in publications, e.g. editors.

EVIDENCE

Q What 2 Questions are applied to any Evidence?

A [a] admissibility; and
[b] weight.

Q What Reasons exist for Excluding Admissible Evidence?

A A trial judge may exclude evidence if he believes its prejudicial effect outweighs its probative value, and in cases of admissions and confessions they may be excluded if obtained by improper or unfair means [inducements and oppression]. Evidence may also be excluded for the following reasons:

[a] the incompetence of the witness;
[b] it relates to previous convictions or character of the accused;
[c] it is hearsay;
[d] it is non-expert opinion evidence;
[e] it is privileged information; or
[f] as a matter of public policy.

Q What is meant by the Facts in Issue?

A The facts which must be proved to establish guilt:

[a] the identity of the defendant;
[b] the actus reus [the physical act]; and
[c] the mens rea [the guilty knowledge - knowingly, wilfully etc].

Q On whom lies the Burden of Proof?

A The prosecution to a standard of *beyond all reasonable doubt*, exceptionally the defence. This standard is known *as the balance of probabilities*.

Q What is a Formal Admission?

A A formal admission dispenses with the need to prove a fact because it is admitted. Any fact may be admitted by the prosecutor or defendant, and admissions:

[a] may be made before or at the proceedings;

EVIDENCE

[b] if not made in court, shall be in writing;
[c] if made by an individual:

    [i] shall be signed; and
    [ii] shall be made by his counsel or solicitor.

S 10 CRIMINAL JUSTICE ACT 1967

Q **What is meant by Drawing Inferences?**

A The courts are permitted to draw 'such inferences as appear proper' against the accused in circumstances relating to the accused's silence. They relate to:

[a] silence when questioned by a constable;
[b] silence when questioned by a person charged with a duty to investigate offences;
[c] silence in court; and
[d] failure to give evidence in his defence.

Q **When can a court draw Such Inferences as Appear Proper?**

A Where in proceedings against a person for an offence evidence is given that he:

[a] on being questioned under caution by a constable; or
[b] on being charged or reported; he

failed to mention any fact relied on in his defence then:

a court or jury may draw such inferences as appear proper.

This does not prejudice:

[a] the admissibility in evidence of the silence of the accused in the face of anything **said in his presence** in so far as evidence would in any case be admissible; or
[b] the drawing of any inference from such silence.

EVIDENCE

Q When can an Inference be Drawn at Court?

A At a trial of a person who has attained 14 years and the court is satisfied that the accused is aware that the stage has been reached at which evidence can be given for the defence

  [a] if he refuses to answer questions; or
  [b] not give evidence;
     the court or jury may draw such inferences as appear proper of his refusal without good cause, to answer questions.

  This does not prejudice:

  [a] the admissibility in evidence of the silence of the accused in the face of anything **said in his presence** in so far as evidence would in any case be admissible; or
  [b] the drawing of any inference from such silence.

Q When must a Special Warning be given?

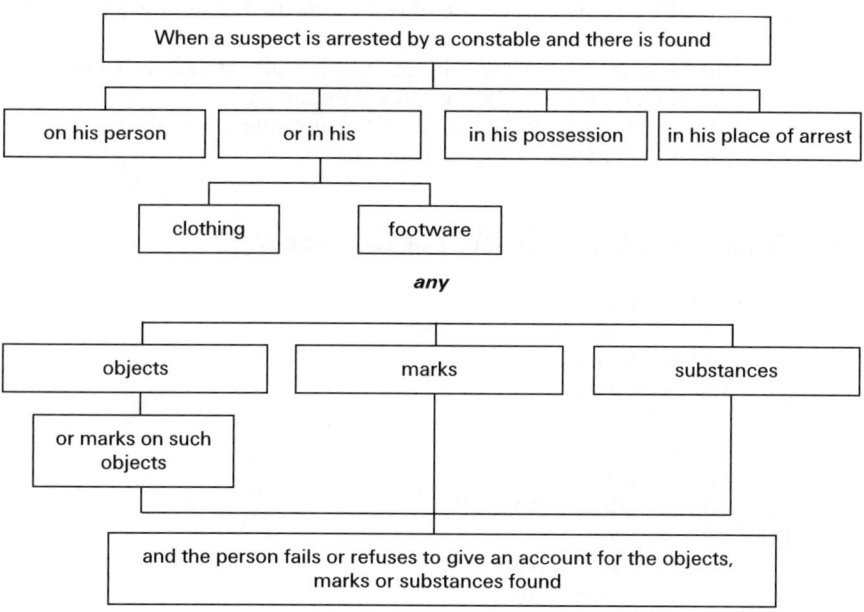

EVIDENCE

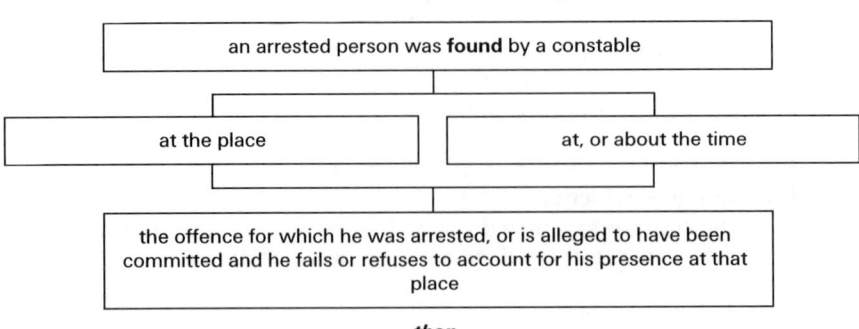

for an inference to be drawn from the suspect's failure or refusal to answer a question about one of the matters, or to answer in a satisfactory manner, the investigating officer must tell the suspect in ordinary language:

[a] what offence he is investigating;
[b] what fact he is asking the suspect to account for;
[c] that he believes this fact may be due to his taking part in the crime;
[d] that a court may draw inferences if he fails or refuses to account for the fact which is being questioned; and
[e] that a record is being made of the interview and that it may be given in evidence if brought to trial.

S 36 - 37 PACE Act 1984

Q What is the Classification of Evidence?

A   Evidence is classified as follows:

[a] original [oral] evidence;
[b] real evidence;
[c] secondary evidence;
[d] documentary evidence;
[e] hearsay evidence;
[f] circumstantial evidence;
[g] presumptions;
[h] evidence of character;
[j] evidence of opinion;
[k] corroboration; and
[l] judicial notice.

EVIDENCE

Original [oral] evidence. Is evidence given to a court from the witness box which is evidence of the first-hand knowledge of the witness, which is subject to cross-examination.

Real evidence. Usually takes the form of a material object, e.g. exhibits.

Secondary evidence. Is evidence which is not the best evidence, e.g. copy of a document.

It may be produced when:

- [a] a party fails to produce evidence in court when required to do so;
- [b] where a stranger to the case lawfully refuses to produce a document, ie where he could claim privilege;
- [c] where a document has been lost or destroyed;
- [d] where the production of the original document is impossible, e.g. painting on a wall;
- [e] where a public document is concerned where it's production would be illegal or inconvenient.

Documentary evidence. e.g. documents, maps, plans, graphs, drawings, photographs, discs, tapes, video tapes and films. They include CCTV video.

Evidence by Certificate of Plan or Drawing. In criminal proceedings, a plan or drawing signed by a constable or person with prescribed qualifications [architect, engineer etc], as a plan or drawing made by him which is drawn to a scale specified shall be evidence of the things shown on the plan or drawing. Before this can be adduced in evidence a copy must be served on the defendant **not less than 7 days** before the hearing and the defendant may serve notice **not less than 3 days** before the hearing that he wishes the witness to attend the trial to give evidence. Otherwise the evidence may be adduced without the witness appearing.

Admissibility of S 9 CJ Act 1967 written statements. Written statements shall be admissible as evidence to the same extent as oral evidence if:

- [a] it is signed by the maker;
- [b] it contains a declaration that it is true to the best of his knowledge and belief and that he made it knowing that, if it were tendered in

EVIDENCE

        evidence, he would be liable to prosecution if he wilfully stated in it anything which he knew to be false or did not believe to be true;
- [c] before the hearing copies are served on the other parties; and
- [d] not of the other parties **within** 7 **days** from the service, serves a notice requiring attendance of the witness. Parties may agree to waive this provision before or during the hearing;
- [e] if under 18, it shall give his age;
- [f] if he cannot read, it shall be read to him before he signs it and contain a declaration by the person who read it to him to that effect;
- [g] exhibits shall be served on the other parties;

Service of S 9 statements. S 9 Statements may be served:

- [a] be delivering it to him or his solicitor;
- [b] by addressing it to him and by leaving it at his usual or last known place of abode or place of business or by addressing it to his solicitor and leaving it at his office;
- [c] by sending it by registered letter or recorded delivery addressed to him at his usual or last known place of abode, or addressed to his solicitor at his office; or
- [d] in the case of a company, addressed to the secretary at their registered office or by registered letter or recorded delivery

Documentary records. A statement made by a person in a document shall be admissible if:

- [a] he is dead or by reason of bodily or mental condition is unfit to attend as a witness
- [b] the person is outside the UK and it is not practicable to secure his attendance; or
- [c] that all reasonable steps have been taken to find him without success; or
- [d] the statement was made to a police officer or person charged with the duty of investigating offences or charging offenders, and that the person does not give evidence through fear or because he is kept out of the way.

Business documents. A statement in a document shall be admissible in criminal proceedings of any fact of which oral evidence would be admissible if:

[a] the document was created or received by a person in the course of a trade, business, profession or other occupation, or as the holder of a paid or unpaid office, and
[b] the information contained in the document was supplied by a person who had personal knowledge of the matter dealt with, but it will only be admissible if:

[i] the information was supplied directly or indirectly, but if indirectly only if each person through whom it was supplied received it in the course of a trade, business, profession or other occupation or is the holder of a paid or unpaid office, or
[ii] a confession which would be inadmissible is not rendered admissible by virtue of the above.

Computer records, In any proceedings a statement in a document produced by a computer shall not be admissible as evidence unless it is shown:

[a] that there are no reasonable grounds for believing that the statements are inaccurate because of improper use of the computer;
[b] that at all material times the computer was operating properly, or if not that any aspect in which it was not operating properly, or was out of operation, was not such as to effect the production of the documents or accuracy of the contents; and
[c] the relevant conditions in the rules of the court are satisfied.

Hearsay evidence. Any statement made out of court is hearsay. Exceptions to the hearsay rule are:

[a] **statement by the accused.** Are admissible as to their factual contents.
[b] **statements made in the presence and hearing of the accused.** To prove the reaction of the accused. The statements do not prove what the author of the statement has said;
[c] **dying declarations.** Are admissible in trials for murder or manslaughter providing that:

[i] the declarant was in 'hopeless expectation of death';
[ii] the death was the subject of the charge; and
[iii] the circumstances of the death were the subject of the declaration. [e.g., identifying who had killed him].

EVIDENCE

[d] **statements made by deceased.** Where the deceased was under a duty to make declarations contemporaneously in the course of his business, written or oral. e.g. a statement by a constable to an inspector that he was going to keep an eye on the prisoner who later killed him.

[e] **entries in public documents.** Are exempted from the hearsay rule, providing:

  [i] the statements and entries have been made by the authorised agents of the public in the course of official duties; and
  [ii] the facts recorded are of public interest, or required to be recorded for the the benefit of the public.

Res gestae. Is evidence which would ordinarily be hearsay but is so *closely connected with a specific event that it ought to be admitted in evidence under the res gestae rule.*

The trial judge must be satisfied that:

[a] the event was so unusual or startling or dramatic as to dominate the thoughts of the victim; and
[b] that very effect on the thoughts of the victim exclude the possibility of their lying or being mistaken; and
[c] the statement was made at approximately the same time as the event.

e.g.: Suppose that 'A' and 'B' are standing drinking at a bar when the door opens. 'A' shouts 'don't shoot Bob' whereupon a shot rings out and 'A' falls to the floor mortally wounded. From 'Bs' position he could not see who fired the shot and the assassin has now made off. Whilst 'B' is comforting 'A' who is dying 'A' says, 'I can't believe it, Bob Russell shot me. Although hearsay, these facts would fit the res gestae rule and be admitted as evidence.

Circumstantial evidence. Is evidence not of the fact to be proved: but from other facts from which that fact may be proved with more or less certainty.

Presumptions. Fall into 3 categories:

[a] **irrebuttable presumption of law.** A child under 10 can be guilty of an offence.

[b] **rebuttable presumption of law.**

  [i] **doli incapax.** A child over 10 but under 14 can be guilty of an offence, It shall be presumed at his trial that he did not have guilty knowledge, and the prosecution **must rebut** the presumption;

  [ii] **presumption of regularity.** Until it is rebutted, it is assumed that officials have been properly appointed, police officers are acting in the execution of their duty, etc.

[c] **presumption of facts.** A court *may* presume, in the absence of evidence to the contrary, a fact from the evidence of other facts. Where evidence that a person was alive on a certain date is given to the court, it may be presumed that the person was still alive on a subsequent date.

Character. A defendant shall not be asked any questions concerning any offence other than the offence for which he is charged, unless:

[a] the proof that he has committed an offence is admissible to show that he is guilty of the offence charged [e.g. disqualified driving];
[b] he has put his own or the defence character in issue; or
[c] he has given evidence against any person charged in the same proceedings.

Previous offences as a juvenile. When a person reaches 21 years any offences he was convicted for when under 14 years shall be disregarded.

Opinion. May be given by non-expert and expert witnesses:

Non-expert evidence. May be given in relation to such matters as, the time of day, temperature, the value of an item, whether a person was drunk etc;

Expert evidence. Usually arises in relation to such issues as:

  [i] medical;
  [ii] science;
  [iii] determining mental illness;
  [iv] handwriting samples;
  [v] facial mapping.

EVIDENCE

Full disclosure requires any party intending to produce an expert to furnish the other party with written statements of the expert's findings.

Corroboration. Must be independent testimony which effects the accused by connecting him with the crime. In other words, it must be evidence which implicates him, that is, which confirms in some material particular that the offence has been committed and that the prisoner committed it.

Corroboration required by law. Involve the offences of treason, perjury and speeding.

Identification evidence. In R v Turnbull [1976] it was held that the factors that should be considered in identification evidence include:

[a] how long did the witness have the accused under observation?
[b] at what distance;
[c] in what light;
[d] was the observation impeded [passing traffic?];
[e] had the witness seen the accused before;
[f] how often;
[g] if only occasionally, had he any special reason for remembering him;
[h] how long elapsed between the original observation and subsequent identification;
[j] was there a material discrepancy between first description and the accused's actual appearance.

Judicial notice. The courts may take notice of facts that are so well known that they need no further proof e.g., night follows day, the grass is green, Glasgow is in Scotland.

SIMILAR FACT EVIDENCE

Q   Define the Similar Fact Principle

A   If you find an 'accident' which benefits a person and you find that the person has been fortunate to have that accident happen a number of times, benefiting each time, you draw a very strong, frequently irresistible inference that the occurrence of so may accidents benefiting him is such a coincidence that it cannot have happened unless it was designed.

Q   What were the facts of R v Smith [1915]

A   A man was charged with the murder of his wife who was found dead in the bath. There was evidence of two further marriages where the former wives had been found dead in a bath, along with other similarities including the defendant's profiting financially from the death on each occasion.

Q   How is Similar Fact Evidence Admissible?

A   **Striking similarity.** This is where the court looks for something *striking* about an offence, e.g., a particular *modus operandi* of a burglary say, who uses black masking tape to break windows without noise being caused or glass falling to the ground.

Multiple offence cases. This was considered in R v Sims [1946] where it was observed that the evidence of a number of accusations taken together is much greater than one alone. Where a jury might think one man might be telling an untruth, three or four are hardly likely to tell the same untruth unless they were conspiring together.

Possession of Objects by the Accused. Where objects are found belonging to the defendant which provides evidence that is more than coincidence, the objects may be admitted under the rule. e.g., an assault occurred whereby an injury was caused by a green beer bottle bearing a French name, allegedly wielded by the defendant. A search of his home reveals a number of green beer bottles all bearing a French name.

Association with an event. This 'association' may not be directly involved with the offence charged but will go to show a background to the offence. e.g., a man whose height is 6' 6 inches was seen leaving a number of burgled houses for which there is no real evidence to implicate him, but he is arrested nearby at the scene of another unlawful entry to a house [no offence yet having been committed] on suspicion of burglary.

Previous sexual conduct and the 'Same Transaction' Rule. Evidence of sexual behaviour which is not the subject of the charge may also be admissible to show the true nature of the relationship between the defendant and victim. In DPP v Boardman [1975] evidence of the accused's *previous* approaches to a boy was admitted. Similar evidence was given by another boy of indecent conduct leading over a period of time to incitement to buggery. Preliminary behaviour is all part of the 'same transaction' and therefore admissible.

Q   When can Confessions be Excluded in Evidence?

A   When they are:

[a]   obtained by oppression; or
[b]   considered unreliable.

Oppression. In any proceedings where the prosecution proposes to give in evidence a confession made by an accused, if it is represented to the court that it may have been obtained by oppression, they court may exclude the evidence. **Oppression is** the exercise of authority or power in a burdensome, harsh or wrongful manner; unjust or cruel treatment...the imposition of unreasonable or unjust burdens.

Unreliable. Means the confession was obtained in consequence of anything said or done which was likely to render it unreliable and the court shall not allow the confession to be given. In R v Fulling [1987] it was suggested that...questioning which by its nature, duration, or other attendant circumstances excites hopes or fears, or so affects the mind of the subject that his will crumbles and he speaks when otherwise he would have stayed silent. Courts have held the following confessions to be unreliable:

[a]   no caution was given, the suspect was not asked if he wanted his solicitor present and he was not shown the notes of the interview;
[b]   flagrant breach of the Codes of Practice;
[c]   interviewing a suspect who had just vomited [should have been seen by a doctor];

- [d] where the appropriate adult had a low IQ and was unable to assist the detained person;
- [e] suggested to a suspect of a sexual assault that it would be better for them to receive treatment than go to prison;
- [f] where a person had been kept in custody for 14 hours, had been interviewed four times before confessing and had been refused any visits from his family;
- [g] where the officers had a 'warm-up chat' with the suspect before the interview and the 'chat' lasted over 2 hours;
- [h] an offer of bail if the suspect admits the offence or conversely telling the suspect that he will be kept in custody until he admits the offence.

Q What is the effect of Excluding Confessions?

A While additional evidence obtained after a confession may be admissible, its value may be lost as S 76 of the PACE Ace 1984 prevents the prosecution from linking the discovery of the additional evidence to any confession which has been excluded.

Q What is the law in relation to the Exclusion of Evidence Generally?

A In any proceedings the court may refuse to allow evidence on which the prosecution rely on to be given if it appears to the court that, having regard to all the circumstances the admission of the evidence would have such an adverse effect on the fairness of the proceedings that the court ought not to admit it.

Evidence that has been excluded:

- [a] informing the suspect [wrongly] that his fingerprints had been found at the scene;
- [b] undercover operations where the police failed to record conversations in accordance with PACE;
- [c] failure by custody officer to inform a detained person of his rights;
- [d] interviewing without informing the detained person of his rights;
- [e] failing to provide the detained person with adequate meals;
- [f] 'off the record' interviews which were not recorded;
- [g] failing to make contemporaneous notes of conversations;
- [h] failing to get an interpreter or appropriate adult.

DISCLOSURE OF EVIDENCE

Q Define a Criminal Investigation

A Is an investigation which police officers or other person have a duty to conduct with a view to it being ascertained:

[a] whether a person should be charged with an offence; or
[b] whether a person charged with an offence is guilty of it.

Q To whom do the Disclosure Provisions apply?

A All not guilty pleas.

Q What is meant by Primary Disclosure?

A Relates to the duty of the prosecutor to disclose material which is in his possession or which he has inspected and which in his opinion **might undermine the case** against the accused. Material is material of any kind, including information and objects which are obtained in the course of a criminal investigation and which may be relevant to the investigation.

Q What is Sensitive Material?

A Material which the disclosure officer believes is **not in the public interest** to disclose.

Q What is Disclosure by the Defence?

A This duty only arises **after** the prosecutions primary disclosure and may be:

[a] compulsory; or
[b] voluntary.

Compulsory. This does not apply to cases being tried at magistrates' court. The statement would outline the defence in general terms. It should include those issues which the accused disputes with the prosecution and any alibi evidence. This must be done **within 14 days of primary disclosure.**

DISCLOSURE OF EVIDENCE

Voluntary. This applies to cases being tried at magistrates' court. This happens where

[a] the defence is not satisfied with the material disclosed at the primary disclosure
[b] where they wish to examine items listed in the schedule of non-sensitive material
[c] they wish to show the strength of their case in order to persuade the prosecution not to proceed.

Q **What is meant by Secondary Disclosure by the Prosecutor?**

A Once a defence statement has been provided [compulsory or voluntarily], the prosecution must disclose any material which:

[a] has not already been disclosed; and
[b] might be reasonably expected to **assist the accused's defence.**

Q **What if the defence are not satisfied about the Level of prosecution disclosure?**

A They may apply to the court for an order requiring them to disclose material which ought reasonably to be disclosed.

Q **What is the Continuing Duty of Prosecution to Disclose?**

A The prosecution must continue to review the disclosure of material right up until the case is completed. The duty falls in two stages:

[a] after primary disclosure the prosecutor **must** review material not disclosed in terms of whether it might undermine the prosecution case; and
[b] after secondary prosecution disclosure.

Q **Outline those with Roles and Responsibilities under the Act**

A **Prosecutor.** Means any person acting as a prosecutor whether an individual or a body.

DISCLOSURE OF EVIDENCE

Officer in charge of the investigation. Is the police officer responsible for directing a criminal investigation. He is also responsible for ensuring that proper procedures are in place for the recording of information, and retaining records of information and other material at the request of the prosecutor.

Disclosure officer. Is the person responsible for examining material retained by the police during the investigation; revealing material to the prosecutor during the investigation and any criminal proceedings resulting from it, and certifying that he has done this, and disclosing material to the accused at the request of the prosecutor.

Supervisor. There must be an officer in charge and a disclosure officer. Where he can no longer perform that task his supervisor must assign another person to take over his duties.

Q   **What are the duties of the disclosure officer in relation to Primary Disclosure?**

A   First, to create a schedule of all *non-sensitive material* and secondly a schedule of *sensitive material*. He must then decide what material might undermine the prosecution case. In addition to the schedules and copies of material which undermine the prosecution case he must provide a copy of material **whether or not it undermines the prosecution case.** This is:

   [a]   first description of the alleged offender;
   [b]   the alleged offender's explanation for the offence;
   [c]   material casting doubt on the reliability of a confession; and
   [d]   any material casting doubt on the reliability of a witness.

Q   **What are the duties of the Disclosure Officer in relation to Secondary Disclosure?**

A   After primary disclosure the defence may provide a defence statement setting out their case, together with reasons why they wish to inspect additional items of the schedule which have not been disclosed. Once the defence statement has been provided, the disclosure officer must:

   [a]   review the material contained in the schedules; and
   [b]   inform the prosecutor of any material which might reasonably be expected **to assist the defence** as disclosed by the defence statement.

Secondary disclosure may then be made to the defence.

DISCLOSURE OF EVIDENCE

Q What is the Continuing Duty of the Disclosure Officer?

A His continuing duty is to review material for items disclosed to the defence **as undermining the prosecution** that should be

Q What are the duties of Investigators?

A Investigators are required to pursue all reasonable lines of inquiry, *whether they point towards* or *away* porn *the suspect*. All material that is relevant to the case must be recorded and retained.

Q What is Sensitive Material?

A Material which is not in the public interest to disclose, e.g.:

[a] material given in confidence;
[b] observation posts;
[c] informants;
[d] police communications, etc.

Q What did The JOHNSON ruling state in relation to Observation Posts?

A In R v Johnson [1988] the following guidance as to the *minimum evidential requirements* was outlined:

[a] The police officer in charge of the observations, not lower than the rank of **sergeant** must be able to give evidence that beforehand he visited all OPs to be used and ascertain the attitude of the occupiers of premises, not only as to the use to be made of them, but also as to the possible **disclosure of their use** and other facts which could lead to the identification of the premises and occupiers;

[b] A police officer of no lower rank than **chief inspector** must be able to testify that, immediately before the trial he visited the places used for observations and ascertained whether the occupiers are the same as when the observations took place and what attitude the current occupiers have as to the **possible disclosure** of the use made of the premises and of other facts which could lead to the identification of the premises and occupiers.

DISCLOSURE OF EVIDENCE

Q **What are the Retention Periods for material?**

A   Material must be retained until a decision is taken whether to prosecute and then until the case has been dealt with. In the event of a conviction it must be retained at least until:

   [a]   the person is released from custody; otherwise
   [b]   6 months from the date of conviction.
          In the case of an appeal, until:

   [a]   the appeal is concluded; or
   [b]   the appeal does not go ahead.

6. What is the Retention Factor? Give examples.

CUSTODY OFFICER DUTIES

Q   Which prisoners must be taken to a Designated Police Station?

A   Person who are to be detained [or likely to be] for **more than 6 hours** must be taken to a designated police station, otherwise they may be taken to a non-designated police station.

S 35 PACE Act 1984

Q   Who shall act as a Custody Officer?

Designated police station
Sft - designated custody officer; or, where the custody officer is not available
any officer

Non-designated police station
Any officer who is not involved in the investigation of the offence, if readily available; or
By the arresting officer who took him to the police station or
any officer
and in all cases
If he is the officer who took him to the station, inform an inspector at a designated police station.

S 36 PACE Act 1984

Q   What is meant by Police Detention?

A   A person is in police detention when:

 [a]   he has been taken to a police station after being arrested for an offence;
 [b]   he is arrested at a police station; or

CUSTODY OFFICER DUTIES

[b] he has been taken to a police station after being arrested under the Prevention of Terrorism Act [Temp provisions] 1989.

and is detained there [or elsewhere] in charge of a constable.

S 118 PACE ACT 1984

Not in detention. A person charged and who is at court is not in police detention. Nor is a person who has been removed to a police station as a place of safety under the Mental Health Act 1983.

Q **What is the Right to Have Someone Informed of Arrest?**

A Any person arrested and held in custody may on request have:

[a] one person known to him; or
[b] who is likely to take an interest in his welfare, informed at public expense of his whereabouts.

S 56 PACE ACT 1984

Alternatives. If the person cannot be contacted 2 alternatives may be chosen, thereafter the custody officer or officer in charge of the investigation has discretion to allow further attempts.

Change of police station. The above rights apply to every move to another police station.

Q **When can an Inspector Delay this right?**

A A person shall be allowed to speak on the telephone and be supplied [on request] with writing materials. Where he is detained for an arrestable offence or serious arrestable offence the right can be denied or delayed if an **inspector** [or above] considers that it would result in:

[a] **interference with or harm** to evidence connected with a serious arrestable offence or interference with, or physical injury to, other people; or
[b] will lead to the **alerting of other people** suspected of having committed such an offence but not yet arrested for it; or
[b] will **hinder the recovery** of property obtained as a result of such an offence.

CUSTODY OFFICER DUTIES

They may also be delayed where the serious arrestable offence is either:

[a] **a drug trafficking offence** and the officer has reasonable grounds or believing that the detained person has benefited from it and that the recovery of the value of that person's proceeds will be hindered; or

[b] an offence covering **confiscation orders** applies and the officer has reasonable grounds for believing that the detained person has benefited from the offence and
that the recovery of the value of the property or anything connected with it will be hindered.

S 56 PACE Act 1984

Superintendents. May also delay, see chapter on superintendents.

Q   What is the right to legal advice?

A   A person arrested and held in custody at a police station or other premises has the right to consult privately with a solicitor free of charge if he requests it and must be informed of the right when he first arrives at the police station.

What if he declines. The custody officer shall ask the reasons.

What if he changes his mind? Where a suspect first requires a solicitor then changes his mind the interview may proceed providing he has given his agreement in writing or on tape to being interviewed without legal advice and an **inspector** or above has inquired into his reasons and given authority to proceed.

Superintendents. May delay access to legal advice, see chapter on Superintendents.

Q   What is meant by a Solicitor?

A   This means a solicitor who holds a current practising certificate, a trainee, a duty solicitor representative or an accredited representative.

Q   Who can refuse to admit a Non-accredited or Probationary representative?

A   Both may give advice unless an officer of **Inspector** or above considers that such a visit will hinder the investigation of crime and directs otherwise. If admitted he should be treated as any other legal adviser.

CUSTODY OFFICER DUTIES

Q What should the Inspector have regard to in deciding whether to Admit?

A [a] his identity and status has been established;
[b] is he a suitable character to give legal advice [a person with a criminal record is unlikely to be suitable, unless minor and not recent]; and
[c] any other matters in a letter of authorisation provided by the solicitor on whose behalf he is acting.

Q Can a person be interviewed in the Absence of a Solicitor who has been Requested?

A No, except [See chapter on Superintendents]

Q What cannot be delayed until a Solicitor arrives?

A It is not necessary to delay taking breath, blood or urine samples.

Q Distinguish Relevant Time from Review Time

A

Relevant time	Review time
Calculates the 24 hours that the detainee is permitted to be kept in police custody and runs from the **time of arrival at the police station**	Calculates the times when reviews of detention must be carried out and runs from the **time detention is authorised**
Note: Invariably the relevant time runs before the review time. This has the effect of having 2 clocks ticking at the same time!	

CUSTODY OFFICER DUTIES

The Relevant time		
Prisoner's status	**Conditions**	**Relevant time begins**
Attends police station voluntarily or accompanies a constable there voluntarily	is arrested at the police station	on arrest
Brought to police station under arrest		on arrival at police station
Arrested outside England and Wales		*the earlier of* time of arrival at the first police station in the police area where the offence is being investigated OR 24 hours **after entry** into England and Wales
Arrested by Force 1 for Force 2	he is not wanted by Force 1 and not questioned about the Force 2 offence	*the earlier of* time of arrival at the police station in the area where he is wanted by Force 2 OR 24 hours **after arrest** by Force 1
Arrested by Force 1 for their offence and is also wanted by Force 2	he is dealt with by Force 1 for their offence and not questioned about the offence in Force 2	*the earlier of* time of arrival at the first police station in the area where he is wanted by Force 2 OR 24 hours **after leaving** the police station where he is detained by Force 1
Hospitals. The relevant clock stops when he is on his way to, whilst at, and on his way back from hospital so long as he is **not questioned** to obtain evidence of the offence.		

CUSTODY OFFICER DUTIES

Suppose that Smith is arrested by Thames Valley Police for an offence and he is being dealt with for that offence by Thames Valley. Before release a PNCcheck reveals he is also wanted for an offence by Devon & Cornwall Constabulary. He is not questioned by Thames Valley about the Devon & Cornwall offence. The relevant time clock for Devon & Cornwall will start at the

earlier time of

| His arrival at the first police where he is wanted in Devon & Cornwall | 24 hours **after leaving** the police station in Thames Valley |

Q   Who is responsible for conducting Reviews of Detention?

A

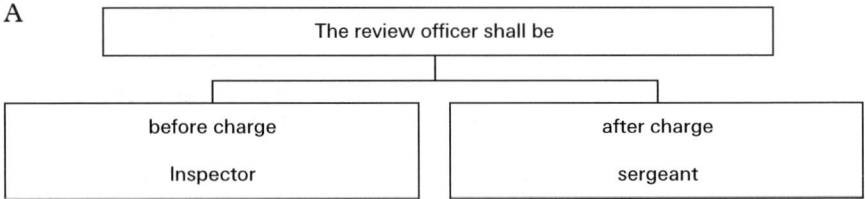

Q   When does the Review Time begin?

A   From the time the custody officer authorises detention.

Q   When shall Review be carried out?

A

Reviews			
1st	not more than	6 hours	from first authorisation
2nd	not more than	9 hours	after the first
3rd	not more than	9 hours	intervals

S 40 PACE Act 1984

CUSTODY OFFICER DUTIES

Q When can a review be Postponed?

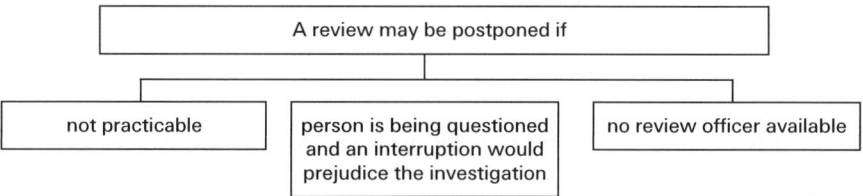

Q Who can make Representation to the review officer?

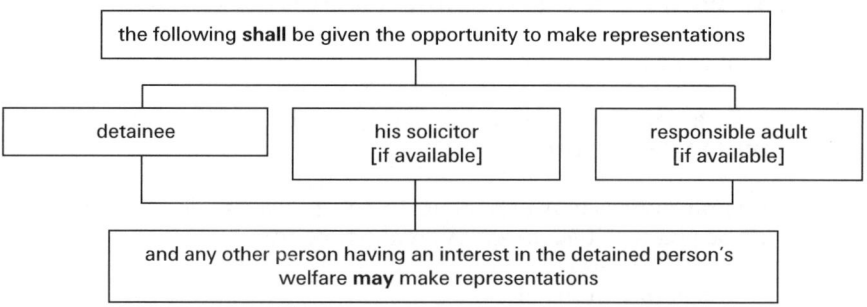

Q Can a review be conducted over the Telephone?

A Yes.

Q What if a review falls at the time when a person is Asleep?

A Bring the review forward.

Q When can detention be authorised beyond 24 hours?

A Detention may be authorised for up to 36 **hours** where the offence is a **serious arrestable offence** and a **superintendent** or above responsible for the station is satisfied:

[a] there is not sufficient evidence to charge; and
[b] the investigation is being conducted diligently and expeditiously; and
[c] the person's detention is necessary to secure or preserve evidence relating to the offence or to obtain evidence by questioning him.

CUSTODY OFFICER DUTIES

Q When can the decision to keep a person in detention for over 24 hours he made?

A [a] within 24 hours of the relevant time; and
[b] not before the 2nd review.

Q Who is the Review Officer during the 24 - 36 hour period?

A The superintendent.

Q How long can a Court Authorise Further detention?

A A total of 96 hours.

Q Outline the Procedure for applying for a Warrant of Further detention

A The application is may under oath in court by the police. The detainee must be present. The information must set out:

[a] the nature of the offence;
[b] the general evidence on which the person was arrested;
[c] what inquiries have been made;
[d] what further inquiries are proposed; and
[e] why it is believed that continuing detention is necessary for the enquiries.

Q When should the application be made?

A Within 36 hours [may be extended by 6 hours if there is no court sitting]. An application for a warrant or its extension should be made between 10 am and 9 pm, and if possible during court hours.

CUSTODY OFFICER DUTIES

Q When can Fingerprints be taken Without Consent?

A

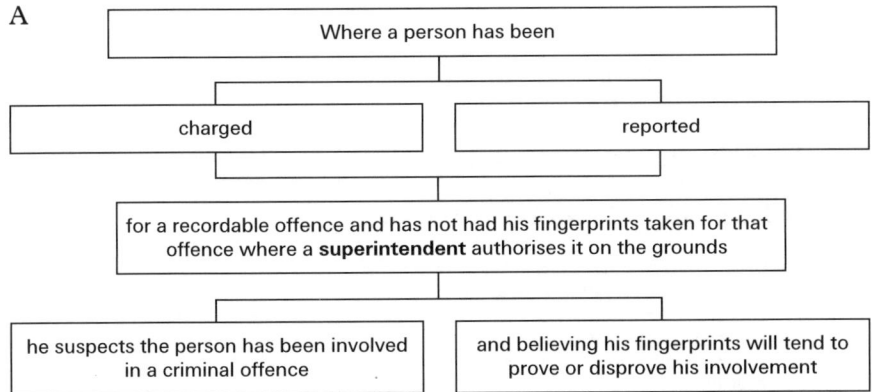

S 61 PACE Act 1984

Q When can Fingerprints be taken Following Conviction?

A

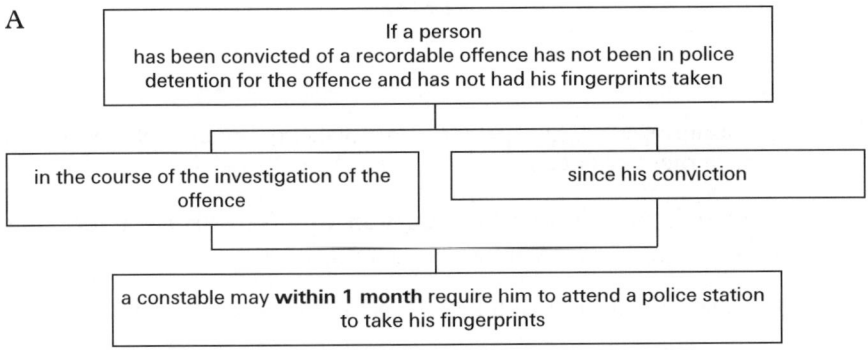

Notice. He must be given 7 **days notice** of the requirement and it may direct that he attends at a specific time of day or between specific times.

Arrest. In the event of failure to comply a constable may arrest.

S 27 PACE Act 1984

Why this power? This power fits the position where a person is reported for an offence say, shoplifting, and is not taken to the police station resulting in fingerprints not being taken, but subsequently being convicted for the offence.

CUSTODY OFFICER DUTIES

Q When can a person be cautioned?

A [a] where there is evidence of guilt with a realistic prospect of conviction; and
[b] he admits the offence; and
[c] he agrees to be cautioned.

Who administers the caution. A uniformed inspector.

Q When can Bail not be granted?

A

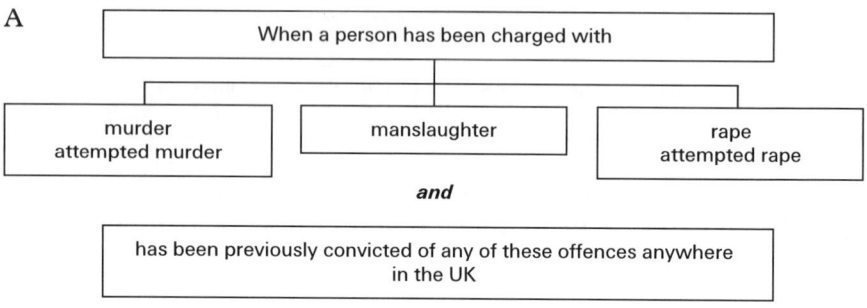

S 25 CJ & Public Order Act 1994

Manslaughter. The person must have been sentenced to imprisonment or detention.

Q What information must be given to a person Refused bail?

A The custody officer must tell the person the reasons why unless he is:

[a] incapable of understanding;
[b] too violent, or likely to become so; or
[c] in need of medical attention.
In any case he must be informed as soon as practicable.

Q When can a custody officer Refuse bail?

A [a] name and address unknown or doubted;
[b] he may fail to appear, based on:

[i] nature and seriousness of the offence;

CUSTODY OFFICER DUTIES

    [ii]   character, antecedents, associations and community ties;
    [iii] his bail record;
    [iv] strength of the evidence.

[c]   detention is necessary to prevent him committing an offence;
[d]   detention is necessary to prevent him interfering with the administration of justice;
[e]   detention is necessary for his own protection;
[f]   in the case of a juvenile, detention is necessary for his own *welfare*.

Q   When can Conditional bail be given?

A   Conditions may be imposed if it appears necessary to do so to prevent him from:

    [a]   failing to surrender;
    [b]   committing offences on bail;
    [c]   interfering with witnesses.

Q   What Conditions may be attached to bail?

A   [a]   to provide sureties to secure surrender to custody;
    [b]   give a security if it appears he is unlikely to remain in the UK;
    [c]   if under 17, a parent or guardian may be bound in the sum of £50
    [d]   and to comply with other requirements.

Q   What is meant by Other Requirements?

A   [a]   residential;
    [b]   inform police of change of address;
    [c]   not to enter a specified building or go within a specified distance of a named address;
    [d]   curfew;
    [e]   not to contact a specified person;
    [f]   surrender a passport;
    [g]   reporting to police station.

Arrest. Failing to surrender without reasonable cause.

S 6 & 7 Bail Act 1976

CUSTODY OFFICER DUTIES

Q What happens to a Juvenile refused bail?

A The custody officer must try to make arrangements for the juvenile to be taken into the care of a local authority, unless:

[a] the custody officer certifies that it is impracticable to do so; or
[b] in the case of a juvenile of at least **12 years old,** no secure accommodation is available *and* there is a risk to the public of serious harm from him which cannot be protected by placing him in local authority accommodation.

The certificate must be produced to the court at the first appearance of the juvenile.

Q Is a person who has been refused bail subject to a Review?

A Yes, within **9 hours** of last being refused bail.

Q When shall a person who has been refused bail be brought to Court?

A As soon as practicable and in any event not later than the first sitting after he has been charged.

Who decides? The clerk of the court decides when the next sitting is to be.

What days are excluded? Sundays, Christmas Day and Good Friday.

Q How can a Surety be relieved of his obligations?

A By informing a constable *in writing* that the person is unlikely to surrender to bail.

Q Outline the custody officer's duties on Arrival of arrested persons

A [a] open custody record;
[b] inform him of his rights;
[c] provide a written notice of rights;
[d] ask for signature on custody record of receipt of rights.

CUSTODY OFFICER DUTIES

Q What must be noted about the author of Entries in the custody record?

A All entries must have the person's name and rank except for officers dealing with Prevention of Terrorist Act offences.

Q What other duties are there in relation to Special Groups?

A [a] if the person is deaf or has difficulty with English, use an interpreter;
[b] if blind or seriously visually impaired, he should have help from his representative;
[c] if a juvenile, obtain an appropriate adult;
[d] if mentally impaired, obtain an appropriate adult.

Q What must be done when Deciding to authorise detention?

A [a] the arresting officer gives the reason for arrest;
[b] record any comment made by that person in response to the officer;
[c] decide whether to authorise detention;
[d] record any comment made by that person.

If detention is authorised inform the detained person unless he is:

[i] violent [likely to become so];
[ii] incapable of understanding what is being said; or
[iii] in need of urgent medical treatment.

Relevant time. If the person is surrendering to S 47 [3] bail the relevant time began at the time of his first arrest. So that if he spent 22 hours in custody before being bailed to re-appear at the police station, then on surrender to bail there are only 2 hours left.

Q Who can authorise a search at the Police Station?

A The custody officer. He shall:

[a] ascertain what property he has on his arrival at the police station;
[b] ascertain what property he might have for a **harmful or unlawful purpose;**

CUSTODY OFFICER DUTIES

[c] decide what property to keep and what to let the detained person keep;
[d] inform him of the reasons why any property is being retained;
[e] record all property in the custody record and have him sign the record.

Sex. The search must be carried out by a person of the same sex.

Force. Reasonable force may be used.

Q What Property cannot be seized?

A Items subject to legal privilege and items found in a body orifice.

Q When does a search become a Strip Search?

A Where the custody officer authorised removal of more than the outer clothing.

Intimate searches. See chapter on superintendents.

Q How often should detainees be Visited in Cells?

A Every hour and drunks every half hour. Drunks should be roused and spoken to on each visit.

Q Can Juveniles be placed in Cells?

A Only if there is no other secure accommodation and the custody officer considers that it is not practicable to supervise him.

Adult/juvenile, same cell? No.

Q Before Handing Over a detainee, what should the custody officer consider?

A [a] whether he is in need of a rest period;
[b] whether he is unfit through drink or drugs; and
[c] whether the right of access to legal advice is being complied with.

CUSTODY OFFICER DUTIES

Q What is meant by Rest Period?

A In any 24 hours he shall have at least **8 hours for rest,** free from questioning, travel or any interruption by police officers in connection with the investigation. His rest may not be interrupted unless there are reasonable grounds for believing that it would:

  [a] involve a risk or harm to people or serious loss of, or damage to property;
  [b] delay unnecessarily the person's release from custody; or
  [c] otherwise prejudice the outcome of the investigation.

Code C 12.2

Q When must an Appropriate Adult be informed?

A In cases where the detained person is:

  [a] a juvenile [under 17];
  [b] mentally handicapped; or
  [c] appears to be suffering from a mental disorder

Juveniles held incommunicado. Must have an appropriate adult.

Q What is meant by an Appropriate Adult?

A **In the case of a juvenile:**

  [a] parent or guardian;
  [b] social worker; or
  [c] failing above an adult [aged 18 or over].

In the case of the mentally ill:

  [a] a relative, guardian or person responsible for his car;
  [b] an person experienced with the mentally ill;
  [c] failing above an adult [aged 18 or over].

What about police employees. A police officer or police employee cannot act as an appropriate adult.

Q Who should Not Act as an appropriate adult?

A Any person who is suspected of involvement in the offence, is a victim, witness or a **person receiving admissions** prior to attending as an appropriate adult. If a juvenile is estranged from a parent and expressly objects to the parent's presence.

IDENTIFICATION

Q Outline identification methods where the Suspect is Known

A
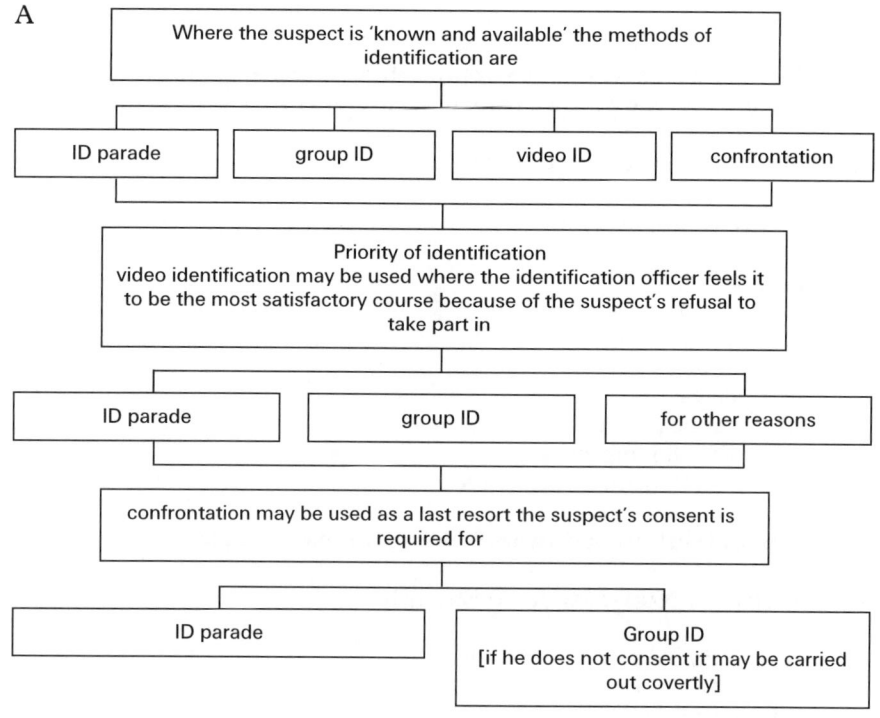

CODE D

Who is the identification officer. A uniformed inspector.

Known and available. Means available for arrest (R v Kitchen [1994]). Do not go to photograph ID if the suspect is known and available.

Q Who may Not take part in the procedures?

A Officers involved in the investigation of the offence.

IDENTIFICATION

Q What is meant by First Description?

A The first description provided of a person suspected of a crime must be recorded. It must be disclosed to the defence in the pre-trial procedure in all cases and, in particular, before any identification procedures take place.

Media publicity. Before any procedures take place, witnesses must be asked if they have seen any material previously released to the media.

Q Define an Intimate Sample

A Intimate sample means:

[a] blood;
[b] semen;
[c] tissue fluid;
[d] urine;
[e] saliva; or
[f] public hair; and
[g] a dental impression;
[h] a swab from a body orifice.

What about mouth swabs? Not an intimate sample.

Q Define a Non-intimate Sample

A Non-intimate samples include:

[a] hair [not pubic];
[b] nails [from a nail or under a nail];
[c] swabs; and
[d] footprints and other impressions of the body [but not his hand].

Q Can an intimate sample be taken Without Consent?

A No.

Q Whose consent is required?

A **Both** the suspect and a superintendent.

IDENTIFICATION

Q   Whose consent is required in the case of Juveniles?

under 14	14 but under 17
parents or guardian only	**both** the juvenile and the parents or guardian
and the superintendent	

Q   What happens where a sample proves 'Insufficient for Analysis'?

A   Retake them [again with both consents].

Q   When can a Superintendent Authorise the taking of Intimate Samples?

A
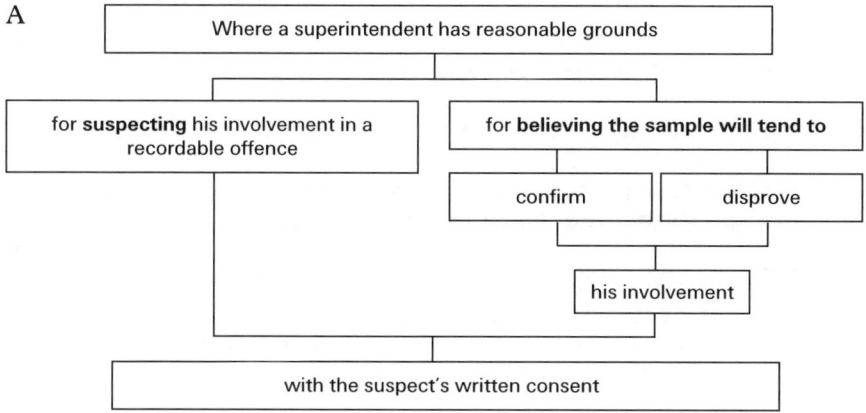

Warning. 'You do nor have to provide a sample but if you refuse without good cause your refusal may harm your case if it comes to trial.'

S 62 PACE Act 1984

Q   What information has to be Recorded?

A   [a]   the authorisation;
    [b]   the grounds;
    [c]   the suspect consented;

IDENTIFICATION

[d] at a police station the suspect was informed the sample would be subject to a speculative search; and
[e] the warning had been given.

Q **Outline the rules regarding an Intimate Search**

A

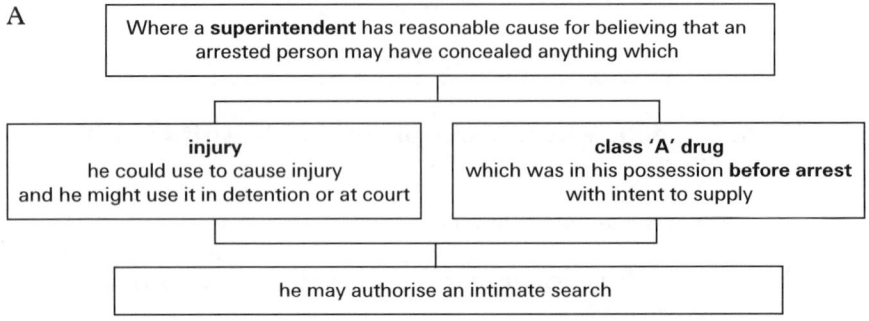

S 55 PACE Act 1984

Drug search. May not be carried out at a police station.

Q **When is a Superintendent's authority Not Required?**

A Where a large number of persons give samples with consent in relation to their **elimination** from a serious crime e.g. rape in a village.

Q **Outline the power to take Non-intimate Samples**

A

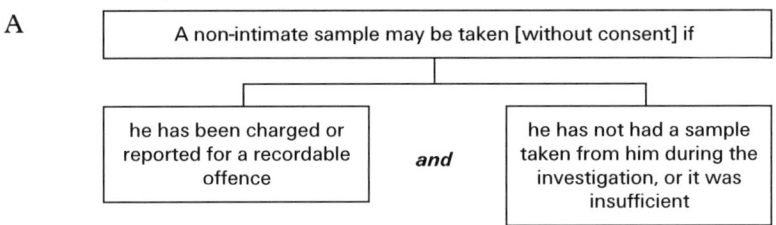

Non attendance at police station. Where a person is convicted not having attended a police stations, e.g. reported, samples may be taken identical to the subsequent taking of fingerprints following conviction.

IDENTIFICATION

Q When should samples be Destroyed?

A [a] where a person is cleared of the offence;
   [b] he is cautioned;
   [c] he is not suspected of the offence.

S 64 PACE Act 1984

Q When can Photographs be taken of an arrested person?

A Photographs can be taken if:

   [a] he is arrested at the same time as other people, or at a time when it is likely that other people will be arrested and a photograph is necessary to establish the who, when and where; or
   [b] he has been charged or reported for a recordable offence; or
   [c] he is convicted and his photograph is not on record as a result of a] or b]; or
   [d] a superintendent authorises it, having reasonable grounds for suspecting his involvement in a criminal offence and where there is identificational evidence.

Arrest. No power to arrest to take photographs but they may be taken during a fingerprint recall.

Can force be used to take photographs? No.

INTERVIEWS

Q   Define an Interview

A   An interview is the questioning of a person regarding his involvement or suspected involvement in a criminal offence.

Questions of identification. Do not amount to an interview e.g., to establish his identity or ownership of a vehicle etc.

Q   When should a person be Cautioned?

A   A caution should be administered to all people who are:

[a]   arrested for an offence;
[b]   whom there are grounds to suspect of an offence,

CODE C

before any questions about it are put to him if his answers or silence may be given in evidence.

The caution. 'You do not have to say anything but it may harm your defence if you do not mention, when questioned, something which you later rely on in court. Anything you say may be given in evidence.

Q   What should be told to a person Cautioned, but not under Arrest?

A   That he is not under arrest and is not obliged to remain with the officer.

Q   When can an arrested person be Interviewed NOT at a Police Station?

A   If the delay in taking him to a police station would be likely to:

[a]   lead to interference with or **harm** to **evidence** connected with an offence or interference with or physical harm to other **people;** or
[b]   lead to the **alerting of others** suspected of having committed an offence but not yet arrested; or
[c]   **hinder the recovery of property** obtained in consequence of the offence.

When must it cease? When the relevant risk has been averted.

INTERVIEWS

Q   When can a person be interviewed AFTER charge?

A   If it is necessary to:

   [a]   prevent or minimise harm or loss to some other person; or
   [b]   clear up an ambiguity in a previous answer or statement; or
   [c]   in the interest of justice to allow him to comment on information that has come to light since he was charged or reported.

Q   When MUST an interview be Taped?

A   [a]   where a person has been cautioned for an indictable offence;
    [b]   when further questions, after charge, are put in relation to a] above;
    [c]   when bringing to the notice of a person at a] the contents of:

        [i]   an interview; or
        [ii]   a statement made by another person.

CODE E

Q   When can a custody officer authorise an interview NOT to be Taped?

A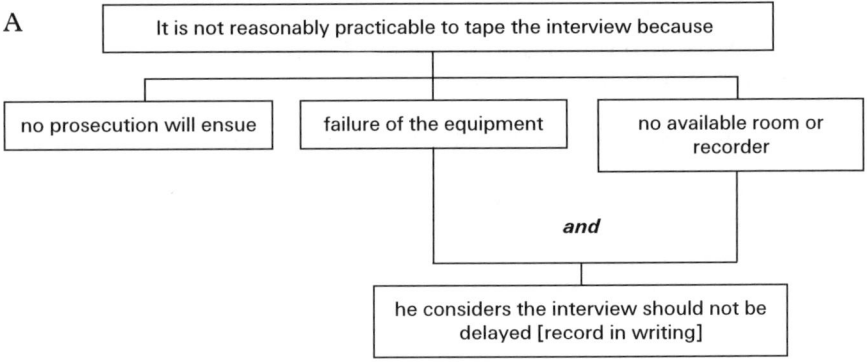

Q   Outline the position of Solicitors and Legal Advice

A   [a]   a suspect must not be dissuaded from obtaining legal advice;
    [b]   if a request for legal advice is made during interview, the interview shall stop and legal advice be sought;

[c]   if a solicitor arrives at a police station to see a suspect, the suspect must be asked if he wants to see the solicitor, regardless of what legal advice has already been received. The custody officer must be informed.

Excluding a solicitor. If the investigating officer considers that a solicitor is acting in a way that he is unable properly to put questions to the suspect he will stop the interview and consult a **superintendent,** and if not available, an **inspector** who will decide whether or not to exclude the solicitor from the interview.

Unacceptable conduct by solicitor. Includes answering questions on his client's behalf and providing written replies for him to quote.

Q   When should questioning Cease?

A   If it is considered that:

    [a]   there is enough evidence to prosecute; and
    [b]   there is enough evidence for a prosecution to succeed; and
    [c]   that the person **has said all he wishes** about the offence,

Q   When is an Interpreter required?

A   An interpreter is required when:

    [a]   he has difficulty in understanding English;
    [b]   the interviewer cannot speak the interviewee's language;
    [c]   the person wishes an interpreter to be present; and
    [d]   the person appears to have a hearing/speaking difficulty, unless he agrees **in writing** to proceed without an interpreter.

Q   When are Special Warnings required?

A   They are required in relation to questions put to suspects about:

    [a]   objects, marks or substances found on them; or
    [b]   in or on their clothing or footwear, or
    [c]   in their possession; or
    [d]   in the place where they were arrested, and in relation to why
    [e]   they were at the scene at or near the time of their arrest; and
    [f]   their failure to account for their presence.

INTERVIEWS

Q **What is the procedure when a person makes a statement in a Foreign Language?**

A [a] the interpreter shall take the statement in the foreign language,
[b] the person making it shall sign it; and
[c] a translation shall then be made.

Q **What inference can be drawn from Silence?**

A Where the person has been arrested; and
[a] is under arrest when interviewed; and
[b] the officer reasonably believes that the presence of the **object, substance or mark** or condition of his clothing/footwear, may be attributable to the person's participation in an offence; and
[c] he is told by the police that he believes the object, substance or mark [clothing/footwear] connects the suspect to the offence; and
[d] the police ask him to account for the object, substance or mark [clothing/footwear]; and
[e] he is warned in ordinary language of the consequences of a failure or refusal to answer such questions.

Q **When can an inference be drawn from a Failure to account for his Presence?**

A The court can draw an inference from a person's silence about his presence at a place at or about the time of the offence if:

[a] the officer found him at a place at or about the time of the offence;
[b] the officer questioning the person reasonably believes that his presence may be attributable to his participation in an offence; and
[c] the officer tells him that he believes his presence connects the suspect to the offence; and
[d] the officer asks him to account for his presence; and
[e] he is warned in ordinary language of the consequences of a failure or refusal to answer such questions.

SUPERINTENDENTS

Q When can a Superintendent authorise an Urgent interview?

A   Where an interview is to take place at a police station and a superintendent considers that delay would result in:

[a]   interference with or harm to evidence connected with an offence, or interference with or physical harm to other people; or
[b]   the alerting of other people suspected of having committed an offence but not yet arrested for it; or
[c]   hindering the recovery of property, then he may authorise the interview of:

   [i]   **drunks.** A person heavily under the intluencc of drink or drugs; or
   [ii] **juveniles.** Or mentally disordered persons in the absence of an appropriate adult; or
   [iii] **difficulty with English.** A person who has difficulty in understanding English or who has a hearing disability, in the absence of an interpreter.

The questioning must end when the risk is averted

Q Who may authorise a Road Check?

A   [a]   a superintendent; or
    [b]   any officer, if it is urgent to do so.

SUPERINTENDENTS

Q Define a Road Check

A

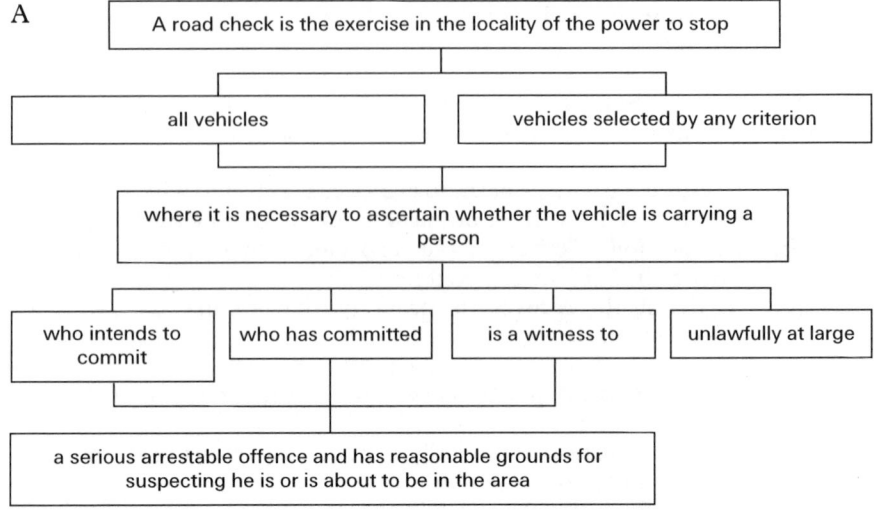

S 4 PACE Act 1984

For how long? Not exceeding **7 days** [renewable in writing]

Continuous? The road check may either be continuous or be conducted at specific times.

Locality. Must be specified.

If authorised by a constable. A record of the authorisation and the time it was given must be recorded and a superintendent informed.

Not a road check. Road traffic offence or vehicle excise offence stops.

Written statements. Are available to the person in charge of the vehicle for a period of 12 months on application. The authorisation shall state:

[a]   the name of the officer giving it;
[b]   the purpose of the check;
[c]   the locality of the check; and
[d]   the serious arrestable offence.

SUPERINTENDENTS

Q When can a superintendent authorise Stop and Search?

A
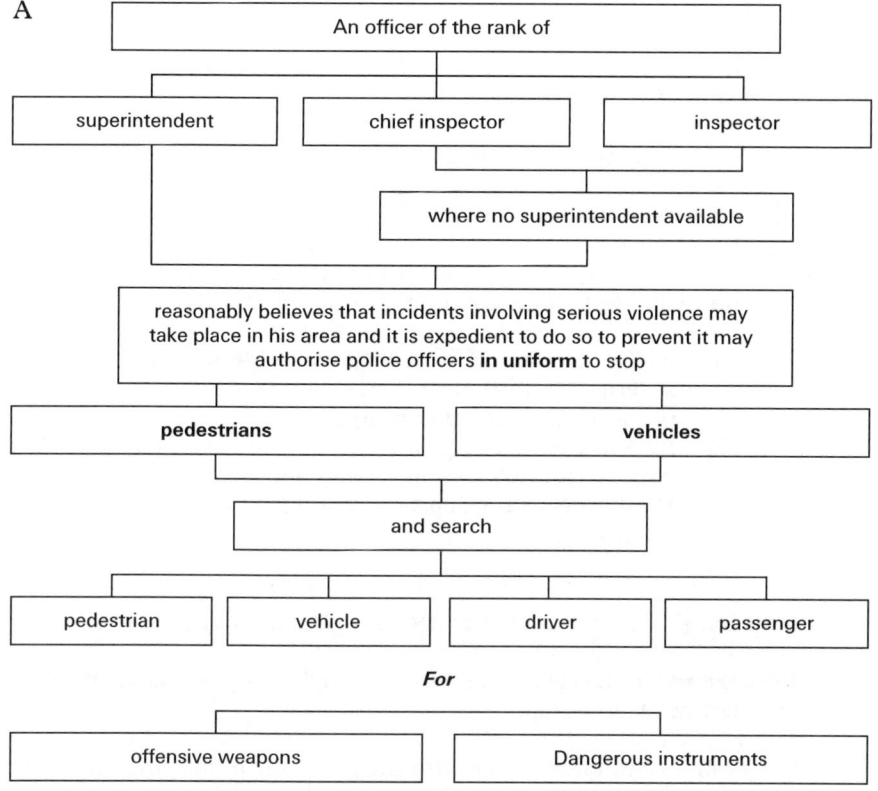

S 60 CJ & Public Order Act 1994

The authorisation, Must be in writing.

How long? It may not exceed **24 hours.** The officer should set the minimum period necessary to deal with the risk.

Extensions? 1 only of up to **6 hours.**

Beyond 30 **hours?** Once the 24 hours and 6 hour [30 hours] extension has expired the authorisation ends. To continue with the power requires a **new authorisation.**

SUPERINTENDENTS

Area of power. The officer should not set a geographical area which is wider than he believes is necessary for preventing the anticipated violence.

Q **When can a superintendent delay Notifying Arrest or Access to Legal Advice?**

A Both rights may be delayed if:

[a] a person is in detention;
[b] the offence is a serious arrestable offence; and
[c] he is not charged, and a superintendent has reasonable grounds for believing that the exercise of either right will:

  [i]   lead to interference with or **harm evidence** connected with a serious arrestable offence or interfere with or cause physical injury to other **people;**
  [ii] lead to the **alerting** of other people suspected of having committed such an offence and not yet arrested for it; or
  [iii] **hinder recovery** of property obtained as a result of such an offence.

Code C

How long? Only for as long as necessary but not beyond **36 hours.**

Terrorism. In the case of terrorism the rights may be detained where the exercise of either right:

1. will lead to interference with the gathering of information about the commission, preparation or instigation of acts of terrorism; or
2. by alerting any person, will make it more difficult to prevent an act of terrorism or secure the apprehension, prosecution or conviction of any person in that connection.

Q **What further restrictions can a superintendent authorise in relation to Legal Advice?**

A If a superintendent has reasonable grounds for believing that:

[a] delay will involve an immediate risk of harm to person, or serious loss of, or damage to property; or

[b] where a solicitor has been contacted and has agreed to attend, awaiting his arrival would cause unreasonable delay to the process of investigation; or
[c] where it is considered necessary to remove a solicitor from an interview because his conduct is such that the investigating officer is unable properly to put questions to the suspect.

Inspectors. Who believe that a firm of solicitors is persistently sending non-accredited or probationary solicitors who are unsuited to provide advice should inform the superintendent.

Q **Who is responsible for Reviews over 24 hours?**

A A superintendent only.

Q **When can a Intimate-search be authorised?**

A When a superintendent has reasonable grounds for believing:

[a] that an article which could cause physical injury to the detained person or others has been concealed; or
[b] that he has concealed a Class A drug which he intended to supply; and
[c] that an intimate search is the only practical means of removing it.

Q **When can a superintendent authorise taking of Fingerprints without consent?**

A A superintendent may authorise the taking of fingerprints from a person over 10 who is in police detention if he has reasonable grounds for suspecting that the fingerprints will tend to confirm or disprove his involvement in a criminal offence.

Q **When can the taking of Intimate Samples be authorised?**

A A superintendent may authorise the taking of intimate samples from a person in police detention if he has reasonable grounds to believe that the sample will tend to confirm or disprove his involvement in a recordable offence. The suspect must consent.

SUPERINTENDENTS

Q When can Non-intimate samples be authorised?

A   A superintendent may authorise the taking of non-intimate samples from a person if he has reasonable grounds to believe that it will tend to confirm or disprove his involvement in a **recordable offence.**

Q Can a Chief Inspector who is Acting-superintendent give authorisations?

A   Yes.

Q Can a sergeant who is Acting-inspector perform the functions of an Inspector?

A   Yes.